Prayer Book Studies Volume Four

Revisiting the Calendar and Eucharist,
Issues XVI-XVII

Edited by
Derek A. Olsen

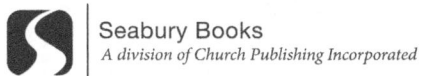

Copyright © 2026 The Domestic and Foreign Missionary Society of the Protestant Episcopal Church in the United States of America

The English text of the liturgies presented in this book is in the public domain and is freely available for quotation without restriction.

Unless otherwise noted, Scripture quotations are from The New Revised Standard Version Bible, copyright © 1989 National Council of the Churches of Christ in the United States of America. Used by permission. All rights reserved worldwide.

Seabury Books
19 East 34th Street
New York, NY 10016
www.churchpublishing.org

Seabury Books is an imprint of Church Publishing Incorporated.

Cover design by Newgen
Typeset by Integra Software Services Pvt. Ltd.

ISBN 978-1-64065-930-8 (paperback)
ISBN 978-1-64065-931-5 (hardback)
ISBN 978-1-64065-932-2 (eBook)

Library of Congress Control Number: 2025945261

CONTENTS

Introduction vii

Prayer Book Studies XVI: The Calendar and the Collects, Epistles, and Gospels for the Lesser Feasts and Fasts

Preface 3

A Review of Recent Proposals 5
  1. The Studies of the Commission 5
  2. Recent Anglican Revisions of the Calendar (With a Note on Calendar Revision in the Roman Catholic Church) 8

Alterations and Additions to the Proper of Saints 12
  1. Names and Dates 12
  2. New Collects 15
  3. Additional Epistles and Gospels 17

Additional Propers for Certain Occasions 18

Appendices 24
  1. Biographical and Bibliographical Notes on the Newly Proposed Black Letter Days 24
  2. A Comparative Table of Calendars 41

The Calendar, Collects, Epistles, and Gospels for the Lesser Feasts and Fasts

The Calendar 66

The Collect, Epistles, and Gospels for the Lesser Feasts and Fasts .. 78
  Advent Season 78
  Lenten Season 81
  Eastertide 99
  The Rogation Days 103
  Whitsuntide 106
  The Autumn Ember Days 110

The Lesser Holy Days	113
The Common of Saints	173

For Special Occasions 180

Indices 199

Alterations in Scripture Lessons	199
Index of Scripture Lessons	202
Movable Days and Seasons	208
Immovable Days	209
Common of Saints and Special Occasions	213

Prayer Book Studies XVII: The Liturgy of the Lord's Supper

Preface 217

Introduction: A Report on Prayer Book Studies IV 219

The Problem of Norms 222

New Perspectives 226

Rationale of Proposed Revision 230

1. The Title	230
2. Rubrics: General and Particular	232
3. The Introduction	237
4. The Ministry of the Word	241
5. The Prayers	245
6. The Offertory	248
7. The Consecration	249
8. The Breaking of the Bread and Communion	254
9. The Final Thanksgiving and Dismissal	257
10. Other Considerations	258

Appendices 261

I. The Structure and Contents of the Eucharistic Liturgy	261
II. Recent Consecration Prayers	263
1. The *Apostolic Tradition* of Hippolytus	263
2. The Church of South India	264
3. The Reformed Church of France	265
4. The Community of Taizé, France	265
5. The Lusitanian Church, Catholic, Apostolic, Evangelical	266
6. The Lutheran Church in America	267
7. The Presbyterian Churches in America	268
8. A Liturgy for Africa	269

      9. Diocese Of Hong Kong and Macao 270
    10. The Church of England 271
    11. "An Experimental Liturgy" 272
    12. "An Order of Holy Communion". 273
    13. The Church of the Province of New Zealand 274
III. A Select Bibliography. 275
    Anglican Rites 275
    Roman Catholic Reforms 278
    Protestant Worship. 279
Acknowledgments 281

The Liturgy of the Lord's Supper 282

The Ministers of the Liturgy. 282
The Liturgy
    The Ministry of the Word 284
    The Offertory 288
    The Consecration 289
    The Breaking of the Bread. 291
The Order for Celebration of Holy Eucharist. 292
The Penitential Order 294
The Offertory Sentences. 295
At The Presentation. 296
Spoken Proper Prefaces 296

INTRODUCTION

The Series as a Whole

The *Prayer Book Studies* (PBS) series documents the 26-year process of study and conversation that led to the adoption of the American 1979 Book of Common Prayer. It falls broadly into two parts, distinguished by the use of Roman numerals and Arabic numerals. PBS I-XVII were published by the members of the Standing Liturgical Commission between 1950 and 1966 to communicate research and draft liturgies leading toward a revision process; PBS 18-29 were published by the various drafting committees between 1970 and 1976 once the revision process was formally begun and the earlier drafts were being transformed into new usable liturgies, leading up to the adoption of the new prayer book in 1979. Finally, PBS 30 and its commentary were added in 1989 to discuss inclusive and expansive language for God for further liturgical efforts.

Context of these Studies

These studies bring to an end the first series–those studies designated with Roman numerals. They sit in an interesting place between what has come before and what will come after. These studies revisit ground already trodden in the first series. Returning to them now is significant because two major shifts have occurred since the original studies were written.

First, the plea of PBS XV succeeded: the change to Article X of the Canons allowing "trial use" passed overwhelmingly by voice vote at the 1961 General Convention (before the publication of PBS XVI) and a second time at the 1964 General Convention (before the publication of PBS XVII). Thus, both of these are written looking forward to or actually receiving the benefits of trial use in actual worshipping congregations.

Second, these studies appeared in the context of the greatest ecclesiastical shift of the 20th century, the Roman Catholic reforms of Vatican II that took place between 1962 and 1965. For the first time in a millennium and a half, the Roman Catholic Mass was revised along 4th-century lines and made available in vernacular languages; for the first time, Roman Catholic and Episcopal laity could compare the liturgies of their co-religionists and discover their similarities.

However, with these publications, The Episcopal Church had not yet turned the corner to full revision; that would not come until the 1967 General Convention. Thus, these two studies are the last words of academically inclined theoretical study. From the publication of PBS I-XV—that is, from 1950 to 1961—the membership of the Standing Liturgical Commission consisted of twenty people, four of whom remained in key roles the entire time. The time from 1961 to 1966 added seven new people to that number. In other words, the first series was governed by disciplined academic and ecclesiastical control that emphasized a cautious and reverent approach to the materials. What will come next will be a radical expansion of voices and authors at the same time that tight deadlines and turnarounds will be demanded from those crafting the new liturgies.

These Studies

PBS XVI

This first study on the calendar draws together the calendrical contents of PBS IX and XII into a usable form. The initial portion describes changes that have occurred within other Anglican calendars as well as sanctoral changes wrought at Vatican II and their impact on the developing Episcopal calendar. The proposed material presents the 12-month calendar of observances, then the collects, epistles, and Gospels for the fasts starting with the Ember Days of Advent and all Wednesdays and Fridays in Lent, the Rogation Days, and the Summer and Fall Ember days. After the fasts come the lesser feasts, starting with Channing Moore Williams on December 2 through the Church Year until Clement on November 23. From there, it takes on the Common of Saints, followed by the Propers for Special Occasions.

This proposed material was accepted for trial use at the 1963 General Convention and published in 1964 as the first *Lesser Feasts and Fasts*.

PBS XVII

Where there was not much change in the sanctoral material from the previous studies, quite a bit was needed for this second study on the Eucharist. Indeed, this volume is explicitly framed as a report on PBS IV. Over 150 responses from groups large and small had been received by the time the drafting of this new study began in 1960—six years before its eventual publication. By that point, it had become clear that a mere revision of the rite of PBS IV would not be acceptable and that work would need to begin again from the ground up. In addition to offering critiques of PBS IV, the study also discusses changes due to Vatican II and includes a selection of consecration prayers from worldwide liturgical efforts through the 1950s and 1960s.

Further changes in later studies would demonstrate that this proposed prayer, too, would be found lacking in several important respects.

PRAYER BOOK STUDIES XVI: THE CALENDAR AND THE COLLECTS, EPISTLES, AND GOSPELS FOR THE LESSER FEASTS AND FASTS

A Supplementary Revision of
Prayer Book Studies IX and XII

The Standing Liturgical Commission
of the Protestant Episcopal Church in the
United States of America

1963

PREFACE

In issuing this Study the Commission has not considered it necessary to repeat either the substance or the arguments of its earlier work on the Calendar and the Propers, as they are presupposed in all that is contained in this volume. One may find them in *Prayer Book Studies* IX (1957) and XII (1958) and in the Supplement to Study XII (1960). We present here only new or amended materials now published for the first time, with some notice of recent developments in Calendar revision that have taken place since 1958 in other provinces of the Church. Several of the tables and indices of the earlier Studies have necessarily been revised to bring them into accord with new information received or with the changes that we ourselves have made.

To our Study is appended a supplementary volume, with all the propers written out in full, comparable to the Supplement to Study XII.

We wish to express our profound gratitude to all the clergy and laity who have given generously of their time and knowledge to help us improve our work by sending us so many helpful comments and suggestions. Their names are too numerous to list here. But we feel a special obligation to mention the careful report sent us by a committee appointed to study our proposals by the diocesan Convention of Louisiana in 1960; a study submitted to us in 1962 by the Liturgical Committee of the American Church Union; an extensive corpus of suggested propers by the Rev. Bonnell Spencer, O.H.C.; and a monograph, with many original translations of Collects, sent to us by Mr. C. T. Ruddick, Jr. of the Hill School, Pottstown, Pennsylvania.

All members of the Commission have been engaged in the preparation of this Study, including those whose term ended with the triennium 1958-61, and also the Rev. Dr. John W. Suter, Jr., who resigned as Custodian and hence as *ex officio* member of the Commission during the past year. Special charge in the preparation of this Study for the press has been in the hands of Dr. Shepherd; and much assistance has been given by Dr. Smith in the consideration of alterations of Scriptural translations taken from the Authorized Version for the proper lections. A list of these appears in the indices of the supplementary volume.

THE STANDING LITURGICAL COMMISSION:

ALBERT R. STUART, *Chairman*
W. R. CHILTON POWELL

MASSEY H. SHEPHERD, JR., *Vice Chairman*
CHARLES W. F. SMITH
LOUIS B. KEITER
H. BOONE PORTER
CHARLES M. GUILBERT, *Custodian*
JOHN W. ASHTON
FRANK ST. CELLIER, *Secretary*
DUPUY BATEMAN, JR.

The Calendar and The Collects, Epistles, and Gospels for the Lesser Feasts and Fasts 5

A Review of Recent Proposals

1. The Studies of the Commission

For almost two decades the Standing Liturgical Commission has been engaged in study and publication with respect to an enrichment of the Calendar and the Propers of the Holy Communion. Our aim has been a more extensive and varied provision of commemoration and teaching in the corporate prayer and devotion of the Church, with particular concern for the needs created by the notable increase in weekday celebrations of the sacrament. With the exception of a relatively few holy days, the Prayer Book at present provides for these occasions only the repetition of the Sunday propers.

An impressive fact of liturgical renewal throughout the Church has been this steady growth of mid-week, or even daily, attendance upon and participation in the Holy Communion, not only in Lent but at all seasons of the year. In innumerable parish churches, mission and school chapels, one or more celebrations of the Eucharist, in addition to those customary on Sundays and holy days, are regularly scheduled every week. Many celebrations are common in connection with meetings of voluntary devotional or study groups; and in recent years frequent celebrations have been characteristic of the numerous conferences of church people held for intensive periods of worship, study, and discussion that normally range in length from several days to two or more weeks.

The rich texture and variety of Scriptural psalmody and lesson contained in the Daily Offices of Morning and Evening Prayer continue, of course, to have their due and appreciated place in the on-going day-to-day corporate worship of the Church. Their unique value in this respect has undoubtedly contributed to the widespread demand for a similar enrichment of the Scriptural propers of the Eucharist, and more particularly for a larger use of Old Testament materials in the lectionary of the Communion rite. Such interest is one of the most welcome fruits of the revival of Bible study and its accompanying emphasis on Biblical theology that are so important a part of the contemporary liturgical renewal.

Another encouraging development has been the increasing appreciation of the heritage the whole Church enjoys in the abiding influence of its heroes and saints who have been "the lights of the world in their several generations." The more objective, and less polemic, study of Church history and the more friendly and sympathetic encounters of ecumenical discussion during the past generation have enlarged our understanding and admiration for the wealth of example and achievement that are ours in the one communion of saints. Along with this enlargement of our sense of the depth and breadth of "the wonderful grace and virtue" that God has bestowed upon us by the witnesses of all times and places, there has come a widespread desire to give acknowledgment and recognition of this heritage in our common worship, both as a thanksgiving to God and as a means of our edification.

As a first step in meeting these new needs and interests, the Commission published in 1957 its Study (No. IX) on the Calendar, in which some ninety-four commemorations of persons and events were proposed to the Church's consideration as suitable "Black Letter Days" for optional observance. This Study contained an historical survey of the development of saints' days from ancient times to the present, with particular consideration of their recent enlargement in the revisions of the Prayer Book in several of our fellow provinces of the Anglican Communion. The principles and criteria of selection of these proposed minor holy days were carefully expounded; and illustrative notes and tables, with select bibliographies, were provided to assist those who were interested in acquainting themselves with the life and achievements of the worthies proposed in our suggested Calendar.

The following year, the Commission issued a second Study (No. XII) on the Propers for the Minor Holy Days. In this volume suggestions were offered for suitable Collects for the saints' days of the proposed Calendar, and appropriate Epistles and Gospels were outlined for certain of the more important ones. In addition, the Commission sought to balance this extension of the "Proper of Saints" with a comparable provision for enriching the "Proper of Time," in particular those days and seasons when celebrations of the Holy Communion are more frequent in many of our churches: namely, the Ember and Rogation days, the weekdays of Lent, and the "vacant" days in the Octaves of Easter and Whitsunday. The proposals for the weekdays of Lent (Wednesdays and Fridays specifically) were part of a more far-reaching scheme that looked ultimately to an overall review of the Lenten propers for Sundays as well, in some future revision of the Prayer Book as a whole.

In 1960 *A Supplement to Prayer Book Studies XII* printed in full the text of the Calendar and proper Collects, Epistles, and Gospels, exactly as they would appear in an authorized Book for optional use, supplementary to the Prayer Book in the same way as *The Book of Offices* for special occasions (Third Edition, 1960), which is authorized by General Convention. Preparatory to the Convention of 1961, the Commission outlined its convictions with regard to "The Problem and Method of Prayer Book Revision" in *Prayer Book Studies* XV. Though concerned with Prayer Book revision as a whole, this Study was particularly addressed to the more immediate problem of how the Church might secure, to best advantage, an adequate evaluation of the materials proposed in Studies IX and XII. To this end, an amendment to Article X of the Church's Constitution was proposed, so that the General Convention could authorize for trial use, under conditions of its own choosing, legal experiment and testing of new observances and forms before admitting them as changes and enrichments of the Book of Common Prayer itself.[1]

The Convention of 1961 passed with overwhelming majorities, by voice vote in both Houses, the proposed amendment to Article X. If this action is ratified in 1964, the General Convention will be able to give canonical sanction to the use of any or all the materials here offered concerning the Calendar and Propers, for experimental and optional use, under whatever conditions and for whatever period of time the Convention may think wise and fitting. Thus the Church would have the opportunity of testing, in the actual context of its due and regular worship, the devotional value of these observances and their new Collects and lessons, and hence be better prepared to decide how much of it may be worthy of inclusion in the Prayer Book at some future revision.

The present Study includes all the Lesser Feasts and Fasts, with the propers both "Of Time" and "Of Saints," which have been proposed in Studies IX and XII. Certain minor changes have been made in them, in response to the helpful criticisms sent to the Commission during the past few years by various individuals and groups, including several diocesan committees appointed to review them. The rationale of this material has been sufficiently discussed in our previous Studies, so that the Commission does not consider it necessary to repeat in detail what it has already published. There are, however, several additional saints' days proposed in this Study; and, in response to many requests from all parts of the Church, a new section of propers for certain "Common" and "Votive" Eucharists. The sources of these new materials, and the reasons for our addition of them, will be outlined below in Chapters II and III.

In a project as extensive as this has become, the Commission has been immensely encouraged and gratified by the goodwill and favorable reaction towards its work that have come from all quarters of the Church. We expected in any case that there would be objections both to the inclusion of certain names in the proposed Calendar and to the omission of others. These have not been wanting, and in each case the Commission has given careful consideration to the suggestions and criticisms made. But there has been no decisive or widespread condemnation of a single one of the "Black Letter Days" that we proposed for the Calendar. We have been faulted more for errors of omission, and these we have tried conscientiously to rectify in the new materials of this Study, but without altering the principles and criteria of selection that we have felt justifiable in our

---

1. The Commission actually proposed this amendment at the Convention of 1958; but the Convention instead voted to approve the saints' days proposed in Study XII, on first reading, as a formal revision of the Prayer Book, The Supplement to Study XII was in part responsive to this action. The Commission has always felt, however, that the new holy days should be introduced to the Church under "trial use" and not as a formal revision of the Prayer Book. The Convention of 1961 consequently did not ratify the revision action taken in 1958, but took up the amendment on trial use.

arguments in Study No. IX. To the best of our knowledge the Church as a whole has accepted these principles and criteria as reasonable and defensible.

A few changes in the phraseology of some of the proposed Collects have been made, for clarification and exactness of meaning. And several errors of inconsistency in the lections, as noted in the studies and schedules of Study XII and its Supplement, have been rectified. What is especially reassuring is the fact that no important objection has been raised to the proposed formularies, either with respect to the doctrinal soundness of the new Collects or to the appropriateness of the new Epistles and Gospels. We trust that the same confidence will be extended to the additional formularies of this Study. We do not for a moment suppose that the proposed forms are incapable of further improvements. And indeed, one of the advantages of a "trial use" of them is the greater flexibility allowed to the Church in making needed changes, without resort to the complicated processes of formal Prayer Book revision. We are, however, much comforted by the fact that our work has commended itself as maintaining the proper balance and rightness of faith as it is expressed in our Prayer Book liturgy; and that it has been as free as possible, in such undertakings, from partisan considerations.

It cannot be emphasized too strongly, however, that we have always intended our proposals of new feasts and fasts, in their entirety, on a basis of optional, trial use. We believe that they are both too vast in scope and too fresh in substance to be considered now, in all their detail, for formal inclusion in the Prayer Book. By making them optional, for any parish or congregation to use at its own discretion any or all of this material, we have sought to commend these observances solely on the basis of their inherent merits for the advancement of the Church's devotion. No one should be under constraint to use them in the same way that the contents of the Prayer Book are expected to be used, wherever and whenever possible as a regular part of the corporate life and discipline of the Church. There is no way of predicting at the present time how much of these proposals will win a place in the heart and mind of the Church. We can only testify that in certain places, where they have been used with special authorization of the Ordinary, the reports sent in to the Commission have uniformly witnessed to their favorable and helpful reception. Others have found through study of them a strong inclination to test them, but have felt restrained from any public use by canonical inhibitions respecting unauthorized formularies that are inherently revisions of the Prayer Book. The final passage of the amendment to Article X should, we trust, make possible a widespread, open, sympathetic, and patient, experiment that may well contribute immeasurably to the wealth of treasure in the Church's liturgical life and common prayer.

2. Recent Anglican Revisions of the Calendar
(With a Note on Calendar Revision in the Roman Catholic Church)

Before describing the modifications and additions that are proposed in this Study for our own Church, it may be well to summarize briefly the developments in

Calendar revision in other provinces of Anglicanism during the past few years. In Study IX we included the pertinent notations of Calendar supplementation in other Anglican Prayer Books, whether completed in formal revisions or projected in proposed revisions. A comparative table of all these Calendars, including also their relation to the Roman and Sarum Calendars, was printed. Modifications since that time, however, necessitate a new comparative table, which the reader will find in the appendices. Specifically, we have received authoritative information with respect to the Calendars officially adopted in the revisions of the Anglican Church of Canada, completed in 1962; the Nippon Sei Ko Kai, in 1959; and the Church of India, Pakistan, Burma, and Ceylon, in 1960.[2]

The Canadian Church was the first province of Anglicanism in modern times (in its revision of 1922) to make an extensive revision of the Black Letter Days inherited from the English Book of 1662, when it dropped 17 names from the older list and added 21 new names. In their preliminary Draft Book of 1955, 54 other names were added; but the Draft Book of 1959, adopted in the two readings of 1959 and 1962, omitted 6 of the earlier list and added 10 others. A few changes of datings were also made. The last additions made were all worthies of the Canadian Church's history, except for a few other Anglicans of modern times, the feasts of our Lord's brothers James and Jude, respectively, and a festival commemorative of the First Council of Nicaea. Only a few individual Collects, Epistles, and Gospels are provided for the new feasts, many of them subsumed under "Common" propers according to various classifications of saints. There are also a number of "Votive" propers, many of them under rubrical direction for use of propers found elsewhere in the Book.

The Japanese Church has a modest listing of additional names to the Red Letter Days, and no provision made as yet for special Collects, Epistles, and Gospels. Most of the names appear on other Anglican Calendars, but a few are particularly appropriate to the heritage of the Church in Japan: a commemoration of all Japanese martyrs on February 5; the organization of the Nippon Sei Ko Kai on February ; Bishop Channing Moore Williams, first Anglican missionary Bishop in Japan, on December 2; and Francis Xavier on December 3. All the entries are pre-Reformation saints and feasts, except Bishop Williams and the 16th century missionaries and martyrs associated with the first preaching of the gospel in Japan.

The Proposed Prayer Book of the C.I.P.B.C. of 1951 contained 66 new names and a rich provision of "Commons" and "Votives." As finally adopted in 1960, twelve of these entries were dropped — including all that were distinctive of the tradition of Indian Christianity, except the feast of St. Thomas on October 6. The Prayer Book itself included the traditional Anglican feasts and propers; but

---

2. The editor wishes to express his gratitude especially to those who have furnished this information: the Rev. Dr. Ramsay Armitage of Maple, Ontario; the Rev. John T. Sakurai, S.S.J.E., of St. Michael's Monastery, Oyama; and the Metropolitan of the C.I.P.B.C., the Most Rev. Dr. H. Lakdasa Jacob de Mel, of Calcutta.

the additional commemorations, with their propers, were issued in a Supplement authorized by the Episcopal Synod. All of these feasts are either ancient or medieval in origin.

The Churches in South Africa and Canada have been to date the most venturesome in enriching their Calendars by extension into and beyond the Reformation period. Our own Church, if it approves our proposals, will join their ranks. Undoubtedly there is some risk in adopting a formal commemoration of worthies who are not universally admitted in the Catholic tradition and whose period of witness has come subsequent to the major divisions of western Christendom. But to deny the fact of Christian heroism and sanctity, even within our own tradition, for the period since the Reformation would seem as illogical, if not more so, as our present Prayer Book Calendar's exclusion of all saints not mentioned in the New Testament.

In the preface of Study IX, we were able to make only a brief reference to the special study made for the Lambeth Conference of 1958 by a commission appointed by the Archbishop of Canterbury, entitled *The Commemoration of Saints and Heroes in the Anglican Communion* (S.P.C.K., 1957). There is much valuable information in this report about the history of holy days as they have developed in the long life of the Church, as well as a useful summary of the steps being taken throughout the Anglican Communion to enrich its commemorations in the various processes of Prayer Book revision going on in many provinces. The report is also forward-looking in its encouragement of this development, including the recognition that our own Anglican tradition has much to contribute. It is not, however, unaware of the problems set for us by the fact that for four hundred years the Anglican Churches have given little or no attention to the continuing supplement of the Calendar, as this has been inherited from the Reformation settlement. It offers certain important warnings regarding overly hasty or extensive constructions, lest there be evident an element of "artificiality" — the danger of producing a set of commemorations "which breathes the study rather than the church." The commission seems a bit fearful of calendars that proceed from "the researches of an historian" rather than from the wider recognition of the faithful as a whole. The report does not give much guidance, however, as to how the popular devotions that develop in the Church about certain individuals may be controlled by a more objective verification of evidences of sanctity.

The resolutions (nos. 77-80) adopted by the bishops at Lambeth in 1958, on the Book of Common Prayer, make specific reference to the problem. They are worth quoting in full, if only by way of comparison with the principles of selection on which our own Studies have been based:

> 77. The Conference holds that the purpose of a Kalendar is to increase our thankfulness to God and to strengthen our faith by recalling regularly the great truths of the Gospel, the principal events in the life of our

Lord, and the lives and examples of men and women who have borne preeminent witness to the power of the Holy Spirit, and are with us in the communion of saints.

78. The Conference considers that the power to revise or amend Kalendars should be exercised by the same authority as is required for the revision of the Book of Common Prayer within each several Church or Province, which authority may allow supplementary commemorations for local use in addition to the Kalendar at the request of a diocese.

79. The Conference is of opinion that the following principles should guide the selection of saints and heroes for commemoration:
    (a) In the case of scriptural saints, care should be taken to commemorate men or women in terms which are in strict accord with the facts made known in Holy Scripture.
    (b) In the case of other names, the Kalendar should be limited to those whose historical character and devotion are beyond doubt.
    (c) In the choice of new names economy should be observed and controversial names should not be inserted until they can be seen in the perspective of history.
    (d) The addition of a new name should normally result from a widespread desire expressed in the region concerned over a reasonable period of time.

80. The Conference recommends that the Church should continue to commemorate the saints in three ways: by Red Letter days, Black Letter days, or a memorial collect alone.

The Commission believes that its work has been faithful to both the spirit and the letter of these recommendations. No doubt some may contest us with respect to the principle enunciated in 79 (d), since it is obvious that our proposals have not come as a result of a poll of the Church that indicates "a widespread desire" for the names on our list. We have had to form our judgments more indirectly — through communications sent in to the Commission, and through the reactions already submitted with respect to our published Studies. But in the last analysis this principle will be adequately upheld if the Church has the opportunity, as we have again and again reiterated, to make a trial use of what is now offered, and thus decide after a period of experimental exposure to the material what it wishes to retain or to amend or to discard.

Calendar Revision in the Roman Catholic Church. Among the many facets of liturgical reform now taking place in the Roman Catholic Church, the Calendar has not been neglected. In fact, the changes made have been radical and bold, according to the *Motu proprio* of Pope John XXIII and the subsequent decree of the Sacred Congregation of Rites in July 1960. Some of these are of especial interest to Anglicans, and may be outlined as follows:

1. A new and simplified classification of feasts, into 1st, 2nd, and 3rd class respectively.
2. Sunday is emphasized; all Sundays are either of 1st or 2nd class, and only a 1st class feast or a and class feast of our Lord has precedence; no permanent assignment of a feast is to be given to a Sunday (excepting a few feasts of our Lord and the feast of the Holy Trinity).
3. Only three Octaves are admitted: those of Christmas, Easter, and Pentecost.
4. Feasts raised to the 1st class are: the Octave of Christmas (which name is to replace Circumcision); All Souls (but if it falls on a Sunday, it is transferred to November 3); Holy Cross.
5. Among the feasts reduced to a mere commemoration are St. George, St. Thomas Becket, and St. Sylvester.
6. Dropped entirely from the Calendar are: Invention of the Holy Cross (May 3); St. John before the Latin Gate (May 6); St. Peters Chains (August 1).
7. Transferred: St. Irenaeus, from June 28 to July 3 (to avoid falling on the Vigil of SS. Peter and Paul); SS. Philip and James to May (this was done in 1955 when the new feast of St. Joseph the Workman was placed on May 1).

(A convenient English translation of the new rubrics affecting the Roman Calendar may be obtained in the pamphlet *Rubrics of the Roman Breviary and Missal*, Collegeville, Minnesota: The Liturgical Press, St. John's Abbey 1960; price 90 cents.)

Alterations and Additions to the Proper of Saints

The Commission has received little comment, and none of it unfavorable, upon its proposals in Prayer Book Studies XII and the Supplement to enlarge the "Proper of Time" with additional lections for the Ember and Rogation days, the Lenten weekdays, and the Easter and Whitsun octaves. In this material we did not propose any Collects that are not already in the Prayer Book, but only a more varied lectionary of Epistles and Gospels. Many of these Epistles are drawn from the Old Testament, as are certain Epistles suggested for some of the new saints' days. There has been frequent and widespread correspondence to the Commission expressing the hope that, in a future revision of the Prayer Book, more of the Old Testament Scriptures might be used in the Eucharistic rite, if not the addition of a regular Old Testament lesson. The Commission hopes that until a revision of the liturgy takes place, this concern may be met in part by our larger use of Old Testament Epistles provided in our proposals.

1. Names and Dates

All of the entries in our proposed Calendar of 1957 have been retained, but several dates have been shifted, both in response to certain suggestions made to the Commission and also in adjustments to the new names now being proposed for the first time. We have changed the date of William Law from April 6 to April 9, since one of our correspondents (the Rev. Arthur M. Sherman) has pointed out that the 9th was the correct date of Law's death and that it is so noted on his tomb. We had taken our original dating from the South African Prayer Book.

We have also shifted John of Damascus from May 6 to December 5, at the request of the Society of St. John the Evangelist and its associates, as they wished to have the date of May 6 free for their patronal festival. One may see from Study IX that various dates were open to us for this commemoration. The Roman Calendar places him on March 27, the Roman Martyrology on May 6. The Eastern Church, which accounts John of Damascus among its most important theologians, commemorates him on December 4 — a date we had already reserved for Clement of Alexandria. Rather than shift Clement's date, we have transferred John of Damascus to the following day.

We have agreed to continue our principle that only one entry be placed on any single day — unlike the Scottish and Canadian Books, which allow concurrent commemorations. Hence it is not always possible to place each worthy on the exact day of his death or on some other day associated with his memory in traditional observance. Where two or more saints would normally fall on the same date, we have adopted a few "rules" of precedence. In general, we have given preference to those entries which have a full set of propers to those which do not, and have usually listed the more ancient worthies before the more modern ones. Because of our new additions, we have made the following adjustments:

Thomas Ken is moved from March 20 to March 21, to make way for Cuthbert on the 20th.

Columba and the commemoration of the First Prayer Book have exchanged dates. Columba's ancient day is June 9, and as such is observed in all the Anglican Calendars that bear his name. The Prayer Book observance commemorates the first use of the 1549 Prayer Book, which was on Whitsunday, a movable feast. It happens that in 1549, Whitsunday fell on June 9.

The Parents of the Blessed Virgin Mary have been placed on July 26 because of a universal association of this day with St. Anne. Because of St. James' day we had already shifted the dates of Thomas a Kempis and William Reed Huntington. The best readjustment seemed to be to place Thomas on July 24, the day preceding his death-day, and leave Huntington unchanged.

Saints Mary and Martha of Bethany, being Scriptural saints with a full set of propers, have taken precedence over William Wilberforce, who has been transferred to July 30.

Henry Martyn, who would normally fall on October 16, has been placed on the 17th, to avoid shifting Bishops Latimer and Ridley.

Richard Hooker, whose proper day is November 2 and is so placed in the Canadian Book, has been moved to November 3, since so many parishes desire a special commemoration of all faithful departed on November 2.

Hugh of Lincoln has been placed on November 17, and Hilda transferred to the 18th. This is the solution of most of the Anglican Calendars — English 1928, Scottish, and South African. The Canadian Calendar places Hugh with Queen Margaret on the 16th, and assigns Hilda to the 17th.

Twenty-three new entries are herewith proposed for the first time. Many of them had been considered by the Commission in preparation for Study IX, and at that time reluctantly omitted. Requests from many of our correspondents for reconsideration have helped us to revise our judgments and have indicated that our earlier caution was apparently not necessary. In fact, only five of our new entries have been really "new" to our discussions since the issuance of Study IX — Joseph of Arimathaea, James of Jerusalem, the Martyrs of Japan, John Donne, and Henry Martyn. The new proposals are spread over all periods and many traditions of the Church's history, and provide a varied selection of contributions to its life and devotion — martyrs, theologians, mystics, missionaries, reformers. Thus our Calendar remains balanced and not overloaded with entries from any one age or any type of saint. As in Study IX, we give in an appendix brief synopses of the newly proposed days, with bibliographical suggestions for further study.

From the New Testament period we have added four feasts, three of them with full propers: The Parents of the Blessed Virgin Mary (a very popular commemoration); Mary and Martha of Bethany, our Lord's closest friends outside the circle of his twelve disciples — friends who made their home His also; Joseph of Arimathaea, the counsellor among the Jews who risked his reputation to give our Lord's body a decent and fitting burial; and James of Jerusalem, our Lord's brother, the leader of the apostolic Church in Jerusalem, and a martyr for his faith. In older traditions, James has been often identified with one of the Twelve, James the son of Alphaeus. But few Biblical scholars today accept that attribution, since there is no clear evidence that James was a believer in or follower of our Lord until the Resurrection. His martyrdom is attested to us not only in Christian sources, but in the Jewish historian Josephus.

Three additions have been made to the roster of saints from the ancient Church of Roman imperial times: one distinguished martyr, Fabian of Rome, the primary witness of the Decian persecution; and two theologians and teachers of the fourth century, Cyril of Jerusalem and Gregory of Nyssa. The latter has been assigned an Epistle and Gospel, comparable to those for his associate "Cappadocian Fathers," Basil of Caesarea and Gregory of Nazianzus.

From the Celtic-Anglo-Saxon Churches, a rich mine of heroic example and witness, we have added Ninian, Chad, and Cuthbert, from the earlier period, and Alphege and Wulfstan from the later. All of them were monks and bishops, with missionary and social concerns. They have remained among the most popular saints of the time. Alphege was the first Archbishop of Canterbury to become a martyr.

The conversion of the Franks from paganism is marked by the entry of Remigius of Rheims, the bishop who baptized Clovis. From later medieval times we have added two distinguished saints and bishops of the English Church, both of whom had popular shrines until they were despoiled by Henry VIII — Hugh of Lincoln, and Richard of Chichester. Clare of Assisi belongs necessarily with the memory of Francis; and Catherine of Siena stands almost in a class by herself as one of the greatest mystics and promoters of reform in the whole history of Christianity.

We are happy to associate ourselves with our brethren in Japan in honoring all the many martyrs of that land on February 5. Anglican additions to the Calendar include Richard Hooker, John Donne, John and Charles Wesley, Henry Martyn, and, from our American Church, James De Koven. These names, even by themselves, are testimony to the richness of our tradition in teaching and preaching, in devotion and missionary zeal.

All of these names, except Donne and De Koven, appear in other Calendars, whether Eastern, medieval Latin, or modern Anglican lists. Two of them, Joseph of Arimathaea and Gregory of Nyssa, have been more prominent in the Eastern tradition than they have been in the Western; although the lovely legends surrounding Joseph and the "Holy Grail" played a prominent role in English medieval piety. Half of them appear on three or more of the current Anglican provincial Calendars. And in addition to the British Isles and our own land, they undergird our links with the Churches, whether ancient or modern, of Palestine, Asia Minor, Italy, France, Japan, India, and Persia.

2. New Collects

The new Collects proposed in Study XII have all been carefully reviewed. The Commission is grateful to the many individuals who have sent in suggestions for their improvement both in clarity of expression and in felicity of style. No objection to the doctrine expressed in these Collects has been received, except for the awkwardness of a phrase in the Collect used for the great theologians of the ancient Church (Hilary, Leo, Athanasius, etc.). This has been corrected by the removal of the phrase "the true faith of" — the obscurity being occasioned by the preposition "of." The Collect for St. Timothy has been somewhat recast, and several changes of phrase have been made in the Collects for St. Mary the Virgin and St. Jerome. Other changes have been minor verbal ones. Often a Collect is clear in meaning when it is read by the eye, but not when it is heard by the ear.

Two Collects have been entirely changed by substitutions. The addition of Ninian (September 16) suggested the use of a Collect appointed for his feast in the Scottish Prayer Book, and this in turn led us to propose that the same Collect also serve, as in the Scottish Book, for Columba (June 9) — thus giving the two evangelizers of Scotland the same proper. The Collect for the Exaltation of the Holy Cross has also been changed. Objection has been made that our proposed Collect is not festal in character, to suit the feast. This is a valid objection, hence we have shifted this Collect to the "votive" propers for the Holy Cross, and substituted for the feast a new Collect based upon one in the Indian Prayer Book.

Most of the new saints' days have been assigned Collects that already appear in our former Study. But the increase in the number of these new days seemed to demand several new Collects, so as to avoid monotony in the overmuch use of the same formulary. Of the new Collects now proposed, and their sources, the following notes may be helpful:

1. The Collect assigned to Wulfstan, Richard, Remigius, and Hugh has been taken, with some alterations, from the Common Collect "Of a Bishop" in the South African and Indian Prayer Books.
2. The Collect appointed for the Wesleys and Clare has been adapted from the Common Collect "Of a Virgin" in the South African and Indian Prayer Books.
3. The Collect for Fabian and Alphege, both of them martyrs, has been taken from the Common Collect for Several Confessors, found in the York Missal, and furnished us in a translation by Mr. C. T. Ruddick, Jr.
4. The Collect for John Donne has been based upon a passage in one of his sermons, preached on Easter Day, April 13, 1628.
5. The Collect for the Parents of the Blessed Virgin Mary has been prepared by the Commission, and is based upon the Prayer "For a Blessing upon the Families of the Land" in the Prayer Book, page 598.
6. The Collect for SS. Mary and Martha of Bethany has been adapted from the Common Collect "Of a Holy Woman" in the South African Prayer Book.
7. The Collect for St. Joseph of Arimathaea has been prepared by the Commission.
8. The Collect for St. James of Jerusalem has been prepared by the Commission on the basis of suggestions given us by the Rev. Francis C. Lightbourn.

For the Common of Saints, the Commission has used some of the special and common Collects of Study XII (Martyr, Missionary, and "A Saint"). The sources of the others are as follows:

1. The Collect for a Theologian or Teacher is a translation of a Collect for St. Ambrose in the Hereford Use, sent to us by Mr. C. T. Ruddick, Jr.
2. The Collect for a Monastic is taken from the Common "Of an Abbot or Abbess" in the South African Prayer Book.

3. The Collect for a Deaconess is adapted from the Common "Of a Holy Woman" in the South African Prayer Book. (Cf. the same Collect for SS. Mary and Martha of Bethany.)

(For the Collects assigned to Eucharists "For Special Occasions," see the Additional Propers for Certain Occasions section on page 18.)

3. Additional Epistles and Gospels

The Epistles and Gospels selected for the three feasts of New Testament saints are, of course, determined by the notices of Scripture itself. This is a simple matter, so far as the Gospels are concerned: Luke to:38-42 for SS. Mary and Martha; Luke 23: 50-56 for St. Joseph of Arimathaea; and Mark 3:31-35 for St. James — our Lord's teaching about "who is my mother, or my brethren?" The Epistles have been chosen so as to give prominence to some outstanding characteristic of the saint. Thus Proverbs 31:20, 26-31, on "a virtuous woman" fits SS. Mary and Martha. It is also the selection of the South African and Indian Prayer Books, as these in turn have drawn it from a similar Common in the Roman Missal. For St. Joseph of Arimathaea we have chosen another passage from Proverbs, 4:10-18, relating the virtues of a just and wise man. St. James of Jerusalem has been assigned his speech in Acts 15 — a speech that in many ways determined the whole future course of Christian missions among the Gentiles. The South African Prayer Book also assigns this lesson for St. James.

The propers for Gregory of Nyssa demanded selections akin to those of his Cappadocian associates. Thus the Epistle from Wisdom 7:22-28 links with the Epistle for Gregory of Nazianzus, which is Wisdom 7:7-14. The Gospel from John 5:19-24 concerns the mystery of the relation of the Son to the Father, and is thus appropriate to one who defended so acutely the Nicene faith.

In the Common of Saints, the following choices were made:

1. Of a Martyr: These are taken from the "commons" in Study XII, for the Collect and Epistle; from the Gospel for St. Perpetua and her Companions, also in Study XII.
2. Of a Missionary: Acts 1:1-9 for the Epistle provides our Lord's commissioning of his disciples to be his witnesses to the end of the earth; Luke 10:2-9 for the Gospel relates our Lord's sending forth of the Seventy to preach the gospel.
3. Of a Theologian or Teacher: The Epistle is the same proposed for Gregory of Nazianzus; the Gospel is from our "commons" in Study XII.
4. Of a Monastic: Philippians 3:7-15 is the same (with one verse added) as that assigned to Antony, and concerns the calling to count all things loss for Christ. The teaching of our Lord on renunciation of material things, and of

unselfish service in expectation of His coming, provides the Gospel, Luke 12:22-37.
5. Of a Deaconess: The Epistle from Romans 15:30 ff. makes mention of the "first" deaconess, Phoebe of Cenchrea; The Gospel from Matthew 9:35-38 relates our Lord's concern for "labourers in the harvest" to follow his own ministry of compassionate service.
6. Of a Saint: These are taken from the Common of Saints in Study XII, and are of a more general nature.

(The Epistles and Gospels for the Eucharists "For Special Occasions" will be discussed below.)

Additional Propers for Certain Occasions

From ancient times the Church has provided for the celebration of the Holy Communion on certain specific occasions and for particular purposes not provided in its regular schedules of seasons and holy days. These additional Eucharists served a great variety of circumstances and interests: marriages, burials, dedication of churches, ordinations, and commemorations of persons and events of more particular concern to local parishes or dioceses. It was only natural and proper that events of primary significance in the lives of individuals, families, and congregations be thus brought into the context of the whole prayer, thanksgiving, and intercession of the Church as a corporate body.

The oldest sacramentaries of the Latin Church exhibit the gradual development of these "votive" celebrations, both of a thanksgiving and of an intercessory character. The Leonine Sacramentary contains masses "in time of drought" and "after illness" in addition to the nuptial, requiem, ordination, and anniversary masses. The Gelasian Sacramentary, a Roman service book enriched with Gallican material, extends the occasions to some sixty votive masses, and includes such items as: when taking a journey, for charity, in time of mortality, against sterility, for rain, for peace, in time of war, for kings, against evil judges, for the irreligious, for the sick, for a deceased priest, etc. Many of these are obviously of communal concerns, but others indicate more personal or "private" interests. The earliest recorded instance of a "private mass" is related in St. Augustine's *City of God* (xxii. 8), — a celebration to rid a house of demons. The popularity of requiem masses for the dead, with special intercession for souls in purgatory, became a noted example of medieval piety, stimulated at first by Pope Gregory the Great's stories in his *Dialogues*.

A new direction in the development of votive, private Eucharists was given by Alcuin, the English "prime minister" of Charlemagne. It fit so admirably into the custom already obtaining in his time, for priests to celebrate more than one mass a day. To increase devotion, Alcuin prepared a little Votive Missal, made up of formularies taken from many sources as well as of his own compositions. This book arranged, for use on a sequence of days of the week, masses in honor of the Holy Trinity, the Blessed Virgin, the Holy Spirit, the Holy Cross, and the Holy Angels. He had many imitators in the following generations, and some of his forms found a place in other contexts. For example, our much beloved Collect for Purity that begins our Holy Communion can be traced to Alcuin's votive mass for the Holy Spirit, and our Collect for Trinity Sunday derives from his votive mass in honor of the Trinity.

Another medieval development was the institution of feasts centered in doctrines, rather than in the commemoration of persons and events. The festival of Trinity Sunday is an early example of this from the late ninth century; Corpus Christi (albeit occasioned by a specific miracle) was another famous one developed in the thirteenth century. Formularies for these feasts were sometimes drawn from private masses (as in the case of Holy Trinity), or specially composed for the new observance (as in the case of Thomas Aquinas' formularies for Corpus Christi). This tendency has been considerably enlarged in modern times in the Roman Catholic Church.

The Reformation swept away entirely the "private" mass, but the Reformers retained certain "votive" celebrations on special occasions. Thus particular propers were provided in the Ordinal for the several ordination rites, and propers were also retained for special services of Communion of the Sick. The 1549 Prayer Book also included propers for a Requiem; and both the 1549 and 1552 Books directed that newly married persons should receive the Holy Communion on "the same day of their marriage," though they did not provide special propers for a Nuptial Eucharist. Our first American Prayer Books, the Proposed Book of 1786 and the first official Book of 1789, made a singular addition to "votive" celebrations, namely, the provision of propers for a celebration on Thanksgiving Day.

Modern Anglican revisions have gradually increased the provisions for special occasions, beginning with the Scottish Book of 1912, which appointed four: Dedication, Thanksgiving for Harvest, Marriage, and Burial. Our own 1928 revision also included these four. (Independence Day propers are, strictly speaking, a commemoration of an event, but they have something of the character of a "votive" for the nation.) The English Proposed Book of 1928 added such observances as "Thanksgiving for the Institution of Holy Baptism," "Thanksgiving for the Institution of Holy Communion," and "For the Missionary Work of the Church overseas." More recent revisions in South Africa, India, and Canada have also made numerous selections for special occasions, sometimes indicating appropriate propers already used for other days. None of these propers of the Anglican Prayer Books has been intended for "private masses" in the medieval sense. They have assumed a public, corporate celebration of the people, but have not imposed them as an obligation in the same way as celebrations on Sundays and major holy days. They are essentially devotional in purpose, and designed for special days of observance or for special groups formed for the work of intercession.

Our Commission has received many requests and suggestions for the enrichment of our propers for such purposes. It is, of course, possible for special intentions to be incorporated in any celebration of the Eucharist. The Prayer Book specifically provides for this by rubric — on page 71, for "authorized prayers and intercessions," and on page 74, for "the secret intercessions . . . for any who have desired the prayers of the Church." Such special intentions are constantly offered in all our churches at the regular celebrations of Sundays and holy days. There is no desire to return to anything like the medieval "private mass."

During the past generation, however, there have developed in the life of our Church many weekday occasions, when the Holy Communion is celebrated in connection with the meetings of various groups associated for a particular purpose of study, prayer, and witness. These may be concerned with missionary, ecumenical, or educational interests, with the witness of Christians to world peace, social justice, or social welfare, or with ministries of healing and the cultivation of the interior life of prayer. In addition, there are the wider meetings of convocations and dioceses, and groups gathered for intensive conferences over one or more days. Another type of gathering is the teaching and preaching missions in our parishes that extend over several if not all the days of a week.

The Prayer Book of 1928 (pp. xlii-xliii) has been generous in listing proper psalms and lessons for special occasions for use in the Daily Offices. These schedules have provided us with a precedent for similar proposals for lessons at the Holy Communion, and we have felt free to draw from them suitable selections for our Eucharistic votives. It is unlikely that this would entail unnecessary duplication, since weekday services for these special interests are not as a rule combinations of both the Office and the Eucharist. More commonly, the weekday service, whether held in the morning or in the evening hours, is either one or the other. Where both the Office and the Holy Communion are used together, however, there is no problem of the overlapping of lessons. For in some cases, such as a Church Convention, there is no duplication at all between our propers and those of the Office lectionary; in others, as in services for missions and education, the Office lectionary provides a number of alternatives. For example, one of our proposed Epistles and Gospels in the votive for Mission (Isa. 49:5-13 and Luke 10:1-9) is also listed in the Office lectionary. But the latter provides seven sets of lessons, and our Eucharistic propers have an alternative Epistle and Gospel that are not included in these seven.

The first eight of our proposed votives are related to doctrinal or devotional themes that may be used individually or as a sequence (though not on a Sunday, in any daily sequence). In the context of a teaching mission or a conference, they would serve to point up significant aspects of Christian faith, devotion, and witness. They might be used in any combination or desired pattern. But we have noted, in three of them, an appropriate commemoration of the three climactic days of Holy Week. Just as Easter is the primary source and origin of meaning for every Sunday, so is Holy Week a similar pattern of commemoration for the "sanctification" of every week. The tradition of this devotion extends back, at least, to the second century, when the "station" days of Wednesday and Friday were related in Christian piety to memories of our Lord's betrayal and crucifixion. Later ages added other associations, notably the recalling of the institution of the Eucharist on Maundy Thursday. There has never been a fixed and unalterable sequence in these weekly memorials, except that Fridays have had a universal association with our Lord's Passion hence the tradition of the Friday "fast" that is noted still in the Prayer Book tables of observances (page li).

The recent Canadian revision of the Prayer Book has listed a comparable sequence of propers, with suggested commemorations for each day of the week, in the following order:

1. Monday and Tuesday: Comparable days in Holy Week, Easter Week, or Whitsun Week;
2. Wednesdays: Ash Wednesday, Wednesday of Holy Week, or Rogation Wednesday;
3. Thursdays: Maundy Thursday or Ascension Day;
4. Fridays: Holy Cross Day, or Good Friday;
5. Saturdays: Easter Even, or a Requiem.

Our proposals have a similar, if not greater, flexibility. For example, Thursdays might be observed not only as a commemoration of the institution of the Holy Eucharist, but also as a commemoration of the Ascension by use of the propers "Of the Reign of Christ." Similarly, Saturdays, which in our suggested scheme links our Lord's burial with all who are baptized into His death, may also be occasion of other types of votives, whether a Requiem (as in the Canadian Book) for all who have died in Christ, or the votive "Of the Reign of Christ" as a sequel to a Friday commemoration of His triumph on the Cross.

Some of these eight votives may also find suitable use as "Commons" in addition to those provided with the Lesser Feasts and Fasts. The one "Of the Holy Spirit" is appropriate for the opening of conventions, conferences, preaching and teaching missions, and other meetings; that "Of the Holy Angels" for days other than Michaelmas associated with the angels, or for patronal festivals of parishes dedicated to the angels; that "Of the Incarnation" for similar patronal feasts, or for special commemorations of St. Mary. Many other uses of these propers will doubtless, upon reflection, come to mind.

A few notes may summarize the rationale of our selections for these eight sets of Collects, Epistles, and Gospels:

1. *Of the Holy Trinity.* The Collect is the one for Trinity Sunday. As we have noted, this Collect was originally designed for a Votive Mass of the Holy Trinity. But the lections for Trinity Sunday are actually propers for the Octave of Pentecost. Hence we have chosen an Epistle that refers to the incomprehensible mystery of the eternal Godhead, and a Gospel that recalls the great commission of our Lord to baptize and teach in the Name of the Trinity.

2. *Of the Holy Spirit.* These propers are the same as those appointed in the Prayer Book for an early celebration on Whitsunday (pages 182-83). They are not required, however, but are optional. We believe that they are appropriate for a much more extended use. The Epistle is appointed in the South African and Indian Prayer Books for a votive at the meeting of Church synods.

3. *Of the Holy Angels.* This is linked to Michaelmas by the Collect. The Epistle recounts the worship of God by the angels in heaven, the Gospel is our Lord's promise of the vision of "the angels of God ascending and descending upon the Son of man."

4. *Of the Incarnation.* The Collect and Gospel are the same as those appointed for the Annunciation. The Epistle from 1 John 4:1-11 is an apostolic injunction concerning the faith in our Lord's having "come in the flesh," with its ethical implication in the love of God and of our neighbor.

5. *Of the Holy Eucharist.* These propers are more festal than those appointed for Maundy Thursday, which necessarily are so closely linked to the passion. The Collect of St. Thomas Aquinas (composed for Corpus Christi) is widely known and used as a post-Communion devotion. The Epistle speaks of the marriage Supper of the Lamb in the Kingdom of God, to which the Eucharist points, and of which it is a foretaste. The Gospel is taken from our Lord's "eucharistic" discourse following upon the feeding of the multitude.

6. *Of the Holy Cross.* As noted above, the Collect has been taken from the one appointed for Holy Cross Day in the Lesser Feasts and Fasts. The Epistle is St. Paul's insistence upon the preaching of the Cross as the center of all Christian proclamation of the gospel. The Gospel is our Lord's own proclamation of the triumph of the Cross. Both the Epistle and the Gospel are the same as those appointed for this votive in the Indian Prayer Book.

7. *For All Baptized Christians.* The Collect is that of Easter Even. Romans 6:3-11, as the Epistle, is the fundamental passage in the New Testament linking our own baptism with our Lord's death and resurrection. The Gospel also presents our Lord's teaching of the relation of Christian discipleship to His baptism into death.

8. *Of the Reign of Christ.* The Collect has been adapted from one sent to the Commission by the Rev. Bonnell Spencer, O.H.C. Both the Epistle and Gospel were suggested by the votive "For the Coming of the Kingdom of God" in the South African Prayer Book. The Epistle is the great Christological

hymn of Colossians celebrating our Lord's universal dominion; the Gospel is our Lord's testimony of His kingship before Pilate.

The other twelve votives (there are two sets for Mission) are all of the intercessory type, and recognize fundamental concerns in the life and work of the Church "at all times and in all places" of its earthly witness. In all but two instances (Church Convention and Peace) we have utilized Collects already included in the Prayer Book. The Collect for a Church Convention has been prepared by the Commission from phrases suggested by prayers for similar occasions in the South African, Indian, and Canadian Prayer Books. The Collect for Peace, well-known in many anthologies of prayer, was written by Bishop Francis Paget of Oxford (d. 1911), and is used in the South African, Indian, and Canadian Books. The selections of the Epistles and Gospels are basically self-explanatory; but a few notes may be of service:

9. *For a Church Convention.* Both of these lections are used for a similar purpose in the South African and Indian Prayer Books. The Epistle teaches the manner and the setting of the mission of the gospel in the world; the Gospel describes the inner unity of the Church and its fruitfulness in Christ.
10. *For Education.* We have chosen for the Epistle one of the second lessons appointed for this theme at the Office. It concerns right teaching as it is based in the Scriptural revelation. The Gospel (used for a "Retreat" in the Canadian Book) is our Lord's prayer and appeal to learn of God through Him, in meekness and humility.
11. *For the Ministry.* These lessons are taken from our selections for Advent Ember Wednesday.
12. *For Mission.* We have provided two sets. Both Epistles are from Isaiah — prophecies of God's purpose and destiny for His people to bring all nations to the knowledge and worship of Him. Both lections are assigned to this theme in the Indian Prayer Book; the selection from 49:5-13 is also appointed in the South African and in the Canadian (Octave of Epiphany) Books; with the Gospel from Luke 10:1-9 it is assigned to Missions in the Office lectionary. The other Gospel, Matthew 9:35-38, is one of the lessons in the Indian Prayer Book. These Gospels relate, respectively, our Lord's commission and His example in mission work.
13. *For the Nation.* Though we have used the Collect for Independence Day, we have selected different lections for the votive. Micah 4:1-5 is a variant of Isaiah 2:2-4, one of the Epistles for Mission. This Epistle is used in the Canadian Book in the votive for Peace. The Gospel contains our Lord's primary teaching on obedience to the State — its Matthean parallel is the Gospel for the Twenty-Third Sunday after Trinity.

14. *For Peace.* The Epistle from Ephesians 2:13-22 is assigned in the Office lectionary to Missions, and to the votive for Missions in the South African and Indian Books. It reminds us of the reconciliation of all sorts and conditions of men in the one Body of Christ. The Johannine Gospel is our Lord's promise of the peace which passes understanding that the disciple has securely in the midst of the tribulations of the world.
15. *For the Sick.* The Epistle from James 5:13-16 is not otherwise used in the Prayer Book for the ministry to the sick. It is also the Epistle for this votive in the Indian Prayer Book. The Gospel describes our Lord's own ministry to the sick.
16. *For Social Justice.* The Epistle proclaims God's justice and its implications in service to the unfortunate and under-privileged; the Gospel reminds us that in all human relations loyalty to Christ comes first.
17. *For Social Service.* The theme of the Epistle is Christian charity and ministry. The Gospel is our Lord's ideal of "service" in His Kingdom, with a specific example of His gracious ministry to the blind Bartimaeus.
18. *For the Unity of the Church.* The Epistle is a fundamental statement of the oneness of the Church in its differentiation of ministries. It is used for this votive in the South African, Indian, and Canadian Books. The Gospel is taken from our Lord's great prayer for the unity of His disciples — and variant selections from the same prayer are assigned as the Gospel in the three other Prayer Books mentioned.
19. *For Vocation in Daily Work.* The Commission took these lessons from its assignments to this theme in The Book of Offices, as revised and approved by General Convention in 1958.

Appendices

1. Biographical and Bibliographical Notes on the Newly Proposed Black Letter Days

Two recent reference works should be added to the General Bibliography in Appendix 4 of *Prayer Book Studies IX: The Calendar*:

Cross, F. L., (ed.), *The Oxford Dictionary of the Christian Church*. New York: Oxford University Press, 1957.

Coulson, John, (ed.), *The Saints, A Concise Biographical Dictionary*. With an Introduction by C. C. Martindale. London: Burns and Oates, 1958.

January 19. WULFSTAN, Bishop of Worcester, 1095

Born in Warwickshire *ca.* 1009; monk and prior at Worcester, and Bishop of the see, 1062-95; died Jan. 18,1095; canonized 1203. Commemorated in the Sarum, English 1928, Scottish, and South African Calendars, on January 19th.

Wulfstan, one of the few Anglo-Saxon bishops to retain his see after the Norman Conquest, throughout his long life as monk and bishop was beloved and respected by all classes of society for his humility, charity, and courage. The Normans at first tended to disparage his lack of learning and his inability to speak "French"; but he remained loyal in support of both William I and II in their work of reform and orderly government. William the Conqueror came to respect his integrity and to appreciate a loyalty based on principle rather than self-seeking subservience. Archbishop Lanfranc also recognized the strength of Wulfstan's character, and the two men worked together harmoniously and successfully to end the traffic at Bristol of kidnapping Englishmen and selling them as slaves in Ireland. The devotion of the English people to his memory was officially sanctioned by the great Pope Innocent III, who canonized Wulfstan in 1203.

The *Life* written by Coleman, a monk of Worcester, was rendered into Latin by William of Malmesbury (and is edited by R. R. Darlington for the Camden Society, 3rd Series, Vol. 40, 1928; English version by J. H. F. Peile, Oxford: Basil Blackwood, 1934). See also John W. Lamb, *Saint Wulstan, Prelate and Patriot, A Study of his Life and Times* (S.P.C.K., 1933).

January 20. FABIAN, Bishop of Rome, and Martyr, 250

In 235 the Roman Emperor Maximin instituted a sudden persecution of the Church in Rome, and banished to Sardinia the Bishop Pontian and the learned presbyter Hippolytus, who there suffered what the Church accounted martyrdom. Pontian's successor lived less than two months, and on January 10, 236, Fabian was elected bishop by acclamation. Eusebius tells us that Fabian's election was a miracle of divine grace, for, being a countryman and not among the distinguished candidates, Fabian was not considered until

> all of a sudden, they relate, a dove flew down from above and settled on his head, in clear imitation of the descent of the Holy Ghost in the form of a dove upon the Saviour; whereupon the whole people, as if moved by one divine inspiration, with all eagerness and with one soul cried out "worthy," and without more ado took him and placed him on the episcopal throne.

We know little of Fabian's pontificate except that he was responsible for the administrative and parochial structure of the Roman Church and the organization of the cultus of the martyrs at their shrines in the catacombs. When the Emperor Decius launched the first general persecution of the Church in the winter of 249-50, Bishop Fabian was his first victim. By his martyrdom he set an example for the whole Church, in what proved to be one of its most terrible ordeals. St. Cyprian, in speaking of it, said that Decius once remarked that he preferred facing a rival for his own imperial office to having a Christian bishop established at Rome. Fabian is commemorated in the Roman, Sarum, English, Scottish, and South African Calendars.

All our information about Fabian is contained in the *Church History* of Eusebius, vi. 29-39, a sixth century history of the popes known as the *Liber Pontificalis*, and passing references in St. Cyprian's correspondence.

February 5. THE MARTYRS OF JAPAN

The Nippon Sei Ko Kai adopted this commemoration in its Calendar (1959) as an inclusive festival of all those who have given their lives for the Christian faith in Japan. Specifically the date is that of the first martyrs, six Spanish Franciscans and twenty of their Japanese converts, who were crucified at Nagasaki on February 5, 1597. The Roman Calendar also includes these martyrs.

The introduction of Christianity into Japan in the 16th century, first by the Jesuits under Francis Xavier, and then by the Franciscans, has left one of the exciting records of heroism and self-sacrifice in the annals of Christian missionary endeavor. Its initial successes were unfortunately soon compromised by a complicated power struggle that involved not only the differing methods of the missionary religious Orders, but also the interplay of power politics both within Japan and between Japan and the western penetration of the Far East by Portuguese and Spanish adventures. After a half century of ambiguous support by some of the powerful Tokugawa shoguns, the Christian enterprise suffered violent and cruel persecution and suppression, partly religious and partly political in motivation. Japan was sealed off from further "foreign" communication until the middle of the 19th century. As told by Miss Leonora Lea:

> Every conceivable kind of torture was employed. The worst persecutions took place in and around Nagasaki, which had been the main stronghold of Christianity. Very few recanted and many simple folk, although instructed very sketchily in the tenets of the faith, died a martyr's death with great courage.
>
> The final blow to Christianity occurred when many Christians joined a civil rebellion in the hope of regaining freedom. The rebellious army was surrounded and defeated, and the remaining Christians went "underground." They were without priests, yet, two hundred and fifty years later, men and women were found who had preserved, although in a corrupted form, the Christian Faith. (*Window on Japan*, Seabury Press, 1956, p. 8.)

In addition to Miss Lea's work, one may find a brief (though less sympathetic) account in Henry St. George Tucker, *The History of the Episcopal Church in Japan* (Scribner's, 1938). A recent Roman Catholic narrative is Joseph Jennes, C.I.C.M., *History of The Catholic Church in Japan* (Missionary Bulletin Series No. 8; Tokyo: The Committee of the Apostolate, 1959). See also K. S. Latourette, *A History of the Expansion of Christianity*, Vol. III (Harpers, 1939), pp. 322-35.

March 2. CHAD, Bishop of Lichfield, 672

Of Anglo-Saxon birth, trained at Lindisfarne by St. Aidan; Abbot of Lastingham, 664, and Bishop of York, 664-69; Bishop of Lichfield, 669 until his death, March 2, 672. Commemorated in the Sarum, English, Scottish, South African, and Canadian Calendars.

Chad is one of the most lovable characters of all the many attractive saints known to us from Bede's history of the evangelization of England. With his brother Cedd (later Bishop of London), he was one of the Anglo-Saxon youths of promise selected by St. Aidan in training an indigenous ministry for the Anglo-Saxons. He succeeded his brother as Abbot of Lastingham, and in the same year (664) King Oswy appointed him Bishop of Northumbria, with his see at York, during the absence of Wilfrid. The see of Canterbury being vacant, Chad was consecrated by the Bishop of Winchester and two British bishops. When Theodore of Tarsus came to England as Archbishop four years later, and engaged himself to the reorganization of the English Church, he removed Chad on the grounds of a defective consecration and as an intruder in the see of York. But he was so impressed by Chad's character and humility that he reconsecrated him to the episcopate and placed him in charge of Mercia, with his see at Lichfield, and gave him a horse to get him about his large diocese. The reply of Chad to Theodore, when the latter questioned his Orders, is famous — and a revealing indication of his saintly character: "If you know I have not duly received episcopal ordination, I willingly resign the office, for I never thought myself worthy of it; but, though unworthy, in obedience submitted to undertake it."

Of Chad's reputation for holiness, and the love and admiration that he won for himself, we are indebted to Bede's narrative, iii. 23 and iv. 2-3. Even Wilfrid's biographer, Eddius Stephanus, who had no special reason to like Chad, testified that he was "a deeply pious servant of God and admirable teacher." See his *Life of Wilfrid*, xiv-xv (edited with translation and notes by B. Colgrave, Cambridge University Press, 1927, pp. 30-33).

March 3. JOHN AND CHARLES WESLEY, Priests, 1791, 1788

John Wesley: Born at Epworth, June 17, 1703, fifteenth child of Rev. Samuel and Susanna Wesley; educated at Charter-house and Christ Church, Oxford;

ordained Deacon, Sept. 19, 1725, Priest, Sept. 22, 1728; Fellow of Lincoln College, Oxford, 1726; curate to his father at Epworth, 1727-29; S.P.G. missionary in Georgia, 1735-37; conversion experience, May 24, 1738; died in London, March 2, 1791.

Charles Wesley: Born at Epworth, Dec. 18, 1707; eighteenth child of Rev. Samuel and Susanna Wesley; educated at Westminster School and Christ Church, Oxford; ordained Deacon and Priest, 1735; in Georgia as secretary to General Oglethorpe, 1736; conversion experience, May 21, 1738; died in London, March 29, 1788.

Both John and Charles Wesley are commemorated in the Canadian Calendar, with Chad, on March 2nd.

The fame of the Wesley brothers is in all the Churches and needs no recounting. Their religious stature increases with the passing years, and the genius of John, in particular, evokes ever-new tributes from Roman Catholic no less than from Anglican and Protestant scholars. Together with their friend George Whitefield, their leadership of the Methodist revival movement revitalized Christianity in 18th century England, and the effects of it are still felt throughout the world and in all Churches.

The lives, fortunes, and interests of the two brothers were closely intertwined throughout their careers. Both men were deeply learned, devout sacramentalists (and accounted High Churchmen by 18th century standards), and extraordinarily effective preachers. Though their theological writings and sermons are still widely read and appreciated, it is in their hymns (and especially those of Charles, who wrote some 6000 of them and more) that their own religious experience and their grasp of basic Christian theology continue to live in the hearts of thousands. Both men were profoundly attached to the doctrine and worship of the Church of England, and both died in this faith. But John in his later years became much more tolerant and open-minded towards other Christian traditions than did his brother. No amount of abuse and opposition to their cause and methods of evangelism, on the part of the established clergy of the Church, ever shook their confidence in and love of the English Church. They lived to see their mission vindicated and their indefatigable itinerancy (John averaged 8000 miles a year travel on horseback) rewarded. At his death, John Wesley was without question the most famous and venerated man in England.

The schism of the Methodists from the Church of England was not desired by John and it was bitterly opposed by Charles; in actuality, the formal break came after their deaths. But John's uncanonical ordinations undoubtedly set the basis for it — and more quickly in America than in England. On the other hand, many of their disciples remained steadfast in the Church of England, to revive the Evangelical tradition; and their piety and sacramentalism were also factors in the background of the 19th century Oxford Movement. The Wesleys always had supporters in high places in the Church; but the explosive character of John's religious genius was too long in being appreciated by the leadership of the Church as a whole.

The withdrawal of the Methodists from the Anglican fold, both in England and in America, must be accounted a judgment upon the established Church.

The literature on the Wesleys is enormous, but all accounts depend primarily upon the writings of the men themselves, especially their Journals. The latest edition of John's Journal has been edited by Nehemiah Curnock, 8 vols., (Epworth Press, 1938). A useful synopsis is *A Compend of Wesley's Theology*, edited by Robert W. Burtner and Robert E. Chiles (Abingdon Press, 1954). A very human and humane biography of both brothers is that of Mabel R. Brailsford, *A Tale of Two Brothers* (London: Rupert Hart-Davis, 1954). Among the many standard studies may be named: John W. Bready, *England Before and After Wesley* (Hodder and Stoughton, 1938); Leslie F. Church, *The Early Methodist People and More About the Early Methodist People* (Epworth Press, 1949) ; Horton Davies, *Worship and Theology in England from Watts and Wesley to Maurice, 1690-1850* (Princeton University Press, 1961); Maximin Piette, *John Wesley in the Evolution of Protestantism* (Sheed and Ward, 1938); J. E. Rattenbury, *The Evangelical Doctrines of Charles Wesley's Hymns* (Epworth Press, 1941), and *The Eucharistic Hymns of John and Charles Wesley* (Epworth Press, 1948); Martin Schmidt, *John Wesley, A Theological Biography*, Vol. 1 (Epworth Press, 1962).

March 9. GREGORY, Bishop of Nyssa, c. 394

Born in Caesarea, Cappadocia, *ca.* 334; consecrated by his brother Basil as Bishop of Nyssa, 372; present at the Second Ecumenical Council of Constantinople, 381; died *ca.* 394. He is commemorated in the Eastern Church on January 10th; in the West he is remembered on March 9th, the date of the Roman Martyrology.

Gregory's name is inevitably linked with that of his older brother Basil and their friend Gregory of Nazianzus — the trio known commonly as the "Cappadocian Fathers," whose writings and labors did more than anything else to assure the triumph of Nicene orthodoxy over the Arian heresy. Gregory had neither the administrative genius of his brother, nor the oratorical power of his friend of Nazianzus. He was a student, not a man of the world, an acute philosopher and a mystical interpreter of Scripture. The Eastern Churches have always accounted him one of their major theological giants. In recent years a revival of interest in and appreciation of Gregory's work has been steadily growing — in part due to the monumental and critical work done on his writings by the late Professor Werner Jaeger of Harvard University and his associates. Another factor has been a better recognition of his deep influence upon Christian mysticism.

An excellent bibliographical guide to the study of Gregory and the many facets of his intellectual and spiritual genius is now available in Johannes Quasten, *Patrology*, Vol. III (Newman Press, 1960), pp. 254-96. The largest collection of his works in English translation continues to be Vol. V of the *Nicene and Post-Nicene Fathers*, Second Series. Two of his works, prefaced by a helpful introduction, have been translated by Prof. C. C. Richardson for *Christology of the Later Fathers*, edited by E. R. Hardy (The Library of Christian Classics, Vol. III; Westminster Press, 1954), pp. 235-325. His classic sermons on the Lord's Prayer have been translated and annotated by Hilda C. Graef (Ancient Christian Writers, 18; Newman Press, 1954); and selections from his mystical writings have recently been published by Jean Danielou and Herbert Musurillo, *From Glory to Glory* (Scribner's, 1962). The old biography of Edmund Venables in the *Dictionary of Christian Biography* (1880), II, 761-68, is still useful and reliable.

March 18. CYRIL, Bishop of Jerusalem, 386

Born *ca.* 315; consecrated Bishop of Jerusalem, 348; three times banished from his see, 357-58, 360-62, 367-78; present at the Second Ecumenical Council of Constantinople, 381; died, March 18, 386. He is commemorated on this date in the Roman, Scottish, South African, Indian, and Japanese Calendars.

Modern study has exonerated Cyril from the taint of Arianism, even though he was made Bishop of Jerusalem by leader of the Arian party. In fact, he was little interested in the partisan conflicts of his time, and his three banishments from his see are indication that he was not accounted a loyal supporter of the Arian cause. However, it is his great series of catechetical lectures on the Creed that prove beyond doubt his soundness in the faith; they are a major monument of fourth century exposition of Catholic truth. Cyril's other great claim to fame rests upon his imaginative development of the liturgy at Jerusalem, where his dramatic services connected with the holy places exercised a powerful influence upon the whole Church by reason of the many pilgrims who flocked to Palestine after the time of Constantine. In particular, many of the observances in Holy Week still in use today go back to Cyril's enrichments of the Church's liturgical practices.

The *Catechetical Lectures* are translated in Vol. VII of the Nicene and Post-Nicene Fathers, Second Series; and selections from them, with a fine introduction, by William Telfer, *Cyril of Jerusalem and Nemesius of Emesa* (The Library of Christian Classics, Vol. IV; Westminster Press, 1955). For his liturgical work, one should also consult the useful edition of the lectures on the sacraments, edited by F. L. Cross (Texts for Students. No. 51; S.P.C.K., 1951), and the relevant pages in Gregory Dix, *The Shape of the Liturgy* (Dacre Press, 1945), pp. 187-203, 349-54. A standard biography is still Edmund Venables in *The Dictionary of Christian Biography* (1880), I, 760-63.

March 20. CUTHBERT, Bishop of Lindisfarne, 687

Born *ca.* 625; monk and prior of Melrose, 651-64; prior of Lindisfarne, 664-76, after which he lived as a recluse on the Isle of Farne, 676-84; appointed Bishop of Hexham, 684, but made his see at Lindisfarne, following his consecration on Easter Day, 685; retired to Farne, 686, where he died March 20, 687. His feast is listed in the Sarum, English 1928, Scottish, South African, and Canadian Calendars.

Cuthbert was the popular saint of the English Church in Anglo-Saxon times; and during the troubled period of the Scandinavian invasions, the monks of Lindisfarne carefully protected his relics during their several wanderings, until they found a final resting place at Durham. There one may see today the surviving treasures of his shrine and tomb.

Though an Anglo-Saxon by birth, Cuthbert's religious training was entirely formed in the austere and learned asceticism of the Celtic tradition, and throughout his life he followed in his personal piety its rigorous discipline. He accepted, however, the decisions of the Synod of Whitby; and by reason of his holiness of life and sweetness of disposition he became a "healer of the breach" that threatened to divide the Church in Northumbria into Celtic and Roman factions. Archbishop Theodore, so different from Cuthbert in his traditions and disciplines, recognized the greatness of Cuthbert's character and capacity, and consecrated him to the episcopate, despite Cuthbert's strong reluctance to undertake the office. His term as bishop, though brief, was diligently and effectively fulfilled, and the whole English Church mourned his death as the loss of a true "Father in God." Even though the ascetic rigor of Cuthbert's life may seem strange and at times bizarre to modern taste, his winsome and utterly unselfish personality remains unsullied and appealing, to our continual edification.

The best edition and translation of the two contemporary accounts of Cuthbert's career, one by Bede, the other anonymous, is that of Bertram Colgrave, *Two Lives of Saint Cuthbert* (Cambridge University Press, 1940). A synopsis of his life is given by Bede in his *Ecclesiastical History*, iv. 27-32. All studies of the English Church of this period devote attention to Cuthbert — the latest is Margaret Deansley, *The Pre-Conquest Church in England* (Oxford University Press, 1961), pp. 114-22. One should not overlook, however, the magnificent commemorative volume edited by C. F. Battiscombe, *The Relics of Saint Cuthbert* (Oxford University Press, 1956).

March 22. JAMES DE KOVEN, Priest, 1879

Born in Middletown, Conn., Sept. 19, 1831; graduate of Columbia College, 1851, and the General Theological Seminary, 1854; Deacon, 1854, Priest, 1855; Rector of St. John Chrysostom's, Delafield, Wis., and Tutor in Ecclesiastical History, Nashotah House, 1855-59; Warden of Racine College, 1859 until his death,

March 19, 1879. He is commemorated by the Sisters of St. Mary at Kenosha and Racine, on March 22nd, the day of his burial at Racine.

Dr. De Koven has left a permanent stamp upon the learning and piety of the Episcopal Church, through his reasoned and compelling defense of its Catholic heritage, especially in the General Conventions of 1868-77. In the troubled conflicts of partisan strife that marred the life of the Church in the generation following the Tractarian Movement, Dr. De Koven more than any other figure achieved acceptance by the Church of its comprehensive principle so as to include the revived Catholic emphases that have so enriched the doctrine, worship, and spirituality of us all. He won his cause through the unquestioned integrity and holiness of his character. Had his views not been so controversial at the time, he would undoubtedly have been made a bishop. He narrowly missed election in Massachusetts in 1873 and in Wisconsin in 1874. The following year he was elected Bishop of Illinois, but the majority of the Standing Committees refused to ratify the choice. His memory is still keenly felt today, especially on the grounds of the old Racine College, which he served with distinction as Warden for twenty years — now known as the De Koven Foundation, an important conference center of the Church.

Dr. De Koven's *Sermons Preached on Various Occasions* were edited with a memoir by Morgan Dix (D. Appleton and Co., 1880). There are brief memoirs by K. J. Gallagher in the *Dictionary of American Biography*, V (1930), 205-06, and by F. C. Morehouse, *Some American Churchmen* (Milwaukee: The Young Churchman Co., 1892), pp. 157-234. One should also consult the pertinent pages in E. C. Chorley, *Men and Movements in the American Episcopal Church* (Scribner's, 1946), and in G. E. DeMille, *The Catholic Movement in the American Episcopal Church* (2nd ed.; Church Historical Society, 1950).

March 31. JOHN DONNE, Priest, 1631

Born in London, 1573; educated at Oxford and Cambridge; ordained Deacon and Priest, 1615; Vicar of Keyston, Hunts., Rector of Sevenoaks, and reader in divinity at Lincoln's Inn, 1616-22; Dean of St. Paul's Cathedral, London, 1622 until his death, March 31, 1631. Donne's name has not hitherto appeared on any Calendar.

Our own generation has witnessed a remarkable revival of interest in Donne, not only as a pre-eminent literary artist of an age that produced many distinguished men of letters, but more especially for the theological and ethical penetration of his poetry and his sermons. His story is of a man drawn as it were by divine grace through intense spiritual suffering from worldliness to holiness. In a way he reminds one of St. Augustine, and especially in his honest wrestling with and psychological insight into the paradoxical and complex predicament of man as he both seeks and yet draws away from the inescapable claim of God upon him. The artistry and learning, indeed the refined contrivance of his style — so characteristic of his period and culture — cannot hide the tremendous passion and exaltation, the compassion and depth of surrender that make his preaching as exciting today as it was to his astounded hearers. Donne cannot be readily classified by neat theological categories. The fashion today is to call him an existentialist. One suspects, however, that there is yet much to be unveiled to our profit from the deep and profound searchings of his mind and heart into the ultimate realities of life and death in the face of judgment and grace.

The Sermons of John Donne have in the past decade received a definitive edition in ten volumes by Evelyn M. Simpson and George R. Potter (Berkeley: University of California Press). A selection of them, with a stimulating introduction, has been edited by Theodore A. Gill in a paperback of Meridian Books, Inc. (Living Age Books, 1958). The standard study of Donne is that of Edmund Gosse, *The Life and Letters of John Donne* (2 vols.; Dodd, Mead and Co., 1899); but enthusiasts will always want to go to the biography of Donne's friend and admirer, Izaak Walton, first published in 1640. See also Evelyn Hardy, *Donne, A Spirit in Conflict* (Constable and Co., 1942); M. F. Moloney, *John Donne, His Flight from Medievalism* (University of Illinois Press, 1944); and W. R. Mueller, *John Donne: Preacher* (Princeton University Press, 1962). Other editions of value: *John Donne: Essays in Divinity*, edited by Evelyn M. Simpson (Oxford, 1952); *John Donne: The Divine Poems*, edited by Helen Gardner (Oxford, 1952).

April 3. RICHARD, Bishop of Chichester, 1253

Born at Wyche (Droitwich), 1197; educated at Oxford and Paris; chancellor of Oxford, 1235, and in same year, of Canterbury diocese; in exile with Archbishop Edmund Rich; elected Bishop of Chichester, 1244, but — due to opposition of the King — consecrated by Pope Innocent IV at Lyons, March 1245; died at Dover, April 3, 1253; canonized by Pope Urban IV, 1262; his tomb in Chichester Cathedral a shrine for pilgrims until destroyed by King Henry VIII. Richard is in the Sarum, English, South African, Canadian, and Japanese Calendars.

Richard of Wyche has been described as one of the models "of the medieval type of saint, severely ascetic, profuse in almsgiving, indifferent to worldly honour, fearless in reproving wickedness and wrong-doing in high places, happiest in seclusion, study, and devotion." Though a scholar of eminence, he was also an excellent administrator, and did much to raise the standards of the clergy in his diocese. The ablest men of the Church in his day, such as Archbishop Rich and the great Bishop Grosseteste of Lincoln, supported him successfully against the King's unworthy and political appointee for the see of Chichester. It was characteristic of his interests that he willed his property to "poor religious houses, hospitals, roads and bridges, widows and orphans."

Good biographies may be found in the *Dictionary of National Biography*, and in Ollard, Crosse, and Bond's *A Dictionary of English Church History*; see also M. R. Capes, *Richard of Wyche* (1913).

April 19. ALPHEGE, Archbishop of Canterbury, and Martyr, 1012

Born 954 — name in Anglo-Saxon, Aelfheah; monk of Deerhurst, then abbot of Bath; Bishop of Winchester, 984-1005; Archbishop of Canterbury, 1005-12; murdered by the Danes at Greenwich, April 19, 1012, and buried in St. Paul's London; body translated to Canterbury, July 1023. His commemoration is in the Sarum, English, Scottish, South African, and Canadian Calendars.

Alphege's leadership in the English Church was set in the troubled time of the second wave of Scandinavian invasion and settlement in England. In 994, when Bishop of Winchester, he was instrumental in bringing the Norse King Olaf Tryggvason (but recently baptized) to King Aethelred at Andover, to make his peace and be confirmed. When the Danes overran Canterbury in 1011, the Archbishop was captured with many other notables, but refused to allow his ransom to be collected from his already over-burdened people. After seven months of imprisonment he was brutally murdered — despite the efforts of the viking commander, Thorkell, who offered all his possessions except his ship for the archbishop's life. The story is given in the Anglo-Saxon Chronicle, which relates that the Danish invaders were "much stirred against the bishop, because he would not promise them any fee, and forbade that any man should give anything for him. They were also much drunken ... Then took they the bishop, and led him to their hustings, on the eve of the Saturday after Easter... and there they then shamefully killed him. They overwhelmed him with bones and horns of oxen; and one of them smote him with an axe-iron on the head; so that he sunk downwards with the blow; and his holy blood fell on the earth, whilst his sacred soul was sent to the realm of God."

Alphege's life may be read in any of the standard dictionaries of biography and church history, or accounts of the Anglo-Saxon Church; see also references in T. D. Kendrick, *A History of the Vikings* (Scribner's, 1930), and in E. S. Duckett, *Saint Dunstan of Canterbury* (W. W. Norton and Co., Inc., 1955) — for Dunstan was instrumental in placing Alphege in the see of Winchester.

April 30. CATHERINE OF SIENA, 1380

Born Catherine Benincasa, in Siena, March 25, 1347; entered the Third Order of St. Dominic as a Sister of Penitence, 1366; died in Rome on the Sunday before Ascension, April 29, 1380; canonized by Pope Pius II, 1461. Catherine is listed on the 30th of April in the Roman, English 1928, Scottish, South African, Indian, Japanese Calendars, and was included in the proposed Calendar for the 1928 American Book. She is the Patron Saint of Italy.

Catherine of Siena, among medieval saints, can only be compared with Bernard of Clairvaux, both in the ardor of her mystical and ascetic devotion and in the strenuous activity in good works both for individuals and for the Church in which she was tirelessly engaged. Her visions began in early childhood, exciting both suspicion and admiration among her family and spiritual directors. The *Dialogue*, or *Book of Divine Doctrine*, one of the supreme works of mystical experience, was dictated in a state of ecstasy; as a literary masterpiece of symbolism, it has been compared with Dante's *Divine Comedy*. Her letters, nearly 400 in number, have also won acclaim as literature, and are a mirror of the political and religious life of her age, being addressed to persons in all ranks from popes and kings to the humblest individuals. She gave many hours of service to the sick, the poor, and the plague-ridden, and many months of labor in embassies on high matters of Church and State. She was largely responsible for persuading Pope Gregory XI to return to Rome and bring an end to the "Avignon Captivity," but the outbreak of the Great Schism, shortly after Gregory's death, broke her heart and hastened her end. Like Francis, she received the stigmata, but revealed the experience only to her confessor.

Her *Life*, by her confessor, Blessed Raymund of Capua, has been translated into English by George Lamb (London: Havrill Press, 1960). The *Dialogue*, translated in an abridged edition by Algar Thorold, was published by The Newman Bookshop in 1943. For the letters, see Vida D. Scudder (ed.), *Saint Catherine of Siena as Seen in Her Letters* (J. M. Dent and Co., 1911). There are many modern biographies — among them: Edmund G. Gardner, *Saint Catherine of Siena* (Dutton, 1907); Alice Curtayne, *Saint Catherine of Siena* (Sheed and Ward, 1935); Johannes Jorgensen, *Saint Catherine of Siena* (Longmans, Green and Co., 1938); and Sigrid Undset, *Catherine of Siena* (Sheed and Ward, 1954). There is a magnificent contemporary portrait of her by Andrea Vanni in the Dominican Church in Siena.

July 26. THE PARENTS OF THE BLESSED VIRGIN MARY

Traditions of SS. Joachim and Anne are first recorded in apocryphal gospels of the second century; in 550 Justinian I dedicated the first church to St. Anne in Constantinople; the cultus became popular in the West from the eighth century, and was fixed on July 26 by Pope Urban in 1378 — the day following the Eastern commemoration. Anne is listed in the Sarum, English, Scottish, Canadian, South African, and Japanese Calendars. The present Roman Calendar assigns Joachim an individual feast on August 16.

The apocryphal accounts of St. Mary's parents are highly legendary and of little historical worth, though the names of Joachim and Anne may rest on good tradition. Actually, these early apocryphal stories are primarily concerned with the life of St. Mary herself, and only incidentally with her parents the legends reflecting in many details the Biblical narratives of the births of Isaac, Samuel, and St. John the Baptist. It is a natural development of Christian piety to surround the memory of our Lord's mother, the chief of all the saints, with the background of a devout and religious home. St. Anne has become one of the most popular of saints, to whom many churches, homes, hospitals, guilds and societies have been dedicated.

The earliest traditions are contained in the apocryphal gospel known as the *Protevangelium of James*, a second century document — English translation in M. R. James, *The Apocryphal New Testament* (Oxford, 1924), pp. 38-49. Brief critical accounts may be found in the *Dictionary of Christian Biography* (1877), I, 116-18, and the *Dictionary of Christian Antiquities* (1880), I, 90-91. There is much incidental information about the history of the cultus of Joachim and Anne in the dissertation of Sister Mary J. Kishpaugh, O.P., *The Feast of the Presentation of the Virgin Mary in the Temple, An Historical and Literary Study* (Catholic University of America Press, 1941).

July 29. SAINTS MARY AND MARTHA OF BETHANY

The origin of the cultus of these friends of our Lord cannot be securely traced. Their names, with that of their brother Lazarus, appear on differing dates in the martyrologies of the seventh—eighth centuries. About the same time, piety began to confuse St. Mary of Bethany with St. Mary Magdalene (July 22). There is no definite evidence of a cult of the latter in Rome before the thirteenth century, the date being that of the Eastern Church. Possibly the commemoration of Martha on the 29th was related to that of the 22nd as a sort of Octave. The modern Roman Calendar has Martha alone on the 29th, and in this is followed by the Indian Calendar. The South African Calendar observes both Mary and Martha on the 30th.

All that we know with certainty about Mary and Martha is found in the Gospels: Luke 10:38-42, and John 11:1-12:8.

There is no warrant for linking Mary either with St. Mary Magdalene or with the "woman that was a sinner" (Luke 7:36-50). John's identification of the woman who anointed Jesus before His Passion (cf. Mark 14:3-9) with Mary of Bethany is accepted by many critics. What is important for devotion is the study of the characters of the two women, so deftly drawn by Luke — less so by John. Yet one should not overly exaggerate them as types of the "active" (Martha) and the "contemplative" (Mary) spirit. Both types of response to Jesus are legitimate, and both need each other for full and complete discipleship. It is perhaps an especially grateful reason for the remembrance of these women, that they provided our Lord with a home where he could find all the refreshment, whether spiritual or physical, that is the gift and blessing of unfeigned and loving friends.

July 31. SAINT JOSEPH OF ARIMATHAEA

St. Joseph occurs in the Eastern Calendar on this date. He is not listed in the Roman, nor in any other Anglican Calendars. The Roman Martyrology records him on March 17.

All that is certainly known about St. Joseph of Arimathaea comes to us from the single narratives in the Gospels of the burial of our Lord. Though St. John speaks of him as a secret "disciple" of Jesus and associates him with Nicodemus — another member of the Jewish Sanhedrin who was drawn to Jesus — we know nothing of any subsequent activity of these eminent men in the early Christian community. Later legends, however, were developed about their leadership in the Church — none more affecting than that of Joseph's coming to the ancient church of Glastonbury in Britain and bringing the Holy Grail. This tradition cannot be traced prior to the thirteenth century. (See J. Armitage Robinson, *Two Glastonbury Legends*, 1926.)

St. Joseph's claim upon our grateful remembrance does not need the embroidery of legend, however beautiful and romantic. At a time when others, even Jesus' most intimate disciples, were in hiding for fear of the authorities, St. Joseph came forward boldly and courageously to do not only what was demanded of Jewish piety but to act generously and humanely in saving our Lord's broken and wounded body from further desecration and in providing for its decent and proper burial.

August 12. CLARE OF ASSISI, Abbess, 1253

Born in Assisi, 1194; joined Francis' movement in 1212, at the Portiuncula, and made a Benedictine nun; became Abbess of the "Poor Clares," 1215; died at Assisi, 7253; canonized two years later by Pope Alexander IV. In addition to her entry in the Roman Calendar on this date, her name has also been adopted in the Japanese Calendar.

The response of Santa Clara to the preaching of Francis, her care and devotion to his ideals, and her valiant life-long (and successful) struggle to maintain those ideals for her order of Poor Clares, form one of the heroic and inspiring chapters in the history of the Friars Minor. None of Francis' disciples showed a more profound understanding of and sympathy with his total renunciation for Christ's sake than did Clare; and her personal relations with him were a model of pure and selfless love in Christ. As Sabatier remarked, it was at Clare's convent of St. Damian's "that St. Francis is the most himself." There "under the shade of its olive-trees, with Clara caring for him, . . . he composes his finest work . . . the 'Canticle of the Sun.'"

All the sources and secondary works concerning Francis provide information about Clare. Her "Life," attributed to Thomas of Celano, the contemporary biographer of Francis, is given in Paschal Robinson's chapter on "St. Clare" in *Franciscan Essays*, edited by Paul Sabatier and others (British Society of Franciscan Studies, Extra Series, Vol. I; Aberdeen University Press, 7972, pp. 31-49). One should also consult Paul Sabatier's gracious chapter on Santa Clara in his standard *Life of St. Francis of Assisi* (Scribner's, 1894), and Miss Vida Scudder's *The Franciscan Adventure* (Dutton, 1931).

September 16. NINIAN, Bishop in Galloway, c. 430

Ninian was never formally canonized, but many church dedications in Scotland attest to his ancient reputation as a saint-founder and missionary among the Celtic peoples of northern Britain. Our principal source of authentic information is a single chapter in Bede's *Ecclesiastical History*, iii. 4, supplemented by an eighth century account of his *Miracula*, and a twelfth century *Life* by Ailred. He is listed in the English, Scottish, South African, and Canadian Calendars.

Ninian's apostolic labors for the gospel covered the area of southern Scotland, south of the Grampian mountains, and antedated by more than a century the work of St. Columba and his Irish associates. Bede places the center of his activity at Candida Casa ("White House" or Whithorn, named from his stone church) in Galloway, dedicated to St. Martin of Tours. From this base much of the tradition and learning of the Church in Gaul and Britain in late Roman times was transmitted to the Celtic and Pictish peoples. When the Anglo-Saxons conquered the area, Whithorn became a bishopric of the English Church. Many of the details of his labors are obscure — and are much debated by historians; but of his significance as a "founder" of Christian mission in Britain at a crucial time of political and cultural transition, there can be no doubt.

Among many modern studies, one may consult W. Douglas Simpson, *Saint Ninian and the Origins of the Christian Church in Scotland* (Oliver and Boyd, 1940); D. D. C. Pochin Mould, *Scotland of the Saints* (Batsford, 1952); and John MacQueen, *St. Nynia, A study of literary and linguistic evidence* (Oliver and Boyd, 1961).

October 1. REMIGIUS, Bishop of Rheims, c. 530

Born *ca.* 438, son of Count of Laon; became Bishop of Rheims at age of twenty-two; baptized the Frankish King Clovis on Christmas Eve, 496. His cult at Rheims is observed on January 13, possibly the day of his death. The date of October 1 in western Calendars derives from a translation of his relics by Pope Leo IX in 1049 to a new abbey-church. He is commemorated in the Roman and Sarum Calendars, and is listed in the English 1928, Scottish, South African, and Canadian Books. "Saint Remi" is one of the three patron saints of France.

Apart from a few extant letters, we know of Remigius' episcopate and early fame chiefly through the Frankish historian, Gregory of Tours (see his *History of the Franks*, ii. 31, translated by O. M. Dalton, Oxford, 1927, II, 69-70). Gregory speaks of his excellent learning, especially in the art of rhetoric, and his exemplary holiness, attested by many miracles. Gregory was sufficiently astute to recognize that Remigius' greatest glory was the baptism of Clovis — an event that changed the religious history not only of France, but of all Europe. By becoming a Catholic instead of an Arian, Clovis was able to unite the Gallo-Roman population and their Christian leaders behind his expanding and expansive hegemony over the Germanic overlords of the West. The conversion also made possible such cooperation as the Franks later gave to Pope Gregory the Great in his evangelistic efforts for the English. The motives behind Clovis' acceptance of Catholic Christianity were doubtless mixed; but there is no doubt about his basic sincerity or the concern given to his preparation for baptism by Bishop Remigius.

A brief but authoritative account of Remigius may be found in the *Dictionary of Christian Biography* IV (1887), 541-42. For the general background see the work of O. M. Dalton on Gregory of Tours, listed above, and also Samuel Dill, *Roman Society in Gaul in the Merovingian Age* (Macmillan, 1926).

October 17. HENRY MARTYN, Priest, and Missionary to India and Persia, 1812

Born at Truro, Feb. 18, 1781; Fellow of St. John's Cambridge, 1802; ordained at Ely, Oct. 22, 1803; chaplain to the East India Company, 1805; died at Tokat, Asia Minor, Oct. 16, 1812. He is commemorated in the South African Calendar.

Henry Martyn was one of the most lovable and dedicated young men whom Charles Simeon inspired to pioneer missionary work in the East. Though his life was cut short, after only seven years of labor in this sphere, his energy and learning left a remarkable legacy for the future in his translations of the Bible and Prayer Book. He made versions of the New Testament in Hindustani, Persian, and Arabic, of the Psalter in Persian, and of the Prayer Book in Hindustani. After his exhausting travels in India and Persia, ill health prevented his going on to Arabia; instead he sought out a better climate in Asia Minor, where he died and was given burial by the Armenian clergy.

His Journals and letters were edited in two volumes by Samuel Wilberforce (1837). There are several biographies, notably that of Constance E. Padwick, *Henry Martyn, Confessor of the Faith* (George H. Doran Co., 1922). For general background, see Eyre Chatterton, *A History of the Church of England in India since the Early Days of the East India Company* (S.P.C.K., 1924).

October 23. SAINT JAMES OF JERUSALEM, Brother of Our Lord Jesus Christ, and Martyr, c. 62

The Eastern Church commemorates our Lord's brother James on this date, and the feast was adopted in the South African and Indian Calendars. The Roman Church, following ancient tradition, identified James with the "other James" among the twelve disciples — James the son of Alphaeus, known often as "St. James the Less," whose feast is associated with Philip on May 1. Modern New Testament scholars are almost unanimous, however, in rejecting this identification, as there is no evidence in the Gospels that our Lord's brother James was a disciple until he became a witness of the Resurrection.

Both the letters of St. Paul and the Book of Acts testify to the pre-eminent position of James in the original Church at Jerusalem in the apostolic age, and his statesmanship in resolving the crucial problem of fellowship between Jew and Gentile in the council held in Jerusalem on this question (cf. Galatians 2 and Acts 15). Though he personally followed Jewish custom and law with great strictness, he accepted without difficulty the freedom of Gentile converts from these traditions, and supported St. Paul in his missionary labors among the heathen. This liberal attitude of James undoubtedly prejudiced the Jews against him, despite his reputation for piety; and James, like other apostles, was a martyr for his faith, being stoned by the Jews about the year 62. (We possess for his martyrdom not only Christian traditions, but the explicit testimony of the Jewish historian Josephus.) Not only an apostle and martyr, James was in fact, if not in name, the first "Bishop" of the Church, and the succession of bishops in the Church at Jerusalem looked back to him as "founder" in the same way that the Roman Church traced its episcopal succession from St. Peter.

November 3. RICHARD HOOKER, Priest, 1600

Born at Heavitree, near Exeter, 1553; admitted to Corpus Christi, Oxford, 1567, and made Fellow, 1577; held living of Drayton-Beauchamp, Bucks., 1582, after ordination; Master of the Temple, 1586; Rector of Boscombe, Salisbury, 1591, and of Bishopsbourne near Canterbury, 1595; died Nov. 2, 1600. Hooker appears in the Canadian Calendar on Nov. 2.

Despite changes of emphasis and perspective that have come since the time of Queen Elizabeth I, the pre-eminence of Hooker among Anglican theologians and apologists shows no sign of losing its place of grandeur. His name would probably stand first in any list of the outstanding writers produced in the Anglican tradition. Even Pope Clement VIII testified to Hooker's *Laws of Ecclesiastical Polity* that the work "had in it such seeds of eternity that it would abide till the last fire shall consume all learning." His *magnum opus* with all its vast learning and vigor of style mirrors nonetheless the moderate, patient, and serene character of the man. As one writer put it, Hooker "rescued theological controversy from the gutter, investing it with a solemn dignity, richness, and grandeur."

There is an inexpensive edition of Hooker's *Polity* in the Everyman Library (2 vols.); the more standard modern edition goes back to John Keble — first edition in 1836 — as revised by Dean Church and Bishop Paget in 1888, in three volumes. Bishop Francis Paget also published *An Introduction to the Fifth Book*, etc. (Oxford, 1899). Among many studies, one may consult: L. S. Thornton, *Richard Hooker, A Study of His Theology* (Macmillan, 1924). F. J. Shirley, *Richard Hooker and Contemporary Political Ideas* (S.P.C.K., i949); Peter Munz, *The Place of Hooker in the History of Thought* (Routledge and Kegan Paul Ltd., 1952); and Gunnar Hillerdal, *Reason and Revelation in Richard Hooker* (Lund: Gleerup, 1962); John S. Marshall, *Hooker and the Anglican Tradition* (Sewanee: The University Press, 1963).

November 17. HUGH, Bishop of Lincoln, 1200

Born at Avalon in Burgundy, *ca.* 1140; canon regular of Grenoble; became Carthusian, 1160, and brought to England by Henry II as prior of Carthusian house at Witham, Somerset; Bishop of Lincoln, 1186 until his death, Nov. 16, 1200. Hugh is listed in the English and Canadian Calendars on the 16th, in the Sarum, Scottish, and South African, on the 17th.

In the later Middle Ages, Hugh's popularity as a saint in England was second only to Becket's. As a Carthusian, he lived, even as a bishop, according to the strictest discipline of his Order. Highly favored and regarded by the crown, Hugh remained absolutely independent of all secular influence — refusing, for example, to raise money from his people for Richard I's wars. Few churchmen of any age have been such stalwart champions of the people, especially the poor and oppressed. His love and care for lepers were noteworthy. He surrounded himself with men of learning as his advisors, and laid the foundations for the noble Gothic cathedral that still stands in Lincoln. King Richard remarked of him, "If only other bishops were like him, no king or prince would ever venture to oppose them!"

The *Magna Vita* of Hugh has recently been edited and translated by Decima L. Dorrie and Dom Hugh Farmer (2 vols.; Thomas Nelson and Sons, 1961-62). There is an older biography by H. Thurston, *The Life of St. Hugh of Lincoln* (1898). and more lately, a gracious sketch by Renee Haynes, in *Saints and Ourselves*, edited by Philip Caraman, S. J. (Second Series; Hollis and Carter, 1955, pp. 18-30). See also the notes in Canon J. H. Srawley's *The Story of Lincoln Minster* (Raphael Tuck and Sons Ltd., 1947); and E. M. Thompson, *The Carthusian Order in England* (S.P.C.K., 1930, pp. 54-70).

2. A Comparative Table of Calendars

The following tables are not a substitute for, but a supplement to and correction of, the tables published in Prayer Book Studies IX. Since that Study was published, the Indian and Canadian Prayer Books have received definitive approval, with certain alterations in the proposed Calendars of their "Draft Books." Meanwhile the Japanese Church has given formal approval to an enlarged Calendar.

In view of these developments, certain of the listings made in the tables of *Prayer Book Studies* IX have been omitted from the following schedules as no longer relevant. In addition we have dropped the listing of additional holy days proposed for the American Book of 1928, as not likely to be revived.

The entries include only those contained in official Anglican Prayer Books (plus the list of the English Proposed Book of 1928), with a comparison of these entries in so far as they may be found also in the Roman and Sarum Calendars. The notations from the Roman Calendar have been brought into accord with the revision of that Calendar promulgated in 1960 (see above, page 10).

JANUARY

Day	Feast	Proposed	English 1928	Scottish 1929	South African 1954	Japanese 1959	Indian 1961	Canadian 1962	Sarum	Roman 1960
1	HOLY NAME OF JESUS	X				X				
	OCTAVE OF CHRISTMAS							X		X
	CIRCUMCISION		X	X	X		X	X	X	
2	Holy name of Jesus [1]									X
3										
4	Titus [2]				X					
5										
6	THE EPIPHANY	X	X	X	X	X	X	X	X	X
7										
8	Lucian								X	
9										
10	William Laud	X			X			X		
11	David of Scotland			X						
12	Benedict Biscop				X			X		
	John Horden							X		
13	Octave of Epiphany							X		
	Institution of Baptism [3]						X			
	Kentigern			X						X
	Hilary		X	X	X			X	X	
14	Hilary	X				X				X

JANUARY (continued)

15									
16									
17	Antony	X	X	X		X		X	
18									
19	Wulfstan	X	X	X				X	
	Henry (of Finland)					X			
20	Fabian [4]	X	X	X	X		X	X	
21	Agnes	X	X	X	X	X	X	X	
22	Vincent	X	X	XX		X	X	X	
23	Phillips Brooks	X							
24	Saint Timothy [5]	X	X	X	X	X	X	X	
25	THE CONVERSION OF ST. PAUL	X	X	X	X	X	X	X	
26	Polycarp	X	X	X	X	X	X		
27	John Chrysostom	X	X	X	X	X	X		
28									
29									
30	King Charles I		X			X			
31									

1. Roman on 2nd Sunday after Christmas or Jan. 2.
2. See Jan. 24 and Feb. 6
3. Roman observes Baptism of Our Lord.
4. With Sebastian, in Roman, Sarum, and South African.
5. With Titus in Canadian.

FEBRUARY

Day	Feast	Proposed	English 1928	Scottish 1929	South African 1954	Japanese 1959	Indian 1961	Canadian 1962	Sarum	Roman 1960
1	Bride			X					X	
2	Ignatius of Antioch [1]	X				X				X
3	PURIFICATION	X	X	X	X	X	X	X	X	X
4	Ansgarius	X	X		X			X		
	Cornelius	X								
	Gilbert of Sempringham				X					
5	Agatha				X				X	X
6	Saint Titus [2]	X		X			X			X
7										
8										
9										
10										
11	Finnian			X						
	Caedmon					X		X		
	Organization Nippon Sei Ko Kai									
12										
13										

The Calendar and The Collects, Epistles, and Gospels for the Lesser Feasts and Fasts 45

FEBRUARY (continued)

Day	Name	1	2	3	4	5	6	7	8	9
14	Valentine			X			X		X	X
15	Thomas Bray	X								
16										
17	Finan		X							
18	Colman		X							
19										
20	African Missionaries and Martyrs			X						
21										
22										
23	Lindel Tsen; Paul Sasaki						X			
24	MATTHIAS	X	X	X		X	X	X	X	
25										
26										
27	George Herbert	X		X			X			
28										
29										

1. See December 17.
2. See Jan. 4 and 24.

MARCH

Day	Feast	Proposed	English 1928	Scottish 1929	South African 1954	Japanese 1959	Indian 1961	Canadian 1962	Sarum	Roman 1960
1	David	X	X	X	X		X	X	X	
	Marnan (Ernin)			X						
2	Chad	X	X	X	X			X	X	
	John and Charles Wesley									
3	John and Charles Wesley	X								
4										
5										
6	Baldred			X						
	Perpetua and Felicitas							X		X
7	Perpetua and Felicitas	X	X	X	X	X	X		X	
	Thomas Aquinas							X		X
8	Thomas Aquinas	X		X	X	X	X			
9	Gregory of Nyssa	X								
10	Kessog			X						
11										
12	Gregory the Great	X	X	X	X	X	X	X	X	X
13										
14										
15										
16										

MARCH (continued)

17	Patrick	X	X	X	X	X	X	X	X	X
18	Cyril of Jerusalem	X		X	X	X	X		X	X
19	Saint Joseph	X		X	X	X	X	X		X
	Thomas Ken [1]					X	X			
20	Cuthbert	X	X	X	X			X	X	
21	Benedict of Nursia [2]		X	X	X	X	X		X	X
	Thomas Cranmer [3]						X			
	Thomas Ken [1]	X								
22	James DeKoven	X								
23	Gregory the Illuminator	X								
24										
25	ANNUNCIATION	X	X	X	X	X	X	X	X	X
26										
27	John of Damascus [4]									X
28										
29	John Keble	X			X			X		
30										
31	John Donne	X								

1. Cf. March 19 and 21.
2. See July 11.
3. See Proposed for June 10.
4. See Dec. 5.

APRIL

Day	Feast	Proposed	English 1928	Scottish 1929	South African 1954	Japanese 1959	Indian 1961	Canadian 1962	Sarum	Roman 1960
1	Gilbert			X						
	J. F. D. Maurice	X								
2	Henry Budd							X		
3	Richard	X	X		X	X		X	X	
	Reginald Heber							X		
4	Ambrose [1]	X	X	X	X	X	X	X	X	
5										
6	William Law [2]				X					
7										
8	William Augustus Muhlenberg	X								
9	William Law [2]	X								
10										
11	Leo the Great [3]	X	X	X	X	X	X	X		X
12	G. A. Selwyn [4]	X			X					
13										
14	Justin Martyr [5]	X		X	X	X	X			X
15										

APRIL (continued)

Day	Name	1	2	3	4	5	6	7	8
16	Magnus			X					
17	Donnan			X					
18									
19	Alphege	X		X	X		X		
20	Serf			X				X	
21	Anselm	X		X	X	X	X		X
	Maelrubha			X					
22									
23	George		X	X	X	X	X	X	X
24	Wilfrid				X			X	
25	MARK	X	X	X	X	X	X	X	X
26									
27									
28									
29									
30	Catherine of Siena	X	X	X	X	X	X		X

1. Roman lists on December 7.
2. Cf. April 6 and 9.
3. Sarum on June 28.
4. S. African on the 11th.
5. Scottish on the 13th; Canadian on June 1.

50 PRAYER BOOK STUDIES XVI

MAY

Day	Feast	Proposed	English 1928	Scottish 1929	South African 1954	Japanese 1959	Indian 1961	Canadian 1962	Sarum	Roman 1960
1	PHILIP AND JAMES [1]	X	X	X	X	X	X	X	X	X
	JAMES OF JERUSALEM [2]							X		
2	Athanasius	X	X	X	X	X	X	X		X
3										
4	Monnica	X	X	X	X	X	X	X		X
5										
6	St. John at Latin Gate		X	X	X	X	X		X	
7										
8										
9	Gregory of Nazianzus	X		X	X	X		X		X
10										
11	Cyril and Methodius [3]	X						X		
12	Florence Nightingale							X		
13	Martyrs of Uganda [4]				X					
14										
15										
16										
17										

MAY (continued)

18									
19	Dunstan	X	X	X		X		X	X
20	Alcuin	X						X	
	Council of Nicaea							X	
21									
22									
23									
24	Jackson Kemper	X							
25	Aldhelm		X	X	X			X	X
26	Augustine of Canterbury [5]	X	X	X	X	X	X	X	X
27	Venerable Bede	X	X	X	X	X	X		
28									
29									
30	Joan of Arc				X			X	
31									

1. Roman on May 11.
2. See Oct. 23.
3. Roman on July 7.
4. See Oct. 29.
5. Roman on the 28th.

JUNE

Day	Feast	Proposed	English 1928	Scottish 1929	South African 1954	Japanese 1959	Indian 1961	Canadian 1962	Sarum	Roman 1960
1	Justin Martyr [1]	X						X		
2	The Martyrs of Lyons				X					
3										
4										
5	Boniface	X	X	X	X	X	X	X	X	X
6										
7										
8										
9	Columba	X	X	X	X	X	X	X		
10	First Prayer Book [2]	X								
	Margaret [3]			X						X
11	BARNABAS	X	X	X	X		X	X	X	X
12	Ternan			X						
13										
14	Basil of Caesarea	X	X	X	X	X	X	X	X	X
15										
16	Joseph Butler	X								

JUNE (continued)

17								
18	Ephrem of Edessa	X						X
19	Bernard Mizeki			X				
20	Fillan		X					
21								
22	Alban	X	X	X	X	X		
23								
24	NATIVITY JOHN BAPTIST	X	X	X	X	X		X
25	Moluag		X					
26								
27								
28	Irenaeus [4]	X	X	X	X	X		X
29	PETER	X	X		X			
29	PETER AND PAUL	X		X	X	X		X
30	PAUL				X		X	

1. See April 14.
2. See Canadian on March 21.
3. See Nov. 16.
4. Romans on July 3.

JULY

Day	Feast	Proposed	English 1928	Scottish 1929	South African 1954	Japanese 1959	Indian 1961	Canadian 1962	Sarum	Roman 1960
1	Octave of John Baptist							X	X	
	Dominion Day							X		
2	Visitation	X	X	X	X	X	X	X	X	X
3										
4	INDEPENDENCE DAY	X								
5										
6	Octave Peter and Paul							X	X	
	Thomas More							X		
7	Palladius			X						
8										
9	Stephen Langton							X		
10										
11	Benedict of Nursia [1]	X							X	
12										
13	Silas				X		X			
14					X					
15	Swithun		X	X	X			X	X	
16	Osmund				X				X	

The Calendar and The Collects, Epistles, and Gospels for the Lesser Feasts and Fasts 55

JULY (continued)

17	William White	X							
18									
19									
20	Margaret of Antioch		X		X		X	X	X
21									
22	Mary Magdalene	X	X		X	X	X	X	
23									
24	Thomas a Kempis	X							
25	JAMES	X	X		X	X	X	X	X
26	Parents B.V.M. [2]	X						X	
26	Anne		X		X		X	X	X
27	W. R. Huntington	X							
28									
29	Olaf		X						
29	Mary and Martha [2]	X		X	X	X	X		X
	William Wilberforce				X		X		
30	William Wilberforce	X							
31	Joseph of Arimathaea	X						X	
	Germanus and Lupus			X					

1. See March 21.
2. Roman observes Joachim on Aug. 16.
3. Roman and Indian observe Martha only; S. African on the 30th.

AUGUST

Day	Feast	Proposed	English 1928	Scottish 1929	South African 1954	Japanese 1959	Indian 1961	Canadian 1962	Sarum	Roman 1960
1	Lammas		X	X				X		
	St. Peter's Chains				X	X	X		X	
2	Maccabean Martyrs							X		X
3										
4	Dominic	X			X	X	X			X
5	Oswald		X	X	X			X	X	
6	TRANSFIGURATION	X	X	X	X	X	X	X	X	X
7	Name of Jesus		X	X	X		X	X	X	
8										
9										
10	Laurence	X	X	X	X	X	X	X	X	X
11	Clare	X								
12	Charles Inglis					X		X		X
13	Hippolytus	X						X	X	X
	Jeremy Taylor							X		
14	Jeremy Taylor	X								

The Calendar and The Collects, Epistles, and Gospels for the Lesser Feasts and Fasts 57

AUGUST (continued)

15	Repose of B.V.M.	X		X		X	X	X	X	X	X
16											
17											
18	Helena					X	X				
19											
20	Bernard of Clairvaux	X	X	X		X	X	X			X
21											
22											
23											
24	BARTHOLOMEW	X	X	X		X	X	X	X	X	X
25	Louis	X									X
	Ebba			X							
26											
27											
28	Augustine of Hippo	X	X	X		X	X	X	X	X	X
	Robert McDonald							X			
29	Beheading of John the Baptist		X	X	X	X	X	X	X	X	X
30			X		X	X	X	X			
31	Aidan	X	X	X			X	X			

SEPTEMBER

Day	Feast	Proposed	English 1928	Scottish 1929	South African 1954	Japanese 1959	Indian 1961	Canadian 1962	Sarum	Roman 1960
1	Giles		X	X	X	X		X	X	X
	Robert Gray				X					
2	Robert Wolfall							X		
3										
4										
5										
6										
7										
8	Nativity of B.V.M.		X	X	X	X	X	X	X	X
9	Boisel; Kiaran			X						
10	E. J. Peck							X		
11										
12	John Henry Hobart	X								
13	Cyprian of Carthage [1]	X	X	X	X		X	X		X
	First General Synod, Canadian Church							X		
14	Holy Cross	X	X	X	X	X	X	X	X	X
15										

The Calendar and The Collects, Epistles, and Gospels for the Lesser Feasts and Fasts

SEPTEMBER (continued)

16	Ninian	X		X			X	
17	Lambert				X			X
18								
19	Theodore of Tarsus	X		X	X	X	X	
20	John C. Patteson	X			X		X	
21	MATTHEW	X	X	X	X	X	X	X
22								
23	Adamnan			X				
24								
25	Sergius	X						
	Finnbar			X				
	Lancelot Andrewes				X		X	
26	Lancelot Andrewes	X						
	Cyprian of Carthage [1]				X			X
27								
28								
29	MICHAELMAS	X	X	X	X	X	X	X
30	Jerome	X	X	X	X	X	X	X

1. Roman on the 16th (with Cornelius); see also the 26th.

OCTOBER

Day	Feast	Proposed	English 1928	Scottish 1929	South African 1954	Japanese 1959	Indian 1961	Canadian 1962	Sarum	Roman 1960
1	Remigius	X	X	X	X			X	X	X
2										
3										
4	Francis of Assisi	X	X	X	X	X	X	X		X
5										
6	Faith		X		X				X	
	Thomas of India						X	X		
	William Tyndale	X								
7										
8										
9	Denys		X	X	X	X		X	X	X
	Grosseteste							X		
10	Paulinus				X			X		
11	Kenneth			X						
	Philip the Deacon				X			X		
12										
13	Edward the Confessor		X	X	X	X		X	X	X
	Congan			X						
14										
15	Schereschewsky	X								

The Calendar and The Collects, Epistles, and Gospels for the Lesser Feasts and Fasts 61

OCTOBER (continued)

16	Latimer and Ridley	X					X	
	Henry Martyn					X		
17	Henry Martyn	X						
18	Etheldreda		X	X			X	
	LUKE	X	X		X		X	X
19	Frideswide			X			X	
20								
21	James Hannington [1]						X	
22								
23	James, Brother of the Lord	X		X		X		
24								
25	Crispin and Crispinian		X	X			X	X
26	King Alfred the Great	X	X	X			X	
	Cedd						X	
27								
28	SIMON AND JUDE	X	X	X	X	X	X	X
29	James Hannington	X		X				
30								
31								

1. See the 29th.

Note: Last Sunday, Feast of Christ the King in Roman and Indian

NOVEMBER

Day	Feast	Proposed	English 1928	Scottish 1929	South African 1954	Japanese 1959	Indian 1961	Canadian 1962	Sarum	Roman 1960
1	ALL SAINTS	X	X	X	X	X	X	X	X	X
2	All Souls		X	X	X	X	X	X	X	X
3	Richard Hooker	X						X		
4	Richard Hooker									
5										
6	Leonard		X	X	X				X	
7	Willibrord	X			X			X		
8	Octave; Anglican Saints		X	X	X		X	X		
9	Gervadius			X						
10										
11	Martin of Tours	X	X	X	X	X	X	X	X	X
12	Machar			X						
13	Charles Simeon	X			X					
13	Charles Simeon							X		
	Devenic			X						
14	Consecration of Samuel Seabury	X								

NOVEMBER (continued)

Day	Name	1	2	3	4	5	6	7	8	9
15	Fergus				X					
16	Edmund	X		X				X		
	Queen Margaret	X		X		X				
16	Hugh of Lincoln		X			X				
17	Hugh of Lincoln	X		X		X		X		
	Hilda		X		X					
18	Hilda	X		X						
19	Elizabeth of Hungary	X		X			X			
20	King Edmund		X	X		X				
21	Columban			X		X				
22	Cecilia		X	X	X	X		X		
23	Clement of Rome	X	X	X	X	X	X	X		
24										
25	Catherine of Alexandria		X	X	X	X		X		
26										
27										
28										
29										
30	ANDREW	X		X	X	X	X	X		X

DECEMBER

Day	Feast	Proposed	English 1928	Scottish 1929	South African 1954	Japanese 1959	Indian 1961	Canadian 1962	Sarum	Roman 1960
1	Nicholas Ferrar				X					
2	Channing Moore Williams	X				X				
3	Birinus				X					
	Francis Xavier						X			X
4	Clement of Alexandria	X	X	X	X	X	X	X		
5	John of Damascus [1]	X								
6	Nicholas of Myra	X	X	X	X	X	X	X	X	X
7	Ambrose [2]									X
8	Conception of B. V. M.		X	X	X			X	X	X
9										
10										
11										
12										
13	Lucy				X	X			X	X
14	Drostan			X						
15				X						
16	O Sapientia		X	X	X			X	X	

DECEMBER (continued)

17	Ignatius of Antioch [3]		X		X		X	
18								
19								
20								
21	THOMAS	X	X	X	X	X	X	X
22								
23								
24								
25	CHRISTMAS DAY	X	X	X	X	X	X	X
26	STEPHEN	X	X	X	X	X	X	X
27	JOHN THE EVANGELIST	X	X	X	X	X	X	X
28	THE HOLY INNOCENTS	X	X	X	X	X	X	X
29	Thomas Becket			X	X		X	X
30	John Wycliffe					X		
31	John West					X		

1. Roman on March 27.
2. See April 4.
3. See Feb. 1.

The Calendar

		JANUARY
1	A	THE HOLY NAME OF OUR LORD JESUS CHRIST
2	b	
3	c	
4	d	
5	e	
6	f	THE EPIPHANY OF OUR LORD JESUS CHRIST
7	g	
8	A	
9	b	
10	c	William Laud, Archbishop of Canterbury, 1645
11	d	
12	e	
13	f	
14	g	*Hilary*, Bishop of Poitiers, 367,
15	A	
16	b	
17	c	*Antony*, Abbot in Egypt, 356
18	d	
19	e	Wulstan, Bishop of Worcester, 1095
20	f	Fabian, Bishop of Rome, and Martyr, 250
21	g	Agnes, Martyr at Rome, 304
22	A	Vincent, Deacon of Saragossa, and Martyr, 304
23	b	Phillips Brooks, Bishop of Massachusetts, 1893
24	c	*Saint Timothy*
25	d	THE CONVERSION OF SAINT PAUL THE APOSTLE
26	e	*Polycarp*, Bishop of Smyrna, and Martyr, 156
27	f	*John Chrysostom*, Bishop of Constantinople, 407
28	g	
29	A	
30	b	
31	c	

The Calendar and The Collects, Epistles, and Gospels for the Lesser Feasts and Fasts

		FEBRUARY
1	d	*Ignatius*, Bishop of Antioch, and Martyr, c. 115
2	e	THE PRESENTATION OF OUR LORD JESUS CHRIST IN THE TEMPLE
3	f	Ansgarius, Archbishop of Hamburg, Missionary to Denmark and Sweden, 865
4	g	*Saint Cornelius*, the Centurion
5	A	The Martyrs of Japan
6	b	*Saint Titus*
7	c	
8	d	
9	e	
10	f	
11	g	
12	A	
13	b	
14	c	
15	d	Thomas Bray, Priest and Missionary, 1730
16	e	
17	f	
18	g	
19	A	
20	b	
21	c	
22	d	
23	e	
24	f	SAINT MATTHIAS THE APOSTLE
25	g	
26	A	
27	b	George Herbert, Priest, 1633
28	c	
29		

			MARCH
	1	d	*David*, Bishop of Menevia, Wales, c. 544
	2	e	Chad, Bishop of Lichfield, 672
	3	f	John and Charles Wesley, Priests, 1791, 1788
	4	g	
	5	A	
	6	b	
	7	c	*Perpetua and her Companions*, Martyrs of Carthage, 202
	8	d	Thomas Aquinas, Friar, 1274
	9	e	*Gregory*, Bishop of Nyssa, c. 394
	10	f	
	11	g	
	12	A	*Gregory the Great*, Bishop of Rome, 604
	13	b	
	14	c	
	15	d	
	16	e	
	17	f	*Patrick*, Bishop and Missionary of Ireland, 461
	18	g	Cyril, Bishop of Jerusalem, 386
	19	A	*Saint Joseph*
	20	b	Cuthbert, Bishop of Lindisfarne, 687
	21	c	Thomas Ken, Bishop of Bath and Wells, 1711
14	22	d	James De Koven, Priest, 1879
3	23	e	Gregory the Illuminator, Bishop and Missionary of Armenia, c. 332
	24	f	
11	25	g	THE ANNUNCIATION OF THE BLESSED VIRGIN MARY
	26	A	
19	27	b	
8	28	c	
	29	d	John Keble, Priest, 1866
16	30	e	
5	31	f	John Donne, Priest, 1631

			APRIL
	1	g	John Frederick Denison Maurice, Priest, 1872
13	2	A	
2	3	b	Richard, Bishop of Chichester, 1253
	4	c	*Ambrose*, Bishop of Milan, 397
10	5	d	
	6	e	
18	7	f	
7	8	g	William Augustus Muhlenberg, Priest, 1877
	9	A	William Law, Priest, 1761
15	10	b	
4	11	c	*Leo the Great*, Bishop of Rome, 461
	12	d	George Augustus Selwyn, Bishop of New Zealand, 1878
12	13	e	
1	14	f	*Justin*, Martyr at Rome, c. 167
	15	g	
9	16	A	
17	17	b	
6	18	c	
	19	d	Alphege, Archbishop of Canterbury, and Martyr, 1012
	20	e	
	21	f	*Anselm*, Archbishop of Canterbury, 1109
	22	g	
	23	A	
	24	b	
	25	c	SAINT MARK THE EVANGELIST
	26	d	
	27	e	
	28	f	
	29	g	
	30	A	Catherine of Siena, 1380

			MAY
1	b		SAINT PHILIP AND SAINT JAMES, APOSTLES
2	c		*Athanasius*, Bishop of Alexandria, 373
3	d		
4	e		Monnica, Mother of Augustine of Hippo, 387
5	f		
6	g		
7	A		
8	b		
9	c		*Gregory of Nazianzus*, Bishop of Constantinople, 389
10	d		
11	e		Cyril and Methodius, Missionary Bishops to the Slavs, 869, 885
12	f		
13	g		
14	A		
15	b		
16	c		
17	d		
18	e		
19	f		Dunstan, Archbishop of Canterbury, 988
20	g		Alcuin, Deacon, and Abbot of Tours, 804
21	A		
22	b		
23	c		
24	d		Jackson Kemper, First Missionary Bishop in the United States, 1870
25	e		
26	f		*Augustine*, First Archbishop of Canterbury, 605
27	g		*Bede*, the Venerable, Priest, and Monk of Jarrow, 735
28	A		
29	b		
30	c		
31	d		

		JUNE
1	e	
2	f	*The Martyrs of Lyons*, 177
3	g	
4	A	
5	b	*Boniface*, Archbishop of Mainz, Missionary to Germany, Martyr, 754
6	c	
7	d	
8	e	
9	f	Columba, Abbot of Iona, 597
10	g	*The First Book of Common Prayer*, 1549
11	A	SAINT BARNABAS THE APOSTLE
12	b	
13	c	
14	d	*Basil the Great*, Bishop of Caesarea, 379
15	e	
16	f	Joseph Butler, Bishop of Durham, 1752
17	g	
18	A	Ephrem of Edessa, Syria, Deacon, 373
19	b	
20	c	
21	d	
22	e	*Alban*, First Martyr of Britain, c. 304
23	f	
24	g	THE NATIVITY OF SAINT JOHN BAPTIST
25	A	
26	b	
27	c	
28	d	*Irenaeus*, Bishop of Lyons, c. 202
29	e	SAINT PETER AND SAINT PAUL, APOSTLES
30	f	

		JULY
1	g	
2	A	*The Visitation of the Blessed Virgin Mary*
3	b	
4	c	INDEPENDENCE DAY
5	d	
6	e	
7	f	
8	g	
9	A	
10	b	
11	c	*Benedict of Nursia,* Abbot of Monte Cassino, c. 540
12	d	
13	e	
14	f	
15	g	
16	A	
17	b	William White, Bishop of Pennsylvania, 1836
18	c	
19	d	
20	e	
21	f	
22	g	*Saint Mary Magdalene*
23	A	
24	b	Thomas a Kempis, Priest, 1471
25	c	SAINT JAMES THE APOSTLE
26	d	The Parents of the Blessed Virgin Mary
27	e	William Reed Huntington, Priest, 1909
28	f	
29	g	*Saints Mary and Martha of Bethany*
30	A	William Wilberforce, 1833
31	b	*Saint Joseph of Arimathaea*

		AUGUST
1	c	
2	d	
3	e	
4	f	Dominic, Friar, 1221
5	g	
6	A	THE TRANSFIGURATION OF OUR LORD JESUS CHRIST
7	b	
8	c	
9	d	
10	e	Laurence, Deacon, and Martyr at Rome, 258
11	f	
12	g	Clare of Assisi, Abbess, 1253
13	A	Hippolytus, Bishop, and Martyr, c. 235
14	b	Jeremy Taylor, Bishop of Down, Connor and Dromore, 1667
15	c	*Saint Mary the Virgin*, Mother of Our Lord Jesus Christ
16	d	
17	e	
18	f	
19	g	
20	A	*Bernard*, Abbot of Clairvaux, 1153
21	b	
22	c	
23	d	
24	e	SAINT BARTHOLOMEW THE APOSTLE
25	f	Louis, King of France, 1270
26	g	
27	A	
28	b	*Augustine*, Bishop of Hippo, 430
29	c	
30	d	
31	e	*Aidan*, Bishop of Lindisfarne, 651

		SEPTEMBER
1	f	
2	g	
3	A	
4	b	
5	c	
6	d	
7	e	
8	f	
9	g	
10	A	
11	b	
12	c	John Henry Hobart, Bishop of New York, 1830
13	d	*Cyprian*, Bishop of Carthage, and Martyr, 258
14	e	*The Exaltation of the Holy Cross*
15	f	
16	g	Ninian, Bishop in Galloway, c. 430
17	A	
18	b	
19	c	*Theodore of Tarsus*, Archbishop of Canterbury, 690
20	d	John Coleridge Patteson, Bishop of Melanesia, and Martyr, 1871
21	e	SAINT MATTHEW, APOSTLE AND EVANGELIST
22	f	
23	g	
24	A	
25	b	Sergius, Abbot of Holy Trinity, Moscow, 1392
26	c	Lancelot Andrewes, Bishop of Winchester, 1626
27	d	
28	e	
29	f	SAINT MICHAEL AND ALL ANGELS
30	g	*Jerome*, Priest, and Monk of Bethlehem, 420

		OCTOBER
1	A	Remigius, Bishop of Rheims, c. 530
2	b	
3	c	
4	d	*Francis of Assisi*, Friar, 1226
5	e	
6	f	William Tyndale, Priest, and Martyr, 1536
7	g	
8	A	
9	b	
10	c	
11	d	
12	e	
13	f	
14	g	
15	A	Samuel Isaac Joseph Schereschewsky, Bishop of Shanghai, 1906
16	b	Hugh Latimer and Nicholas Ridley, Bishops and Martyrs, 1555
17	c	Henry Martyn, Priest, and Missionary to India and Persia, 1812
18	d	SAINT LUKE THE EVANGELIST
19	e	
20	f	
21	g	
22	A	
23	b	*Saint James of Jerusalem*, Brother of Our Lord Jesus Christ, and Martyr, c. 62
24	c	
25	d	
26	e	*Alfred the Great*, King of England, 899
27	f	
28	g	SAINT SIMON AND SAINT JUDE, APOSTLES
29	A	James Hannington and his Companions, Bishop and Martyrs of Uganda, 1885
30	b	
31	c	

		NOVEMBER
1	d	ALL SAINTS
2	e	
3	f	Richard Hooker, Priest, 1600
4	g	
5	A	
6	b	
7	c	Willibrord, Archbishop of Utrecht, Missionary to Frisia, 738
8	d	
9	e	
10	f	
11	g	*Martin*, Bishop of Tours, 397
12	A	Charles Simeon, Priest, 1836
13	b	
14	c	*Consecration of Samuel Seabury*, First American Bishop, 1784
15	d	
16	e	Margaret, Queen of Scotland, 1093
17	f	Hugh, Bishop of Lincoln, 1200
18	g	Hilda, Abbess of Whitby, 680
19	A	Elizabeth, Princess of Hungary, 1231
20	b	
21	c	
22	d	
23	e	Clement, Bishop of Rome, c. 100
24	f	
25	g	
26	A	
27	b	
28	c	
29	d	
30	e	SAINT ANDREW THE APOSTLE

The Calendar and The Collects, Epistles, and Gospels for the Lesser Feasts and Fasts

		DECEMBER
1	f	
2	g	Channing Moore Williams, Missionary Bishop in China and Japan, 1910
3	A	
4	b	*Clement of Alexandria*, Priest, c. 210
5	c	John of Damascus, Priest, c. 760
6	d	Nicholas, Bishop of Myra in Lycia, c. 342
7	e	
8	f	
9	g	
10	A	
11	b	
12	c	
13	d	
14	e	
15	f	
16	g	
17	A	
18	b	
19	c	
20	d	
21	e	SAINT THOMAS THE APOSTLE
22	f	
23	g	
24	A	
25	b	THE NATIVITY OF OUR LORD JESUS CHRIST
26	c	SAINT STEPHEN, DEACON AND MARTYR
27	d	SAINT JOHN, APOSTLE AND EVANGELIST
28	e	THE HOLY INNOCENTS
29	f	
30	g	
31	A	

The Collect, Epistles, and Gospels for the Lesser Feasts and Fasts

Advent Season

WEDNESDAY IN THE THIRD WEEK OF ADVENT EMBER DAY

The Collect

ALMIGHTY God, the giver of all good gifts, who of thy divine providence hast appointed divers Orders in thy Church: Give thy grace, we humbly beseech thee, to all those who are to be called to any office and administration in the same; and so replenish them with the truth of thy doctrine, and endue them with innocency of life, that they may faithfully serve before thee, to the glory of thy great Name, and the benefit of thy holy Church; through Jesus Christ our Lord. *Amen.*

ALMIGHTY God, give us grace that we may cast away the works of darkness, and put upon us the armour of light, now in the time of this mortal life, in which thy Son Jesus Christ came to visit us in great humility; that in the last day, when he shall come again in his glorious majesty to judge both the quick and the dead, we may rise to the life immortal, through him who liveth and reigneth with thee and the Holy Ghost, now and ever. *Amen.*

¶ *This Collect is to be repeated every day, after the other Collects in Advent, until Christmas Day.*

The Epistle. 1 Corinthians 3:5-11

WHO then is Paul, and who is Apollos, but ministers by whom ye believed, even as the Lord gave to every man? I have planted, Apollos watered; but God gave the increase. So then neither is he that planteth any thing, neither he that watereth; but God that giveth the increase. Now he that planteth and he that watereth are equal: and every man shall receive his own reward according to his own labour. For we are labourers together with God: ye are God's husbandry, ye are God's building. According to the grace of God which is given unto me, as a wise masterbuilder, I have laid the foundation, and another buildeth thereon. But let every man take heed how he buildeth thereupon. For other foundation can no man lay than that is laid, which is Jesus Christ.

The Gospel. St. John 4:31-38

IN the meanwhile his disciples prayed him, saying, Master, eat. But he said unto them, I have meat to eat that ye know not of. Therefore said the disciples one to another, Hath any man brought him ought to eat? Jesus saith unto them, My meat is to do the will of him that sent me, and to finish his work. Say not ye, There are yet four months, and then cometh harvest? behold, I say unto you Lift up your eyes, and look on the fields; for they are white already to harvest. And he that reapeth receiveth wages, and gathereth fruit unto life eternal: that both he that soweth and he that reapeth may rejoice together. At herein is that saying true, One soweth, and another reapeth I sent you to reap that whereon ye bestowed no labour. other men laboured, and ye are entered into their labours

FRIDAY IN THE THIRD WEEK OF ADVENT
EMBER DAY

The Collect

ALMIGHTY God, the giver of all good gifts, who thy divine providence hast appointed divers Orders in thy Church: Give thy grace, we humbly beseech thee, to all those who are to be called to any office and administration in the same; and so replenish them with the truth of thy doctrine, and endue them with innocency of life, that they may faithfully serve before thee, to the glory of thy great Name, and the benefit of thy holy Church; through Jesus Christ our Lord. *Amen.*

The Epistle. 1 Peter 4:7-11

THE end of all things is at hand: be ye therefore sober, and watch unto prayer. And above all things have fervent charity among yourselves: for charity shall cover the multitude of sins. Use hospitality one to another without grudging. As every man hath received the gift, even so minister the same one to another, as good stewards of the manifold grace of God. If any man speak, let him speak as the oracles of God, if any man minister, let him do it as of the ability which God giveth: that God in all things may be glorified through Jesus Christ to whom be praise and dominion for ever and ever. *Amen.*

The Gospel. St. Luke 12:25-44

JESUS said: Which of you by being anxious can add a cubit to his span of life? If ye then be not able to do that thing which is least, why are ye anxious for the rest? Consider the lilies how they grow: they toil not, they spin not; and yet I say unto you, that Solomon in all his glory was not arrayed like one of these. If then God so clothe the grass, which is to day in the field, and to morrow is cast into the oven; how much more will he clothe you, O ye of little faith? And seek not ye what ye shall eat, or what ye shall drink, neither be ye of doubtful mind. For all these things do the nations of the world seek after: and your Father knoweth that ye have need of these things. But rather seek ye the kingdom of God; and all these things shall be added unto you.

Fear not, little flock; for it is your Father's good pleasure to give you the kingdom. Sell that ye have, and give alms; provide yourselves bags which wax not old, a treasure in the heavens that faileth not, where no thief approacheth, neither moth corrupteth. For where your treasure is, there will your heart be also. Let your loins be girded about, and your lights burning; and ye yourselves like unto men that wait for their lord, when he will return from the wedding; that when he cometh and knocketh, they may open unto him immediately. Blessed are those servants, whom the lord when he cometh shall find watching: verily I say unto you, that he shall gird himself, and make them to sit down to meat, and will come forth and serve them. And if he shall come in the second watch, or come in the third watch, and find them so, blessed are those servants. And this know, that if the goodman of the house had known what hour the thief would come, he would have watched, and not have suffered his house to be broken through. Be ye therefore ready also: for the Son of man cometh at an hour when ye think not.

Then Peter said unto him, Lord, speakest thou this parable unto us, or even to all? And the Lord said, Who then is that faithful and wise steward, whom his lord shall make ruler over his household, to give them their portion of meat in due season? Blessed is that servant, whom his lord when he cometh shall find so doing. Of a truth I say unto you, that he will make him ruler over all that he hath.

SATURDAY IN THE THIRD WEEK OF ADVENT
EMBER DAY

The Collect

ALMIGHTY God, the giver of all good gifts, who thy divine providence halt appointed divers Orders in thy Church: Give thy grace, we humbly beseech thee, to all those who are to be called to any office and administration in the same; and so replenish them with the truth of thy doctrine, and endue them with innocency of life, that they may faithfully serve before thee, to the glory of thy great Name, and the benefit of thy holy Church; through Jesus Christ our Lord. *Amen.*

The Epistle. 1 Timothy 1:12-17

I THANK Christ Jesus our Lord, who hath enabled me, for that he counted me faithful, putting me into the ministry; who was before a blasphemer, and a persecutor, and injurious: but I obtained mercy, because I did it ignorantly in unbelief. And the grace of our Lord was exceeding abundant with faith and love which is in Christ Jesus. This is a faithful saying, and worthy of all acceptation, that Christ Jesus came into the world to save sinners; of whom I am chief. Howbeit for this cause I obtained mercy, that in me first Jesus Christ might shew forth all longsuffering, for a pattern to them which should hereafter believe on him to life everlasting. Now unto the King eternal, immortal, invisible, the only wise God, be honour and glory for ever and ever. Amen.

The Gospel. St. Matthew 16:24-27

THEN said Jesus unto his disciples, If any man will come after me, let him deny himself, and take up his cross, and follow me. For whosoever will save his life shall lose it: and whosoever will lose his life for my sake shall find it. For what is a man profited, if he shall gain the whole world, and lose his own soul? or what shall a man give in exchange for his soul? For the Son of man shall come in the glory of his Father with his angels; and then he shall reward every man according to his works.

Lenten Season

¶ *The Collect, Epistle, and Gospel herewith appointed for Wednesday and Fridays of each week of Lent may, at the discretion of the Priest be used on any day of the same week, except on Sundays and such other Holy Days for which a proper Collect, Epistle, and Gospel assigned.*

FRIDAY AFTER ASH WEDNESDAY

The Collect

ALMIGHTY and everlasting God, who hatest nothing that thou hast made, and dost forgive the sins of all those who are penitent: Create and make in us new and contrite hearts, that we, worthily lamenting our sins and acknowledging our wretchedness, may obtain of thee, the God of all mercy, perfect remission and forgiveness; through Jesus Christ our Lord. *Amen.*

¶ *This Collect is to be said every day in Lent, after the Collect appointed for the day, until Palm Sunday.*

The Epistle. Isaiah 58:1-12

CRY aloud, spare not, lift up thy voice like a trumpet, and shew my people their transgression, and the house of Jacob their sins. Yet they seek me daily, and delight to know my ways, as a nation that did righteousness, and foresook not the ordinance of their God: they ask of me the ordinances of justice; they take delight in approaching to God. Wherefore have we fasted, say they, and thou seest not? wherefore have we afflicted our soul, and thou takes no knowledge?

Behold, in the day of your fast ye find pleasure, and exact all your labours. Behold, ye fast for strife and debate, and to smite with the fist of wickedness: ye shall not fast as ye do this day, to make your voice to be heard on high. Is it such a fast that I have chosen? a day for a man to afflict his soul? is it to bow down his head as bulrush, and to spread sackcloth and ashes under him? wilt thou call this a fast, and an acceptable day to the LORD?

Is not this the fast that I have chosen? to loose the bands of wickedness, to undo the heavy burdens, and to let the oppressed go free, and that ye break every yoke? Is it not to deal thy bread to the hungry, and that thou bring the poor that are cast out to thy house? when thou seest the naked, that thou cover him; and that thou hide not thyself from thine own flesh? Then shall thy light break forth as the morning, and thine health shall spring forth speedily: and thy righteousness shall go before thee; the glory of the LORD shall be thy rear guard. Then shalt thou call, and the LORD shall answer; thou shalt cry, and he shall say, Here I am.

If thou take away from the midst of thee the yoke, the putting forth of the finger, and speaking vanity; and if thou draw out thy soul to the hungry, and satisfy the afflicted soul; then shall thy light rise in obscurity, and thy darkness be as the noon day: and the LORD shall guide thee continually, and satisfy thy soul in drought, and make fat thy bones: and thou shalt be like a watered garden, and like a spring of water, whose waters fail not. And they that shall be of thee shall build the old waste places: thou shalt raise up the foundations of many generations; and thou shalt be called, The repairer of the breach, The restorer of paths to dwell in.

The Gospel. St Matthew 5:43-6:8

YE have heard that it hath been said, Thou shalt love thy neighbour, and hate thine enemy. But I say unto you, Love your enemies, bless them that curse you, do good to them that hate you, and pray for them which despitefully use you, and persecute you; that ye may be the children of your Father which is in heaven: for he maketh his sun to rise on the evil and on the good, and sendeth rain on the just and on the unjust. For if ye love them which love you, what reward have ye? do not even the publicans the same? And if ye salute your brethren only, what do ye more than others? do not even the publicans so? Be ye therefore perfect, even as your Father which is in heaven is perfect.

Take heed that ye do not your alms before men, to be seen of them: otherwise ye have no reward of your Father which is in heaven. Therefore when thou doest thine alms do not sound a trumpet before thee, as the hypocrites do in the synagogues and in the streets, that they may have glory of men. Verily I say unto you, They have their reward. But when thou doest alms, let not thy left hand know what thy right hand doeth: that thine alms may be in secret and thy Father which seeth in secret himself shall reward thee openly.

And when thou prayest, thou shalt not be as the hypocrites are: for they love to pray standing in the synagogues and in the corners of the streets, that they may be seen of men. Verily I say unto you, They have their reward. But thou, when thou prayest, enter into thy closet, and when thou hast shut thy door, pray to thy Father which is in secret; and thy Father which seeth in secret shall reward thee openly. But when ye pray, use not vain repetitions, as the heathen do: for they think that they shall be heard for their much speaking. Be not ye therefore like unto them: for your Father knoweth what things ye have need of, before ye ask him.

WEDNESDAY IN THE FIRST WEEK OF LENT
EMBER DAY

The Collect

O ALMIGHTY God, who hast committed to the hand of men the ministry of reconciliation: We humbly beseech thee, by the inspiration of thy Holy Spirit, to put into the hearts of many to offer themselves for this ministry that thereby mankind may be drawn to thy blessed kingdom; through Jesus Christ our Lord. *Amen.*

The Epistle. Exodus 24:12-18

THE LORD said unto Moses, Come up to me into the mount, and be there: and I will give thee tables of stone, and a law, and commandments which I have written; that thou mayest teach them. And Moses rose up, and his minister Joshua: and Moses went up into the mount of God. And he said unto the elders, Tarry ye here for us, until we come again unto you: and, behold, Aaron and Hur are with you: if any man have any matters to do, let him come unto them. And Moses went up into the mount, and a cloud covered the mount. And the glory of the LORD abode upon mount Sinai, and the cloud covered it six days: and the seventh day he called unto Moses out of the midst of the cloud. And the sight of the glory of the LORD was like devouring fire on the top of the mount in the eyes of the children of Israel. And Moses went into the midst of the cloud, and gat him up into the mount: and Moses was in the mount forty days and forty nights.

The Gospel. St. Matthew 20:17-28

JESUS going up to Jerusalem took the twelve disciples apart in the way, and said unto them, Behold, we go up to Jerusalem; and the Son of man shall be betrayed unto the chief priests and unto the scribes, and they shall condemn him to death, and shall deliver him to the Gentiles to mock, and to scourge, and to crucify him: and the third day he shall rise again.

Then came to him the mother of Zebedee's children with her sons, worshipping him, and desiring a certain thing of him. And he said unto her, What wilt thou? She saith unto him, Grant that these my two sons may sit, the one on thy right hand, and the other on the left, in thy kingdom. But Jesus answered and said, Ye know not what ye ask. Are ye able to drink of the cup that I shall drink of, and to be baptized with the baptism that I am baptized with? They say unto him, We are able. And he saith unto them, Ye shall drink indeed of my cup, and be baptized with the baptism that I am baptized with: but to sit on my right hand, and on my left, is not mine to give, but it shall be given to the for whom it is prepared of my Father. And when the ten heard it, they were moved with indignation against the two brethren. But Jesus called them unto him, and said, Ye know that the princes of the Gentiles exercise dominion over them, and they that are great exercise authority upon them. But it shall not be so among you: but whosoever will be great among you, let him be your minister; and whosoever will be chief among you, let him be your servant: even as the Son of man came not to be ministered unto, but minister, and to give his life a ransom for many.

FRIDAY IN THE FIRST WEEK OF LENT
EMBER DAY

The Collect

O ALMIGHTY God, who hast committed to the hand of men the ministry of reconciliation: We humbly beseech thee, by the inspiration of thy Holy Spirit, to put it into the hearts of many to offer themselves for this ministry; that thereby mankind may be drawn to thy blessed kingdom; through Jesus Christ our Lord. *Amen.*

The Epistle. 1 Kings 19:1-8

AHAB told Jezebel all that Elijah had done, and withal how he had slain all the prophets with the sword. Then Jezebel sent a messenger unto Elijah, saying, So let the gods do to me, and more also, if I make not thy life as the life of one of them by tomorrow about this time. An when he saw that, he arose, and went for his life, and came to Beer-Sheba, which belongeth to Judah, and left his servant there.

But he himself went a day's journey into the wilderness, and came and sat down under a broom tree: and he requested for himself that he might die; and said, It is enough; now, O Lord, take away my life; for I am not better than my fathers. And as he lay and slept under a broom tree, behold, then an angel touched him, and said unto him, Arise and eat. And he looked, and, behold, there was a cake baken on the coals, and a cruse of water at his head. And he did eat and drink, and laid him down again. And the angel of the Lord came again the second time, and touched him, and said, Arise and eat; because the journey is too great for thee. And he arose, and did eat and drink, and went in the strength of that meat forty days and forty nights unto Horeb the mount of God.

The Gospel. St. Matthew 21:33-44

JESUS said: There was a certain householder, which planted a vineyard, and hedged it round about, and digged a wine-press in it, and built a tower, and let it out to husbandmen, and went into a far country: and when the time of the fruit drew near, he sent his servants to the husbandmen, that they might receive the fruits of it. And the husbandmen took his servants, and beat one, and killed another, and stoned another. Again, he sent other servants more than the first: and they did unto them likewise. But last of all he sent unto them his son, saying, They will reverence my son. But when the husbandmen saw the son, they said among themselves, This is the heir; come, let us kill him, and let us seize on his inheritance. And they caught him, and cast him out of the vineyard, and slew him. When the lord therefore of the vineyard cometh, what will he do unto those husbandmen? They say unto him, He will miserably destroy those wicked men, and will let out his vineyard unto other husbandmen, which shall render him the fruits in their seasons. Jesus saith unto them, Did ye never read in the scriptures,

> The stone which the builders rejected,
> the same is become the head of the corner:
> this is the Lord's doing,
> and it is marvellous in our eyes?

Therefore say I unto you, The kingdom of God shall I taken from you, and given to a nation bringing forth the fruits thereof. And whosoever shall fall on this stone shall be broken: but on whomsoever it shall fall, it will grind him to powder.

SATURDAY IN THE FIRST WEEK OF LENT
EMBER DAY

The Collect

O ALMIGHTY God, who hast committed to the hand of men the ministry of reconciliation: We humbly beseech thee, by the inspiration of thy Holy Spirit, to put it into the hearts of many to offer themselves for this ministry; that thereby mankind may be drawn to thy blessed kingdom; through Jesus Christ our Lord. *Amen.*

The Epistle. 2 Corinthians 3:4-18

SUCH confidence have we through Christ to God-ward: not that we are sufficient of ourselves, to account anything as from ourselves; but our sufficiency is from God; who also made us sufficient as ministers of a new covenant not of the letter, but of the spirit: for the letter killeth, but the Spirit giveth life. But if the ministration of death written, and engraven on stones, came with glory, so that the children of Israel could not look stedfastly upon the face of Moses for the glory of his face; which glory was passing away: how shall not rather the ministration of the spirit be with glory? For if the ministration of condemnation is glory, much rather doth the ministration of righteousness exceed in glory. For verily that which hath been made glorious hath not been made glorious in this respect, by reason of the glory that surpasseth. For if that which passeth away was with glory, much more that which remaineth is in glory.

Having therefore such a hope, we use great boldness of speech, and are not as Moses, who put a veil upon his face, that the children of Israel should not look stedfastly on the end of that which was passing away: but their minds were hardened: for until this very day at the reading of the old covenant the same veil remaineth unlifted; which veil is done away in Christ. But unto this day, whensoever Moses is read, a veil lieth upon their heart. But whensoever a man shall turn to the Lord, the veil is taken away. Now the Lord is the Spirit: and where the Spirit of the Lord is, there is liberty. But we all, with unveiled face reflecting as a mirror the glory of the Lord, are transformed into the same image from glory to glory, even as from the Lord the Spirit.

The Gospel. St. Luke 9:28-36

AND it came to pass about an eight days after these sayings, he took Peter and John and James, and went up into a mountain to pray. And as he prayed, the fashion of his countenance was altered, and his raiment was white and glistering. And, behold, there talked with him two men, which were Moses and Elias: who appeared in glory, and spake of his decease which he should accomplish at Jerusalem. But Peter and they that were with him were heavy with sleep: and when they were awake, they saw his glory, and the two men that stood with him. And it came to pass, as they departed from him, Peter said unto Jesus, Master, it is good for us to be here: and let us make three tabernacles; one for thee, and one for Moses, and one for Elias: not knowing what he said. While he thus spake, there came a cloud, and overshadowed them: and they feared as they entered into the cloud. And there came a voice out of the cloud, saying, This is my beloved Son: hear him. And when the voice was past, Jesus was found alone. And they kept it close, and told no man in those days any of those things which they had seen.

WEDNESDAY IN THE SECOND WEEK OF LENT

The Collect

ALMIGHTY God, who seest that we have no power of ourselves to help ourselves: Keep us both outwardly in our bodies, and inwardly in our souls;

that may be defended from all adversities which may happen to the body, and from all evil thoughts which may assault and hurt the soul; through Jesus Christ our Lord. *Amen.*

The Epistle. Jeremiah 2:4-13

HEAR ye the word of the Lord, O house of Jacob, and all the families of the house of Israel: Thus saith the Lord, What iniquity have your fathers found in me, that they are gone far from me, and have walked after vanity, and are become vain? Neither said they, Where is the Lord that brought us up out of the land of Egypt, that led us through the wilderness, through a land of deserts and of pits, through a land of drought, and of the shadow of death, through a land that no man passed through, and where no man dwelt? And I brought you into a plentiful country, to eat the fruit thereof and the goodness thereof; but when ye entered, ye defiled my land, and made mine heritage an abomination. The priests said not, Where is the Lord? and they that handle the law knew me not: the shepherds also transgressed against me, and the prophets prophesied by Baal, and walked after things that do not profit.

Wherefore I will yet plead with you, saith the Lord, and with your children's children will I plead. For pass over the isles of Chittim, and see; and send unto Kedar, and consider diligently, and see if there be such a thing. Hath a nation changed their gods, which are yet no gods? but my people have changed their glory for that which doth not profit. Be astonished, O ye heavens, at this, and be horribly afraid, be ye very desolate, saith the Lord. For my people have committed two evils; they have forsaken me the fountain of living waters, and hewed them out cisterns, broken cisterns, that can hold no water.

The Gospel. St. John 4:5-26

THEN cometh Jesus to a city of Samaria, which is called Sychar, near to the parcel of ground that Jacob gave to his son Joseph. Now Jacob's well was there. Jesus therefore, being wearied with his journey, sat thus on the well: and it was about the sixth hour.

There cometh a woman of Samaria to draw water: Jesus saith unto her, Give me to drink. (For his disciples were gone away unto the city to buy meat.) Then saith the woman of Samaria unto him, How is it that thou, being a Jew, askest drink of me, which am a woman of Samaria? for the Jews have no dealings with the Samaritans. Jesus answered and said unto her, If thou knewest the gift of God, and who it is that saith to thee, Give me to drink; thou wouldest have asked of him, and he would have given thee living water. The woman saith unto him, Sir, thou hast nothing to draw with, and the well is deep: from whence then hast thou that living water? Art thou greater than our father Jacob, which gave us the well, and drank thereof himself, and his children, and his cattle? Jesus answered and said unto her, Whosoever drinketh of this water shall thirst again: but whosoever drinketh of the water that I shall give him shall never thirst; but the water that I shall give him shall be in him a well of water springing up into everlasting life. The woman saith unto him, Sir, give me this water, that I thirst not, neither come hither to draw.

Jesus saith unto her, Go, call thy husband, and come hither. The woman answered and said, I have no husband. Jesus said unto her, Thou hast well said, I have no husband: for thou hast had five husbands; and he whom thou now hast is not thy husband: in that saidst thou truly. The woman saith unto him, Sir, I perceive that thou art a prophet. Our fathers worshipped in this mountain; and ye say, that in Jerusalem is the place where men ought to worship. Jesus saith unto her, Woman, believe me, the hour cometh, when ye shall neither in this mountain, nor yet at Jerusalem, worship the Father. Ye worship ye know not what: we know what we worship: for salvation is of the Jews. But the hour cometh, and now is, when the true worshippers shall worship the Father in spirit and in truth: for the Father seeketh such to worship him. God is a Spirit: and they that worship him must worship him in spirit and in truth. The woman saith unto him, I know that Messias cometh, which is called Christ: when he is come, he will tell us all things. Jesus saith unto her, I that speak unto thee am he.

FRIDAY IN THE SECOND WEEK OF LENT

The Collect

ALMIGHTY God, who seest that we have no power ourselves to help ourselves: Keep us both outward in our bodies, and inwardly in our souls; that we may defended from all adversities which may happen to t body, and from all evil thoughts which may assault a hurt the soul; through Jesus Christ our Lord. *Amen.*

The Epistle. Numbers 20:1-13

THEN came the children of Israel, even the whole congregation, into the desert of Zin in the first month: and the people abode in Kadesh; and Miriam died there, and was buried there.

And there was no water for the congregation: and they gathered themselves together against Moses and against Aaron. And the people chode with Moses, and spake, saying, Would God that we had died when our brethren died before the Lord! And why have ye brought up the congregation of the Lord into this wilderness, that we and our cattle should die there? And wherefore have ye made us to come up out of Egypt, to bring us in unto this evil place? it is no place of seed, or of figs, or of vines, or of pomegranates; neither is there any water to drink.

And Moses and Aaron went from the presence of the assembly unto the door of the tabernacle of the congregation, and they fell upon their faces: and the glory of the LORD appeared unto them. And the LORD spake unto Moses, saying, Take the rod, and gather thou the assembly together, thou, and Aaron thy brother, and speak ye unto the rock before their eyes; and it shall give forth his water, and thou shalt bring forth to them water out of the rock: so thou shalt give the congregation and their beasts drink. And Moses took the rod from before the LORD, as he commanded him.

And Moses and Aaron gathered the congregation together before the rock, and he said unto them, Hear now, ye rebels; must we fetch you water out of this rock? And Moses lifted up his hand, and with his rod he smote the rock twice: and the water came out abundantly, and the congregation drank, and their beasts also. And the LORD spake unto Moses and Aaron, Because ye believed me not, to sanctify me in the eyes of the children of Israel, therefore ye shall not bring this congregation into the land which I have given them. This is the water of Meribah; because the children of Israel strove with the LORD, and he showed himself holy among them.

The Gospel. St. John 5:1-16

AFTER this there was a feast of the Jews; and Jesus went up to Jerusalem. Now there is at Jerusalem by the sheep market a pool, which is called in the Hebrew tongue Bethesda, having five porches. In these lay a great multitude of crippled folk, of blind, halt, withered, waiting for the moving of the water. For an angel went down at a certain season into the pool, and troubled the water: whosoever then first after the troubling of the water stepped in was made whole of whatsoever disease he had. And a certain man was there, which had an infirmity thirty and eight years. When Jesus saw him lie, and knew that he had been now a long time in that case, he saith unto him, Wilt thou be made whole? The crippled man answered him, Sir, I have no man, when the water is troubled, to put me into the pool: but while I am coming, another steppeth down before me. Jesus saith unto him, Rise, take up thy bed, and walk. And immediately the man was made whole, and too up his bed, and walked: and on the same day was the sabbath.

The Jews therefore said unto him that was cured, It is the sabbath day: it is not lawful for thee to carry thy bed. He answered them, He that made me whole, the same said unto me, Take up thy bed, and walk. Then asked they him What man is that which said unto thee, Take up thy bed and walk? And he that was healed wist not who it was: for Jesus had conveyed himself away, a multitude being in that place. Afterward Jesus findeth him in the temple, and said unto him, Behold, thou art made whole: sin no more, lest a worse thing come unto thee. The man departed, and told the Jews that it was Jesus, which had made him whole. And therefore did the Jews persecute Jesus, and sought to slay him, because he had done these things on the sabbath day.

WEDNESDAY IN THE THIRD WEEK OF LENT

The Collect

WE beseech thee, Almighty God, look upon the hearty desires of thy humble servants, and stretch forth the right hand of thy Majesty, to be our defence against all our enemies; through Jesus Christ our Lord. *Amen.*

The Epistle. 2 Samuel 22:1-15

AND the Lord sent Nathan unto David. And he came unto him, and said unto him, There were two men in one city; the one rich, and the other poor. The rich man had exceeding many flocks and herds: but the poor man had nothing, save one little ewe lamb, which he had bought and nourished up: and it grew up together with him, and with his children; it did eat of his own meat, and drank of his own cup, and lay in his bosom, and was unto him as a daughter. And there came a traveller unto the rich man, and he spared to take of his own flock and of his own herd, to dress for the wayfaring man that was come unto him; but took the poor man's lamb, and dressed it for the man that was come to him. And David's anger was greatly kindled against the man; and he said to Nathan, As the LORD liveth, the man that hath done this thing shall surely die: and he shall restore the lamb fourfold, because he did this thing, and because he had no pity.

And Nathan said to David, Thou art the man. Thus saith the LORD God of Israel, I anointed thee king over Israel, and I delivered thee out of the hand of Saul; and I gave thee thy master's house, and thy master's wives into thy bosom, and gave thee the house of Israel and of Judah; and if that had been too little, I would moreover have given unto thee such and such things. Wherefore hast thou despised the commandment of the LORD, to do evil in his sight? thou hast killed Uriah the Hittite with the sword, and hast taken his wife to be thy wife, and hast slain him with the sword of the children of Ammon. Now therefore the sword shall never depart from thine house; because thou hast despised me, and hast taken the wife of Uriah the Hittite to be thy wife. Thus saith the LORD, Behold, I will raise up evil against thee out of thine own house, and I will take thy wives before thine eyes, and give them unto thy neighbour, and he shall lie with thy wives in the sight of this sun. For thou didst it secretly: but I will do this thing before all Israel, and before the sun. And David said unto Nathan, I have sinned against the LORD. And Nathan said unto David, The LORD also hath put away thy sin; thou shalt not die. Howbeit, because by this deed thou hast given great occasion to the enemies of the LORD to blaspheme, the child also that is born unto thee shall surely die. And Nathan departed unto his house.

The Gospel. St. John 8:12, 28-36

THEN spake Jesus again unto them, saying, I am the light of the world: he that followeth me shall not walk in darkness, but shall have the light of life. When ye have lifted up the Son of man, then shall ye know that I am he, and that I do nothing of myself; but as my Father hath taught me, I speak these things. And he that sent me is with me: the Father hath not left me alone; for I do always those things that please him. As he spake these words, many believed on him.

Then said Jesus to those Jews which believed on him, If ye continue in my word, then are ye my disciples indeed; and ye shall know the truth, and the truth shall make you free. They answered him, We be Abraham's seed, and were never in bondage to any man: how sayest thou, Ye shall be made free? Jesus answered them, Verily, verily, I say unto you, Whosoever committeth sin is the servant of sin. An the servant abideth not in the house for ever: but the Son abideth ever. If the Son therefore shall make you free, ye shall be free indeed.

FRIDAY IN THE THIRD WEEK OF LENT

The Collect

WE beseech thee, Almighty God, look upon the heart desires of thy humble servants, and stretch forth the right hand of thy Majesty, to be our defence against all our enemies; through Jesus Christ our Lord. *Amen.*

The Epistle. 1 Kings 21:1-20

AND it came to pass after these things, that Naboth the Jezreelite had a vineyard, which was in Jezreel, hard by the palace of Ahab king of Samaria. And Ahab spake unto Naboth, saying, Give me thy vineyard, that I may have it for a garden of herbs, because it is near unto my house: and I will give thee for it a better vineyard than it; or, if it seem good to thee, I will give thee the worth of it in money. And Naboth said to Ahab, The LORD forbid it me, that I should give the inheritance of my fathers unto thee. And Ahab came into his house heavy and displeased because of the word which Naboth the Jezreelite had spoken to him: for he had said, I will not give thee the inheritance of my fathers. And he laid him down upon his bed, and turned away his face, and would eat no bread.

But Jezebel his wife came to him and said unto him, Why is thy spirit so sad, that thou eatest no bread? And he said unto her, Because I spake unto Naboth the Jezreelite, and said unto him, Give me thy vineyard for money; or else, if it please thee, I will give thee another vineyard for it: and he answered, I will not give thee my vineyard. And Jezebel his wife said unto him, Dost thou now govern the kingdom of Israel? arise, and eat bread, and let thine heart be merry: I will give thee the vineyard of Naboth the Jezreelite. So she wrote letters in Ahab's name, and sealed them with his seal, and sent the letters unto the elders and to the nobles that were in his city, dwelling with Naboth. And she wrote in the letters, saying, Proclaim a fast, and set Naboth on high among the people: and set two men, sons of Belial, before him, to bear witness against him, saying, Thou didst blaspheme God and the king. And then carry him out, and stone him, that he may die.

And the men of his city, even the elders and the nobles who were the inhabitants in his city, did as Jezebel had sent unto them, and as it was written in the letters which she had sent unto them. They proclaimed a fast, and set Naboth on high among the people. And there came in two men, children of Belial, and sat before him: and the men of Belial witnessed against him, even against Naboth, in the presence of the people, saying, Naboth did blaspheme God and the king. Then they carried him forth out of the city, and stoned him with stones, that he died. Then they sent to Jezebel, saying, Naboth is stoned, and is dead. And it came to pass, when Jezebel heard that Naboth was stoned, and was dead, that Jezebel said to Ahab, Arise, take possession of the vineyard of Naboth the Jezreelite, which he refused to give thee for money: for Naboth is not alive, but dead. And it came to pass, when Ahab heard that Naboth was dead, that Ahab rose up to go down to the vineyard of Naboth the Jezreelite, to take possession of it.

And the word of the LORD came to Elijah the Tishbit, saying, Arise, go down to meet Ahab king of Israel, which is in Samaria: behold, he is in the vineyard of Naboth, whither he is gone down to possess it. And thou shalt speak unto him, saying, Thus saith the LORD, Hast thou killed, and also taken possession? And thou shalt speak unto him, saying, Thus saith the LORD, In the place where dogs licked the blood of Naboth shall dogs lick thy blood, even thine. And Ahab said to Elijah, Hast thou found me, O mine enemy? And he answered, I have found thee: because thou hast sold thyself to work evil in the sight of the LORD.

The Gospel. St. John 7:14-18,25-30

NOW about the midst of the feast Jesus went up into the temple, and taught. And the Jews marvelled saying, How knoweth this man letters, having never learned? Jesus answered them, and said, My doctrine is not mine, but his that sent me. If any man will do his will, he shall know of the doctrine, whether it be of God, or whether I speak of myself. He that speaketh of himself seeketh his own glory: but he that seeketh his glory that sent him, the same is true, and no unrighteousness is in him.

Then said some of them of Jerusalem, Is not this he, whom they seek to kill? But, lo, he speaketh boldly, and they say nothing unto him. Do the rulers know indeed that this is the very Christ? Howbeit we know this man whence he is: but when Christ cometh, no man knoweth whence he is. Then cried Jesus in the temple as he taught, saying, Ye both know me, and ye know whence I am: and I am not come of myself, but he that sent me is true, whom ye know not. But I know him: for I am from him, and he hath sent me. Then they sought to take him: but no man laid hands on him, because his hour was not yet come.

WEDNESDAY IN THE FOURTH WEEK OF LENT

The Collect

GRANT, we beseech thee, Almighty God, that we, who for our evil deeds do worthily deserve to be punished, by the comfort of thy grace may mercifully be relieved; through our Lord and Saviour Jesus Christ. *Amen.*

The Epistle. Jeremiah 31:31-34

BEHOLD, the days come, saith the Lord, that I will make a new covenant with the house of Israel, and with the house of Judah: not according to the covenant that I made with their fathers in the day that I took them by the hand to bring them out of the land of Egypt; which my covenant they brake, although I was an husband unto them, saith the Lord: but this shall be the covenant that I will make with the house of Israel; After those days, saith the Lord, I will put my law in their inward parts, and write it in their hearts; and will be their God, and they shall be my people. And they shall teach no more every man his neighbour, and every man his brother, saying, Know the Lord: for they shall all know me, from the least of the unto the greatest of them, saith the Lord: for I will forgive their iniquity, and I will remember their sin no more.

The Gospel. St. John 9:1-38

AS Jesus passed by, he saw a man which was blind from his birth. And his disciples asked him, saying, Master, who did sin, this man, or his parents, that he was born blind? Jesus answered, Neither hath this man sinned, nor his parents: but that the works of God should be made manifest in him. I must work the works of him that sent me, while it is day: the night cometh, when no man can work. As long as I am in the world, I am the light of the world. When he had thus spoken, he spat on the ground, and made clay of the spittle, and he anointed the eyes of the blind man with the clay, and said unto him, Go, wash in the pool of Siloam, (which is by interpretation, Sent.) He went his way therefore, and washed, and came seeing. The neighbours therefore, and they which before had seen him that he was blind, said, Is not this he that sat and begged? Some said, This is he others said, He is like him: but he said, I am he. Therefore said they unto him, How were thine eyes opened? He answered and said, A man that is called Jesus made clay, and anointed mine eyes, and said unto me, Go to the pool of Siloam, and wash: and I went and washed, and I received sight. Then said they unto him, Where is he? He said, I know not.

They brought to the Pharisees him that aforetime was blind. And it was the sabbath day when Jesus made the clay, and opened his eyes. Then again the Pharisees also asked him how he had received his sight. He said unto them, He put clay upon mine eyes, and I washed, and do see. Therefore said some of the Pharisees, This man is not of God, because he keepeth not the sabbath day. Others said, How can a man that is a sinner do such miracles? And there was a division among them. They say unto the blind man again, What sayest thou of him, that he hath opened thine eyes? He said, He is a prophet.

But the Jews did not believe concerning him, that he had been blind, and received his sight, until they called the parents of him that had received his sight. And they asked them, saying, Is this your son, who ye say was born blind? how then doth he now see? His parents answered them and said, We know that this is our son, and that he was born blind: but by what means he now seeth, we know not; or who hath opened his eyes, we know not: he is of age; ask him: he shall speak for himself. These words spake his parents, because they feared the Jews: for the Jews had agreed already, that if any man did confess that he was Christ, he should be put out of the synagogue. Therefore said his parents, He is of age; ask him.

Then again called they the man that was blind, and said unto him, Give God the praise: we know that this man is a sinner. He answered and said, Whether he be a sinner or no, I know not: one thing I know, that, whereas I was blind, now I see. Then said they to him again, What did he to thee? how opened he thine eyes? He answered them, I have told you already, and ye did not hear: wherefore would ye hear it again? will ye also be his disciples? Then they reviled him, and said, Thou art his disciple; but we are Moses' disciples. We know that God spake unto Moses: as for this fellow, we know not from whence he is. The man answered and said unto them, Why herein is a marvellous thing, that ye know not from whence he is, and yet he hath opened mine eyes. Now we know that God heareth not sinners: but if any man be a worshipper of God, and doeth his will, him he heareth. Since the world began was it not heard that any man opened the eyes of one that was born blind. If this man were not of God, he could do nothing. They answered and said unto him, Thou wast altogether born in sins, and dost thou teach us? And they cast him out.

Jesus heard that they had cast him out; and when he had found him, he said unto him, Dost thou believe on the Son of man? He answered and said, Who is he, Lord, that I might believe on him? And Jesus said unto him, Thou hast both seen him, and it is he that talketh with thee. And he said, Lord, I believe. And he worshipped him.

FRIDAY IN THE FOURTH WEEK OF LENT

The Collect

GRANT, we beseech thee, Almighty God, that we, who for our evil deeds do worthily deserve to be punished, by the comfort of thy grace may mercifully be relieved; through our Lord and Saviour Jesus Christ. *Amen.*

The Epistle. Ezekiel 34:1-16

FOR thus saith the Lord God; Behold, I, even I, will both search my sheep, and seek them out. As a shepherd seeketh out his flock in the day that he is among his sheep, that are scattered; so will I seek out my sheep, and will deliver them out of all places where they have been scattered in the cloudy and dark day. And I will bring them out from the people, and gather them from the countries, and will bring them to their own land, and feed them upon the mountains of Israel by the rivers, and in all the inhabited places of the country. I will feed them in a good pasture, and upon the high mountains of Israel shall their fold be: there shall they lie in a good fold, and in a fat pasture shall they feed upon the mountains of Israel. I will feed my flock, and I will cause them to lie down, saith the Lord God. I will seek that which was lost, and bring again that which was driven away, and will bind up that which was broken, and will strengthen that which was sick: but I will watch over the fat and the strong; I will feed them with judgment.

The Gospel. St. John 10:17-31

THEREFORE doth my Father love me, because I lay down my life, that I might take it again. No man taketh it from me, but I lay it down of myself. I have power to lay it down, and I have power to take it again. This commandment have I received of my Father. There was a division therefore again among the Jews for these sayings. And many of them said, He hath a devil, and is mad; why hear ye him? Others said, These are not the words of him that hath a devil. Can a devil open the eyes of the blind?

And it was at Jerusalem the feast of the dedication, and it was winter. And Jesus walked in the temple in Solomon's porch. Then came the Jews round about him, and said unto him, How long dost thou make us to doubt? If thou be the Christ, tell us plainly. Jesus answered them, I told you, and ye believed not: the works that I do in my Father's name, they bear witness of me. But ye believe not, because ye are not of my sheep, as I said unto you. My sheep hear my voice, and I know them, and they follow me: and I give unto them eternal life; and they shall never perish, neither shall any man pluck them out of my hand. My Father, which gave them me, is greater than all; and no man is able to pluck them out of my Father's hand. I and my Father are one. Then the Jews took up stones again to stone him.

WEDNESDAY IN THE FIFTH WEEK OF LENT

The Collect

WE beseech thee, Almighty God, mercifully to look upon thy people; that by thy great goodness they may be governed and preserved evermore, both in body and soul; through Jesus Christ our Lord. *Amen.*

The Epistle. Isaiah 49:1-6

LISTEN, O isles, unto me; and hearken, ye people, from far; The Lord hath called me from the womb; from the bowels of my mother hath he made mention of my name. And he hath made my mouth like a sharp sword; in the shadow of his hand hath he hid me, and made me a polished arrow; in his quiver hath he hid me; and said unto me, Thou art my servant, O Israel, in whom I will be glorified. Then I said, I have laboured in vain, I have spent my strength for nought, and in vain: yet surely my judgment is with the Lord, and my work with my God. And now, saith the Lord that formed me from the womb to be his servant, to bring Jacob again to him, Though Israel be not gathered, yet shall I be glorious in the eyes of the Lord, and my God shall be my strength. And he said, It is a light thing that thou shouldest be my servant to raise up the tribes of Jacob, and to restore the preserved of Israel: I will also give thee for a light to the Gentiles, that thou mayest be my salvation unto the end of the earth.

The Gospel. St. John 11:1-46

NOW a certain man was sick, named Lazarus, of Bethany, the town of Mary and her sister Martha. (It was that Mary which anointed the Lord with ointment, and wiped his feet with her hair, whose brother Lazarus was sick.) Therefore his sisters sent unto him, saying, Lord, behold, he whom thou lovest is sick. When Jesus heard that, he said, This sickness is not unto death, but for the glory of God, that the Son of God might be glorified thereby.

Now Jesus loved Martha, and her sister, and Lazarus. When he had heard therefore that he was sick, he abode two days still in the same place where he was. Then after that saith he to his disciples, Let us go into Judaea again. His disciples say unto him, Master, the Jews of late sought to stone thee; and goest thou thither again? Jesus answered Are there not twelve hours in the day? If any man walk in the day, he stumbleth not, because he seeth the light of this world. But if a man walk in the night, he stumbleth, because there is no light in him. These things said he: and after that he saith unto them, Our friend Lazarus sleepeth; but I go, that I may awake him out of sleep. Then said his disciples, Lord, if he sleep, he shall do well. Howbeit Jesus spake of his death: but they thought that he had spoken of taking of rest in sleep. Then said Jesus unto them plainly Lazarus is dead. And I am glad for your sakes that I was not there, to the intent ye may believe; nevertheless let us go unto him. Then said Thomas, which is called Didymus, unto his fellowdisciples, Let us also go, that we may die with him.

Then when Jesus came, he found that he had lain in the grave four days already. Now Bethany was nigh unto Jerusalem, about fifteen furlongs off: and many of the Jews came to Martha and Mary, to comfort them concerning their brother. Then Martha, as soon as she heard that Jesus was coming, went and met him: but Mary sat still in the house. Then said Martha unto Jesus, Lord, if thou hadst been here, my brother had not died. But I know, that even now, whatsoever thou wilt ask of God, God will give it thee. Jesus saith unto her, Thy brother shall rise again. Martha saith unto him, I know that he shall rise again in the resurrection at the last day. Jesus said unto her, I am the resurrection, and the life: he that believeth in me, though he were dead, yet shall he live: and whosoever liveth and believeth in me shall never die. Believest thou this? She saith unto him, Yea, Lord: I believe that thou art the Christ, the Son of God, which should come into the world.

And when she had so said, she went her way, and called Mary her sister secretly, saying, The Master is come, and calleth for thee. As soon as she heard that, she arose quickly, and came unto him. Now Jesus was not yet come into the town, but was in that place where Martha met him. The Jews then which were with her in the house, and comforted her, when they saw Mary, that she rose up hastily and went out, followed her, saying, She goeth unto the grave to weep there. Then when Mary was come where Jesus was, and saw him, she fell down at his feet, saying unto him, Lord, if thou hadst been here, my brother had not died. When Jesus therefore saw her weeping, and the Jews also weeping which came with her, he groaned in the spirit, and was troubled, and said, Where have ye laid him? They said unto him, Lord, come and see. Jesus wept. Then said the Jews, Behold how he loved him! And some of them said, Could not this man, which opened the eyes of the blind, have caused that even this man should not have died?

Jesus therefore again groaning in himself cometh to the grave. It was a cave, and a stone lay upon it. Jesus said, Take ye away the stone. Martha, the sister of him that was dead, saith unto him, Lord, by this time he stinketh: for he hath been dead four days. Jesus saith unto her, Said I not unto thee, that, if thou wouldest believe, thou shouldest see the glory of God? Then they took away the stone from the place where the dead was laid. And Jesus lifted up his eyes, and said, Father, I thank thee that thou hast heard me. And I knew that thou hearest me always: but because of the people which stand by I said it, that they may believe that thou hast sent me. And when he thus had spoken, he cried with a loud voice, Lazarus, come forth. And he that was dead came forth, bound hand and foot with graveclothes: and his face was bound about with a napkin. Jesus saith unto them, Loose him, and let him go. Then many of the Jews which came to Mary, and had seen the things which Jesus did, believed on him. But some of them went their ways to the Pharisees, and told them what things Jesus had done.

FRIDAY IN THE FIFTH WEEK OF LENT

The Collect

WE beseech thee, Almighty God, mercifully to look upon thy people; that by thy great goodness they may be governed and preserved evermore, both in body and soul; through Jesus Christ our Lord. *Amen.*

The Epistle. Isaiah 52:13-53:12

BEHOLD, my servant shall prosper, he shall be exalted and extolled, and be very high. As many were astonished at thee; his visage was so marred more than any man, and his form more than the sons of men: so shall he startle many nations; the kings shall shut their mouths at him: for that which had not been told them shall they see; and that which they had not heard shall they consider.

Who hath believed our report? and to whom is the arm of the LORD revealed? For he grew up before him as a tender plant, and as a root out of a dry ground: he hath no form nor comeliness, that we should look at him, and no beauty that we should desire him. He is despised and rejected of men; a man of sorrows, and acquainted with grief: and we hid as it were our faces from him; he was despised, and we esteemed him not.

Surely he hath borne our griefs, and carried our sorrows: yet we did esteem him stricken, smitten of God, and afflicted. But he was wounded for our transgressions, he was bruised for our iniquities: the chastisement of our peace was upon him; and with his stripes we are healed. All we like sheep have gone astray; we have turned every one to his own way; and the LORD hath laid on him the iniquity of us all.

He was oppressed, and he was afflicted, yet he opened not his mouth: he is brought as a lamb to the slaughter, and as a sheep before her shearers is dumb, so he openeth not his mouth. He was taken from prison and from judgment: at who shall declare his generation? for he was cut off out of the land of the living: for the transgression of my people was he stricken. And he made his grave with the wicked and with the rich in his death; although he had done no violence, neither was any deceit in his mouth.

Yet it pleased the LORD to bruise him; he hath put him to grief: when thou shalt make his soul an offering for sin, he shall see his seed, he shall prolong his days, and the pleasure of the LORD shall prosper in his hand. He shall see of the travail of his soul, and shall be satisfied: by his knowledge shall my righteous servant justify many; for he shall bear their iniquities. Therefore will I divide him a portion with the great, and he shall divide the spoil with the strong; because he hath poured out his soul unto death: and he was numbered with the transgressors; and he bare the sin of many, and made intercession for the transgressors.

The Gospel. St. John 12:23-32

JESUS answered them, saying, The hour is come, that the Son of man should be glorified. Verily, verily, I say unto you, Except a corn of wheat fall into the ground and die, it abideth alone: but if it die, it bringeth forth much fruit. He that loveth his life shall lose it; and he that hateth his life in this world shall keep it unto life eternal. If any man serve me, let him follow me; and where I am, there shall also my servant be: if any man serve me, him will my Father honour. Now is my soul troubled; and what shall I say? Father, save me from this hour: but for this cause came I unto this hour. Father, glorify thy name. Then came there a voice from heaven, saying, I have both glorified it, and will glorify it again. The people therefore, that stood by, and heard it, said that it thundered: others said, An angel spake to him. Jesus answered and said, This voice came not because of me, but for your sakes. Now is the judgment of this world: now shall the prince of this world be cast out. And I, if I be lifted up from the earth, will draw all men unto me.

Eastertide

WEDNESDAY IN EASTER WEEK

The Collect

ALMIGHTY God, who through thine only-begotten Son Jesus Christ hast overcome death, and opened unto us the gate of everlasting life: We humbly beseech thee that, as by thy special grace preventing us thou dost put into our minds good desires, so by thy continual help we may bring the same to good effect; through the same Jesus Christ our Lord, who liveth and reigneth with thee and the Holy Ghost ever, one God, world without end. *Amen.*

The Epistle. Acts 3:13-5, 17-19, 26

AND Peter said: The God of Abraham, and of Isaac, and of Jacob, the God of our fathers, hath glorified his Son Jesus; whom ye delivered up, and denied him in the presence of Pilate, when he was determined to let him go. But ye denied the Holy One and the Just, and desired a murderer to be granted unto you; and killed the Prince of life, whom God hath raised from the dead; whereof we are witnesses. And now, brethren, I know that through ignorance ye did it, as did also your rulers. But those things, which God before had shewed by the mouth of all his prophets, that Christ should suffer, he hath so fulfilled.

Repent ye therefore, and be converted, that your sins may be blotted out, when the times of refreshing shall come from the presence of the Lord. Unto you first God, having raised up his Son Jesus, sent him to bless you, in turning away every one of you from his iniquities.

The Gospel. St. John 21:1-14

AFTER these things Jesus shewed himself again to the disciples at the sea of Tiberias; and on this wise shewed he himself. There were together Simon Peter, and Thomas called Didymus, and Nathaniel of Cana in Galilee, and the sons of Zebedee, and two other of his disciples. Simon Peter saith unto them, I go a fishing. They say unto him, We also go with thee. They went forth, and entered into a ship immediately; and that night they caught nothing.

But when the morning was now come, Jesus stood on the shore: but the disciples knew not that it was Jesus. Then Jesus saith unto them, Children, have ye any meat? They answered him, No. And he said unto them, Cast the net on the right side of the ship, and ye shall find. They cast therefore, and now they were not able to draw it for the multitude of fishes. Therefore that disciple whom Jesus loved saith unto Peter, It is the Lord. Now when Simon Peter heard that it was the Lord, he girt his fisher's coat unto him, (for he was naked,) and did cast himself into the sea. And the other disciples came in a little ship; (for they were not far from land, but as it were two hundred cubits,) dragging the net with fishes.

As soon then as they were come to land, they saw a fire of coals there, and fish laid thereon, and bread. Jesus saith unto them, Bring of the fish which ye have now caught. Simon Peter went up, and drew the net to land full of great fishes, an hundred and fifty and three: and for all there were so many, yet was not the net broken. Jesus saith unto them, Come and dine. And none of the disciples durst ask him, Who art thou? knowing that it was the Lord. Jesus then cometh, and taketh bread, and giveth them, and fish likewise. This is now the third time that Jesus shewed himself to his disciples, after that he was risen from the dead.

THURSDAY IN EASTER WEEK

The Collect

ALMIGHTY God, who through thine only-begotten Son Jesus Christ hast overcome death, and opened unto us the gate of everlasting life: We humbly beseech thee that, as by thy special grace preventing us thou dost put into our minds good desires, so by thy continual help we may bring the same to good effect; through the same Jesus Christ our Lord, who liveth and reigneth with thee and the Holy Ghost ever, one God, world without end. *Amen.*

The Epistle. Colossians 1:18-23

HE is the head of the body, the church: who is the beginning, the firstborn from the dead; that in all things he might have the preeminence. For it pleased the Father that in him should all fulness dwell; and, having made peace through the blood of his cross, by him to reconcile all things unto himself; by him, I say, whether they be things in earth, or things in heaven. And you, that were sometime alienated and enemies in your mind by wicked works, yet now hath he reconciled in the body of his flesh through death, to present you holy and unblameable and unreproveable in his sight: if ye continue in the faith grounded and settled, and be not moved away from the hope of the gospel, which ye have heard, and which was preached to every creature which is under heaven.

The Gospel. St. Luke 24:1-12

NOW upon the first day of the week, very early in the morning, they came unto the sepulchre, bringing the spices which they had prepared, and certain others with them. And they found the stone rolled away from the sepulchre. And they entered in, and found not the body of the Lord Jesus. And it came to pass, as they were much perplexed thereabout, behold, two men stood by them in shining garments: and as they were afraid, and bowed down their faces to the earth, they said unto them, Why seek ye the living among the dead? He is not here, but is risen: remember how he spake unto you when he was yet in Galilee, saying, The Son of man must be delivered into the hand of sinful men, and be crucified, and the third day rise again. And they remembered his words, and returned from the sepulchre, and told all these things unto the eleven, and to all the rest. It was Mary Magdalene, and Joanna, and Mary the mother of James, and other women that were with them, which told these things unto the apostles. And their words seemed to them as idle tales, and they believed them not. Then arose Peter, and ran unto the sepulchre; and stooping down, he beheld the linen clothes laid by themselves, and departed, wondering in himself at that which was come to pass.

FRIDAY IN EASTER WEEK

The Collect

ALMIGHTY God, who through thine only-begotten Son Jesus Christ hast overcome death, and opened unto us the gate of everlasting life: We humbly beseech thee that, as by thy special grace preventing us thou do put into our minds good desires, so by thy continual help we may bring the same to good effect; through the same Jesus Christ our Lord, who liveth and reigneth with the and the Holy Ghost ever, one God, world without end. *Amen.*

The Epistle. Colossians 2:10-15

YE are complete in him, which is the head of all principality and power: in whom also ye are circumcised with the circumcision made without hands, in putting on the body of the sins of the flesh by the circumcision of Christ: buried with him in baptism, wherein also ye are risen with him through the faith of the operation of God, who hath raised him from the dead. And you, being dead in your sins and the uncircumcision of your flesh, hath he quickened together with him, having forgiven you all trespasses; blotting out the handwriting of ordinances that was against us, which was contrary to us, and took it out of the way, nailing it to his cross; and having spoiled principalities and powers, he made a shew of them openly, triumphing over them in it.

The Gospel. St. Matthew 28:1-10

IN the end of the sabbath, as it began to dawn toward the first day of the week, came Mary Magdalene and the other Mary to see the sepulchre. And, behold, there was a great earthquake: for the angel of the Lord descended from heaven, and came and rolled back the stone from the door, and sat upon it. His countenance was like lightning, and his raiment white as snow: and for fear of him the keepers did shake, and became as dead men. And the angel answered and said unto the women, Fear not ye: for I know that ye seek Jesus, which was crucified. He is not here: for he is risen, as he said. Come, see the place where the Lord lay. And go quickly, and tell his disciples that he is risen from the dead; and, behold, he goeth before you into Galilee; there shall ye see him: lo, I have told you. And they departed quickly from the sepulchre with fear and great joy; and did run to bring his disciples word. And as they went to tell his disciples, behold, Jesus met them, saying, All hail. And they came and held him by the feet, and worshipped him. Then said Jesus unto them, Be not afraid: go tell my brethren that they go into Galilee, and there shall they see me.

SATURDAY IN EASTER WEEK

The Collect

ALMIGHTY God, who through thine only-begotten Son Jesus Christ hast overcome death, and opened unto us the gate of everlasting life: We humbly beseech thee that, as by thy special grace preventing us thou dost put into our minds good desires, so by thy continual help we may bring the same to good effect; through the same Jesus Christ our Lord, who liveth and reigneth with thee and the Holy Ghost ever, one God, world without end. *Amen.*

The Epistle. 1 Peter 1:3-5, 13-21

BLESSED be the God and Father of our Lord Jesus Christ, which according to his abundant mercy hath begotten us again unto a lively hope by the resurrection of Jesus Christ from the dead, to an inheritance incorruptible, and undefiled, and that fadeth not away, reserved in heaven for you, who are kept by the power of God through faith unto salvation ready to be revealed in the last time.

Wherefore gird up the loins of your mind, be sober, and hope to the end for the grace that is to be brought unto you at the revelation of Jesus Christ; as obedient children, no fashioning yourselves according to the former lusts in your ignorance: but as he which hath called you is holy, so be ye holy in all manner of conversation; because it is written, Be ye holy; for I am holy. And if ye call on the Father, who without respect of persons judgeth according to every man's work, pass the time of your sojourning here in fear: forasmuch as ye know that ye were not redeemed with corruptible things, as silver and gold, from your vain conversation received by tradition from your fathers; but with the precious blood of Christ, as of a lamb without blemish and without spot: who verily was foreordained before the foundation of the world, but was manifest in these last times for you, who by him do believe in God, that raised him up from the dead, and gave him glory; that your faith and hope might be in God.

The Gospel. St. John 20:11-18

MARY stood without at the sepulchre weeping: and as she wept, she stooped down, and looked into the sepulchre, and seeth two angels in white sitting, the one at the head, and the other at the feet, where the body of Jesus had lain. And they say unto her, Woman, why weepest thou? She saith unto them, Because they have taken away my Lord, and I know not where they have laid him. And when she had thus said, she turned herself back, and saw Jesus standing, and knew not that it was Jesus. Jesus saith unto her, Woman, why weepest thou? whom seekest thou? She, supposing him to be the gardener, saith unto him, Sir, if thou have borne him hence, tell me where thou hast laid him, and I will take him away. Jesus saith unto her, Mary. She turned herself, and saith unto him, Rabboni; which is to say, Master. Jesus saith unto her, Touch me not; for I am not yet ascended to my Father: but go to my brethren, and say unto them, I ascend unto my Father, and your Father; and to my God, and your God. Mary Magdalene came and told the disciples that she had seen the Lord, and that he had spoken these things unto her.

The Rogation Days
Being the Three Days before Ascension Day

MONDAY

The Collect

ALMIGHTY God, Lord of heaven and earth: We beseech thee to pour forth thy blessing upon this land, and to give us a fruitful season; that we, constantly receiving thy bounty, may evermore give thanks unto thee in thy holy Church; through Jesus Christ our Lord. *Amen.*

The Epistle. Ezekiel 34:2 5-31

I WILL make with them a covenant of peace, and will cause the evil beasts to cease out of the land: and they shall dwell safely in the wilderness, and sleep in the woods. And I will make them and the places round about my hill a blessing; and I will cause the shower to come down in his season; there shall be showers of blessing. And the tree of the field shall yield her fruit, and the earth shall yield her increase, and they shall be safe in their land, and shall know that I am the Lord, when I have broken the bands of their yoke, and delivered them out of the hand of those that served themselves of them. And they shall no more be a prey to the heathen, neither shall the beast of the land devour them; but they shall dwell safely, and none shall make them afraid. And I will raise up for them a plant of renown, and they shall be no more consumed with hunger in the land, neither bear the shame of the heathen any more. Thus shall they know that I the Lord their God am with them, and that they, even the house of Israel, are my people, saith the Lord God. And ye my flock, the flock of my pasture, are men, and I am your God, saith the Lord God.

The Gospel. St. Luke 11:5-13

JESUS said unto them, Which of you shall have a friend, and shall go unto him at midnight, and say unto him, Friend, lend me three loaves; for a friend of mine in his journey is come to me, and I have nothing to set before him? and he from within shall answer and say, Trouble me not: the door is now shut, and my children are with me in bed; I cannot rise and give thee. I say unto you, Though he will not rise and give him, because he is his friend, yet because of his importunity he will rise and give him as many as he needeth. And I say unto you, Ask, and it shall be given you; seek, and ye shall find; knock, and it shall be opened unto you. For every one that asketh receiveth; and he that seeketh findeth; and to him that knocketh it shall be opened. If a son shall ask bread of any of you that is a father, will he give him a stone? or if he ask a fish, will he for a fish give him a serpent? or if he shall ask an egg, will he offer him a scorpion? If ye then, being evil, know how to give good gifts unto your children: how much more shall your heavenly Father give the Holy Spirit to them that ask him?

TUESDAY

The Collect

ALMIGHTY God, Lord of heaven and earth: We beseech thee to pour forth thy blessing upon this land, and to give us a fruitful season; that we, constantly receiving thy bounty, may evermore give thanks unto thee in thy holy Church; through Jesus Christ our Lord. *Amen.*

The Epistle. Joel 2:21-27

FEAR not, O land; be glad and rejoice: for the Lord will do great things. Be not afraid, ye beasts of the field: for the pastures of the wilderness do spring, for the tree beareth her fruit, the fig tree and the vine do yield their strength. Be glad then, ye children of Zion, and rejoice in the Lord your God: for he hath given you the former rain moderately, and he will cause to come down for you the rain, the former rain, and the latter rain, as before. And the floors shall be full of wheat, and the vats shall overflow with wine and oil. And I will restore to you the years that the locust hath eaten, the cankerworm, and the caterpiller, and the palmerworm, my great army which I sent among you. And ye shall eat in plenty, and be satisfied, and praise the name of the LORD your God, that hath dealt wondrously with you: and my people shall never be ashamed. And ye shall know that I am in the midst of Israel, and that I am the Lord your God, and none else: and my people shall never ashamed.

The Gospel. St. Mark 11:22-26

JESUS saith unto them, Have faith in God. For verily I say unto you, That whosoever shall say unto this mountain, Be thou removed, and be thou cast into the sea; and shall not doubt in his heart, but shall believe that those things which he saith shall come to pass; he shall have whatsoever he saith. Therefore I say unto you, What things soever ye desire, when ye pray, believe that ye receive them, and ye shall have them. And when ye stand praying, forgive, if ye have ought against any: that your Father also which is in heaven may forgive you your trespasses. But if ye do not forgive, neither will your Father which is in heaven forgive your trespasses.

WEDNESDAY

The Collect

ALMIGHTY God, Lord of heaven and earth: We beseech thee to pour forth thy blessing upon this land, and to give us a fruitful season; that we, constantly receiving thy bounty, may evermore give thanks unto thee in thy holy Church; through Jesus Christ our Lord. *Amen.*

The Epistle. Micah 6:6-8

HEREWITH shall I come before the LORD, and bow myself before the high God? shall I come before him with burnt offerings, with calves of a year old? Will the LORD be pleased with thousands of rams, or with ten thousands of rivers of oil? shall I give my firstborn for my transgression, the fruit of my body for the sin of my soul? He hath shewed thee, O man, what is good; and what doth the LORD require of thee, but to do justly, and to love mercy, and to walk humbly with thy God?

The Gospel. St. Matthew 6:5-8

WHEN thou prayest, thou shalt not be as the hypocrites are: for they love to pray standing in the synagogues and in the corners of the streets, that they may be seen of men. Verily I say unto you, They have their reward. But thou, when thou prayest, enter into thy closet, and when thou hast shut thy door, pray to thy Father which is in secret; and thy Father which seeth in secret shall reward thee openly. But when ye pray, use not vain repetitions, as the heathen do: for they think that they shall be heard for their much speaking. Be not ye therefore like unto them: for your Father knoweth what things ye have need of, before ye ask him.

Whitsuntide

WEDNESDAY IN WHITSUN WEEK
EMBER DAY

The Collect

ALMIGHTY God, our heavenly Father, who hast purchased to thyself an universal Church by the precious blood of thy dear Son: Mercifully look upon the same, and at this time so guide and govern the minds of thy servants the Bishops and Pastors of thy flock, that they may lay hands suddenly on no man, but faithfully and wisely make choice of fit persons, to serve in the sacred Ministry of thy Church. And to those who shall be ordained to any holy function, give thy grace and heavenly benediction; that both by their life and doctrine they may show forth thy glory, and set forward the salvation of all men; through Jesus Christ our Lord. *Amen.*

O GOD, who as at this time didst teach the hearts thy faithful people, by sending to them the light thy Holy Spirit: Grant us by the same Spirit to have right judgment in all things, and evermore to rejoice his holy comfort; through the merits of Christ Jesus o Saviour, who liveth and reigneth with thee, in the unity the same Spirit, one God, world without end. *Amen.*

¶ *This Collect is to be said daily throughout Whitsun Week.*

The Epistle. 2 Corinthians 3:17-4:6

NOW the Lord is that Spirit: and where the Spirit of the Lord is, there is liberty. But we all, with open face beholding as in a glass the glory of the Lord, are changed into the same image from glory to glory, even as by the Spirit of the Lord. Therefore seeing we have this ministry, as we have received mercy, we faint not; but have renounced the hidden things of dishonesty, not walking in craftiness, nor handling the word of God deceitfully; but by manifestation of the truth commending ourselves to every man's conscience in the sight of God. But if our gospel be hid, it is hid to them that are lost: in whom the god of this world hath blinded the minds of them which believe not, lest the light of the glorious gospel of Christ, who is the image of God, should shine unto them. For we preach not ourselves, but Christ Jesus the Lord; and ourselves your servants for Jesus' sake. For God, who commanded the light to shine out of darkness, hath shined in our hearts, to give the light of the knowledge of the glory of God in the face of Jesus Christ.

The Gospel. St. Luke 4:16-2.1

JESUS came to Nazareth, where he had been brought up: and, as his custom was, he went into the synagogue on the sabbath day, and stood up for to read. And there was delivered unto him the book of the prophet Esaias. And when he had opened the book, he found the place where it was written.

> The Spirit of the Lord is upon me,
> because he hath anointed me to preach the gospel to the poor;
> he hath sent me to heal the broken-hearted, to preach
> deliverance to the captives,
> and recovering of sight to the blind,
> to set at liberty them that are bruised,
> to preach the acceptable year of the Lord.

And he closed the book, and he gave it again to the minister, and sat down. And the eyes of all them that were in the synagogue were fastened on him. And he began to say unto them, This day is this scripture fulfilled in your ears.

THURSDAY IN WHITSUN WEEK

The Collect

O GOD, who as at this time didst teach the hearts of thy faithful people, by sending to them the light of thy Holy Spirit: Grant us by the same Spirit to have a right judgment in all things, and evermore to rejoice in his holy comfort; through the merits of Christ Jesus our Saviour, who liveth and reigneth with thee, in the unity of the same Spirit, one God, world without end. *Amen.*

The Epistle. Romans 8:

THERE is therefore now no condemnation to them which are in Christ Jesus, who walk not after the flesh, but after the Spirit. For the law of the Spirit of life in Christ Jesus hath made me free from the law of sin and death. For what the law could not do, in that it was weak through the flesh, God sending his own Son in the likeness of sinful flesh, and for sin, condemned sin in the flesh: that the righteousness of the law might be fulfilled in us, who walk not after the flesh, but after the Spirit. For they that are after the flesh do mind the things of the flesh; but they that are after the Spirit the things of the Spirit. For to be carnally minded is death; but to be spiritually minded is life and peace. Because the carnal mind is enmity against God: for it is not subject to the law of God, neither indeed can be. So then they that are in the flesh cannot please God. But ye are not in the flesh, but in the Spirit, if so be that the Spirit of God dwell in you. Now if any man have not the Spirit of Christ, he is none of his. And if Christ be in you, the body is dead because of sin; but the Spirit is life because of righteousness. But if the Spirit of him that raised up Jesus from the dead dwell in you, he that raised up Christ from the dead shall also quicken your mortal bodies by his Spirit that dwelleth in you.

The Gospel. St. John 16:12-15

I HAVE yet many things to say unto you, but ye cannot bear them now. Howbeit when he, the Spirit of truth, is come, he will guide you into all truth: for he shall not speak of himself; but whatsoever he shall hear, that shall he speak: and he will shew you things to come. He shall glorify me: for he shall receive of mine, and shall shew it unto you. All things that the Father hath are mine: therefore said I, that he shall take of mine, and shall shew it unto you.

FRIDAY IN WHITSUN WEEK
EMBER DAY

The Collect

ALMIGHTY God, our heavenly Father, who hast purchased to thyself an universal Church by the precious blood of thy dear Son: Mercifully look upon the same, and at this time so guide and govern the minds of thy servants the Bishops and Pastors of thy flock, that they may lay hands suddenly on no man, but faithfully and wisely make choice of fit persons, to serve in the sacred Ministry of thy Church. And to those who shall be ordained to any holy function, give thy grace and heavenly benediction; that both by their life and doctrine they may show forth thy glory, and set forward the salvation of all men; through Jesus Christ our Lord. *Amen.*

The Epistle. Titus 3:4-8

AFTER that the kindness and love of God our Saviour toward man appeared, not by works of righteousness which we have done, but according to his mercy he saved us, by the washing of regeneration, and renewing of the Holy Ghost; which he shed on us abundantly through Jesus Christ our Saviour; that being justified by his grace, we should be made heirs according to the hope of eternal life. This is a faithful saying, and these things I will that thou affirm constantly, that they which have believed in God might be careful to maintain good works. These things are good and profitable unto men.

The Gospel. St. Matthew 28:16-20

THEN the eleven disciples went away into Galilee, into a mountain where Jesus had appointed them. And when they saw him, they worshipped him: but some doubted. And Jesus came and spake unto them, saying, All power is given unto me in heaven and in earth. Go ye therefore, and teach all nations, baptizing them in the name of the Father, and of the Son, and of the Holy Ghost: teaching them to observe all things whatsoever I have commanded you: and, lo, I am with you alway, even unto the end of the world. Amen.

SATURDAY IN WHITSUN WEEK
EMBER DAY

The Collect

ALMIGHTY God, our heavenly Father, who hast purchased to thyself an universal Church by the precious blood of thy dear Son: Mercifully look upon the same, and at this time so guide and govern the minds of thy servants the Bishops and Pastors of thy flock, that they may lay hands suddenly on no man, but faithfully and wisely make choice of fit persons, to serve in the sacred Ministry of thy Church. And to those who shall be ordained to any holy function, give thy grace and heavenly benediction; that both by their life and doctrine they may show forth thy glory, and set forward the salvation of all men; through Jesus Christ our Lord. *Amen.*

The Epistle. Ephesians 2:13-22

NOW in Christ Jesus ye who sometimes were far off are made nigh by the blood of Christ. For he is our peace, who hath made both one, and hath broken down the middle wall of partition between us; having abolished in his flesh the enmity, even the law of commandments contained in ordinances; for to make in himself of twain one new man, so making peace; and that he might reconcile both unto God in one body by the cross, having slain the enmity thereby: and came and preached peace to you which were afar off, and to them that were nigh. For through him we both have access by one Spirit unto the Father. Now therefore ye are no more strangers and foreigners, but fellowcitizens with the saints, and of the household of God; and are built upon the foundation of the apostles and prophets, Jesus Christ himself being the chief corner stone; in whom all the building fitly framed together groweth unto an holy temple in the Lord: in whom ye are also builded together for an habitation of God through the Spirit.

The Gospel. St. John 20:19-23

THE same day at evening, being the first day of the week, when the doors were shut where the disciples were assembled for fear of the Jews, came Jesus and stood in the midst, and saith unto them, Peace be unto you. And when he had so said, he shewed unto them his hands and his side. Then were the disciples glad, when they saw the Lord. Then said Jesus to them again, Peace be unto you: as my Father hath sent me, even so send I you. And when he had said this, he breathed on them, and saith unto them, Receive ye the Holy Ghost: whose soever sins ye remit, they are remitted unto them; and whose soever sins ye retain, they are retained.

The Autumn Ember Days

WEDNESDAY

The Collect

O ALMIGHTY God, look mercifully upon the world which thou hast redeemed by the blood of thy dear Son, and incline the hearts of many to dedicate themselves to the sacred Ministry of thy Church; through the same thy Son Jesus Christ our Lord. *Amen.*

The Epistle. Ephesians 4:11-16

AND he gave some, apostles; and some, prophets; and some, evangelists; and some, pastors and teachers; for the perfecting of the saints, for the work of the ministry, for the edifying of the body of Christ: till we all come in the unity of the faith, and of the knowledge of the Son of God, unto a perfect man, unto the measure of the stature of the fulness of Christ: that we henceforth be no more children, tossed to and fro, and carried about with every wind of doctrine, by the sleight of men, and cunning craftiness, whereby they lie in wait to deceive; but speaking the truth in love, may grow up into him in all things, which is the head, even Christ: from whom the whole body fitly joined together and compacted by that which every joint supplieth, according to the effectual working in the measure of every part, maketh increase of the body unto the edifying of itself in love.

The Gospel. St. John 15:1-8

I AM the true vine, and my Father is the husbandman. Every branch in me that beareth not fruit he taketh away: and every branch that beareth fruit, he pruneth it, that it may bring forth more fruit. Now ye are clean through the word which I have spoken unto you. Abide in me, and I in you. As the branch cannot bear fruit of itself, except it abide in the vine; no more can ye, except ye abide in me. I am the vine, ye are the branches: he that abideth in me, and I in him, the same bringeth forth much fruit: for without me ye can do nothing. If a man abide not in me, he is cast forth as a branch, and is withered; and men gather them, and cast them into the fire, and they are burned. If ye abide in me, and my words abide in you, ye shall ask what ye will, and it shall be done unto you. Herein is my Father glorified, that ye bear much fruit; so shall ye be my disciples.

FRIDAY

The Collect

O ALMIGHTY God, look mercifully upon the world which thou hast redeemed by the blood of thy dear Son, and incline the hearts of many to dedicate themselves to the sacred Ministry of thy Church; through the same thy Son Jesus Christ our Lord. *Amen.*

The Epistle. Acts 13:44-49

THE next sabbath day came almost the whole city together to hear the word of God. But when the Jews saw the multitudes, they were filled with envy, and spake against those things which were spoken by Paul, contradicting and blaspheming. Then Paul and Barnabas waxed bold, and said, It was necessary that the word of God should first have been spoken to you: but seeing ye put it from you, and judge yourselves unworthy of everlasting life, lo, we turn to the Gentiles. For so hath the Lord commanded us, saying, I have set thee to be a light of the Gentiles, that thou shouldest be for salvation unto the ends of the earth. And when the Gentiles heard this, they were glad, and glorified the word of the Lord: and as many as were ordained to eternal life believed. And the word of the Lord was published throughout all the region.

The Gospel. St. Matthew 10:24-32

THE disciple is not above his master, nor the servant above his lord. It is enough for the disciple that he be as his master, and the servant as his lord. If they have called the master of the house Beelzebub, how much more shall they call them of his household? Fear them not therefore: for there is nothing covered, that shall not be revealed; and hid, that shall not be known. What I tell you in darkness, that speak ye in light: and what ye hear in the ear, that preach ye upon the housetops. And fear not them which kill the body, but are not able to kill the soul: but rather fear him which is able to destroy both soul and body in hell. Are not two sparrows sold for a farthing? and one of them shall not fall on the ground without your Father. But the very hairs of your head are all numbered. Fear ye not therefore, ye are of more value than many sparrows.

Whosoever therefore shall confess me before men, him will I confess also before my Father which is in heaven.

SATURDAY

The Collect

O ALMIGHTY God, look mercifully upon the world which thou hast redeemed by the blood of thy dear Son, and incline the hearts of many to dedicate themselves to the sacred Ministry of thy Church; through the same thy Son Jesus Christ our Lord. *Amen.*

The Epistle. Acts 20:28-32

TAKE heed therefore unto yourselves, and to all the flock, over the which the Holy Ghost hath made you overseers, to feed the church of God, which he hath purchased with his own blood. For I know this, that after my departing shall grievous wolves enter in among you, not sparing the flock. Also of your own selves shall men arise, speaking perverse things, to draw away disciples after them. Therefore watch, and remember, that by the space of three years I ceased not to warn every one night and day with tears. And now, brethren, I commend you to God, and to the word of his grace, which is able to build you up, and to give you an inheritance among all them which are sanctified.

The Gospel. St. John 10:1-10

VERILY, verily, I say unto you, He that entereth not by the door into the sheepfold, but climbeth up some other way, the same is a thief and a robber. But he that entereth in by the door is the shepherd of the sheep. To him the porter openeth; and the sheep hear his voice: and he calleth his own sheep by name, and leadeth them out. And when he putteth forth his own sheep, he goeth before them. and the sheep follow him: for they know his voice. And a stranger will they not follow, but will flee from him: for they know not the voice of strangers. This parable spake Jesus unto them: but they understood not what things they were which he spake unto them.

Then said Jesus unto them again, Verily, verily, I say unto you, I am the door of the sheep. All that ever came before me are thieves and robbers: but the sheep did not hear them. I am the door: by me if any man enter in, he shall be saved, and shall go in and out, and find pasture. The thief cometh not, but for to steal, and to kill, and to destroy: I am come that they might have life, and that they might have it more abundantly.

The Lesser Holy Days

CHANNING MOORE WILLIAMS
Missionary Bishop in China and Japan
[December 2.]

The Collect

ALMIGHTY and everlasting God, we thank thee for thy servant Channing Moore Williams, whom thou didst call to preach the Gospel to the people of China and Japan: Raise up, we pray thee, in this and every land, heralds and evangelists of thy kingdom, that thy Church may make known the unsearchable riches of Christ, and may increase with the increase of God; through the same thy Son Jesus Christ our Lord. *Amen.*

CLEMENT OF ALEXANDRIA
Priest
[December 4.]

The Collect

O GOD, who hast enlightened thy Church by the teaching of thy servant Clement: Enrich us evermore, we beseech thee, with thy heavenly grace, and raise up faithful witnesses who by their life and doctrine will set forth the truth of thy salvation; through Jesus Christ our Lord. *Amen.*

The Epistle. 2 Peter 1:2-8

GRACE and peace be multiplied unto you through the knowledge of God, and of Jesus our Lord, according as his divine power hath given unto us all things that pertain unto life and godliness, through the knowledge of him that hath called us to glory and virtue: whereby are give unto us exceeding great and precious promises: that by these ye might be partakers of the divine nature, having escaped the corruption that is in the world through lust. And beside this, giving all diligence, add to your faith virtue; and to virtue knowledge; and to knowledge temperance; and to temperance patience; and to patience godliness; and to godliness brotherly kindness; and to brotherly kindness charity. For if these things be in you, and abound, they make you that ye shall neither be barren nor unfruitful in the knowledge of our Lord Jesus Christ.

The Gospel. St. John 6:57-63

AS the living Father hath sent me, and I live by the Father: so he that eateth me, even he shall live by me. This is that bread which came down from heaven: not as your fathers did eat manna, and are dead: he that eateth of this bread shall live for ever. These things said he in the synagogue, as he taught in Capernaum. Many therefore of his disciples, when they had heard this, said, This is an hard saying; who can hear it? When Jesus knew in himself that his disciples murmured at it, he said unto them, Doth this offend you? What and if ye shall see the Son of man ascend up where he was before? It is the spirit that quickeneth; the flesh profiteth nothing: the words that I speak unto you, they are spirit, and they are life.

JOHN OF DAMASCUS
Priest
[December 5.]

The Collect

ALMIGHTY God, who hast enriched thy Church with the singular learning and holiness of thy servant John: Grant us to hold fast the true doctrine of thy Son our Saviour Jesus Christ, and to fashion our lives according to the same, to the glory of thy great Name and the benefit of thy holy Church; through the same Jesus Christ our Lord. *Amen.*

NICHOLAS
Bishop of Myra
[December 6.]

The Collect

ALMIGHTY and everlasting God, who didst enkindle the flame of thy love in the heart of thy servant Nicholas: Grant to us, thy humble servants, the same faith and power of love; that, as we rejoice in his triumph, we may profit by his example; through Jesus Christ our Lord. *Amen.*

WILLIAM LAUD
Archbishop of Canterbury
[January 10]

The Collect

ACCEPT, O Lord, our thanksgiving this day for thy servant William Laud; and grant unto us such constancy and zeal in thy service, that we may obtain with him and thy servants everywhere a good confession and the crown of everlasting life; through Jesus Christ our Lord. *Amen.*

HILARY
Bishop of Poitiers
[January 14.]

The Collect

ALMIGHTY, everlasting God, whose servant Hilary steadfastly confessed thy Son our Saviour Jesus Christ to be Very God and Very Man: Grant that we may hold fast to this faith, and evermore magnify his holy Name; through the same thy Son Jesus Christ our Lord, who liveth and reigneth with thee and the Holy Spirit ever, one God, world without end. *Amen.*

The Epistle. 2 Timothy 4:1-8

I CHARGE thee therefore before God, and the Lord Jesus Christ, who shall judge the quick and the dead at his appearing and his kingdom; preach the word; be instant in season, out of season; reprove, rebuke, exhort with all longsuffering and doctrine. For the time will come when they will not endure sound doctrine; but after their own lusts shall they heap to themselves teachers, having itching ears; and they shall turn away their ears from the truth, and shall be turned unto fables. But watch thou in all things, endure afflictions, do the work of an evangelist, make full proof of thy ministry. For I am now ready to be offered, and the time of my departure is at hand. I have fought a good fight, I have finished my course, I have kept the faith: henceforth there is laid up for me a crown of righteousness, which the Lord, the righteous judge, shall give me at that day: and not to me only, but unto all them also that love his appearing.

The Gospel. St. Luke 12:8-12

ALSO I say unto you, Whosoever shall confess me before men, him shall the Son of man also confess before the angels of God: but he that denieth me before men shall be denied before the angels of God. And whosoever shall speak a word against the Son of man, it shall be forgiven him: but unto him that blasphemeth against the Holy Ghost it shall not be forgiven. And when they bring you unto the synagogues, and unto magistrates, and powers, do not be anxious how or what thing ye shall answer, or what ye shall say: for the Holy Ghost shall teach you in the same hour what ye ought to say.

ANTONY
Abbot in Egypt
[January 17.]

The Collect

O GOD, who by thy Holy Spirit didst enable thy servant Antony to withstand the temptations of the world, the flesh, and the devil: Grant that we by the same Spirit may with pure hearts and minds follow thee, the only God; through Jesus Christ our Lord. *Amen.*

The Epistle. Philippians 3:7-14

HOWBEIT what things were gain to me, these have I counted loss for Christ. Yea verily, and I count all things to be loss for the excellency of the knowledge of Christ Jesus my Lord: for whom I suffer the loss of all things, and do count them but dung, that I may gain Christ, and be found in him, not having a righteousness of mine own, even that which is of the law, but that which is through faith in Christ, the righteousness which is of God by faith: that I may know him, and the power of his resurrection, and the fellowship of his sufferings, becoming conformed unto his death; if by any means I may attain unto the resurrection of the dead. Not that I have already obtained, or am already made perfect: but I press on, if so be that I may apprehend that for which also I was apprehended by Christ Jesus. Brethren, I count not myself yet to have apprehended: but one thing I do, forgetting the things which are behind, and stretching forward to the things which are before, I press on toward the goal unto the prize of the high calling of God in Christ Jesus.

The Gospel. St. Luke 2:32-34

FEAR not, little flock; for it is your Father's good pleasure to give you the kingdom. Sell that ye have, and give alms; provide yourselves bags which wax not old, a treasure in the heavens that faileth not, where no thief approacheth, neither moth corrupteth. For where your treasure is, there will your heart be also.

WULFSTAN
Bishop of Worcester
[January 19.]

The Collect

O GOD, the light of the faithful and shepherd of souls, who didst call thy servant Wulfstan to feed thy sheep by his word, and guide them by his example: Grant us, we pray thee, to keep the faith which he taught, and to follow in his footsteps; through Jesus Christ our Lord. *Amen.*

FABIAN
Bishop of Rome, and Martyr
[January 20.]

The Collect

O GOD, who dost support and defend us with the glorious witness of thy blessed martyr Fabian: Grant us to go forward in his footsteps, and ever to rejoice in fellowship with him; through Jesus Christ our Lord. *Amen.*

AGNES
Martyr at Rome
[January 21.]

The Collect

ALMIGHTY and everlasting God, with whom thy meek ones go forth as the mighty: Grant us so to cherish the memory of thy blessed martyr Agnes, that we may share her pure and steadfast faith in thee; through Jesus Christ our Lord. *Amen.*

VINCENT
Deacon of Saragossa, and Martyr
[January 22.]

The Collect

ALMIGHTY God, by whose grace and power thy holy Deacon and martyr Vincent triumphed over suffering and despised death: Grant, we beseech thee, that enduring hardness, and waxing valiant in fight, we may with the noble army of martyrs receive the crown of everlasting life; through Jesus Christ our Lord. *Amen.*

PHILLIPS BROOKS
Bishop of Massachusetts
[January 23.]

The Collect

ALMIGHTY and everlasting God, the source and perfection of all virtues, who didst inspire thy servant Phillips Brooks both to do what is right and to preach what is true: Grant that all ministers and stewards of thy mysteries may afford to thy faithful people, by word and example, the instruction which is of thy grace; through Jesus Christ our Lord. *Amen.*

SAINT TIMOTHY
[January 24.]

The Collect

ALMIGHTY and merciful God, who didst call Saint Timothy to endure hardship, as a good soldier of thy Son: Strengthen us in like manner to stand firm in adversity, that we may obtain salvation with eternal glory; through the grace of Christ Jesus our Lord, who liveth and reigneth with thee and the Holy Ghost ever, one God, world without end. *Amen.*

The Epistle. 2 Timothy 1:1-7

PAUL, an apostle of Jesus Christ by the will of God, according to the promise of life which is in Christ Jesus, To Timothy, my dearly beloved son: Grace, mercy, and peace, from God the Father and Christ Jesus our Lord. I thank God, whom I serve from my forefathers with pure conscience, that without ceasing I have remembrance of thee in my prayers night and day; greatly desiring to see thee, being mindful of thy tears, that I may be filled with joy; when I call to remembrance the unfeigned faith that is in thee, which dwelt first in thy grandmother Lois, and thy mother Eunice; and I am persuaded that in thee also. Wherefore I put thee in remembrance that thou stir up the gift of God, which is in thee by the putting on of my hands. For God hath not given us the spirit of fear; but of power, and of love, and of self-control.

The Gospel. St. John 10:7-10

THEN said Jesus unto them again, Verily, verily, I say unto you, I am the door of the sheep. All that ever came before me are thieves and robbers: but the sheep did not hear them. I am the door: by me if any man enter in, he shall be saved, and shall go in and out, and find pasture. The thief cometh not, but for to steal, and to kill, and to destroy: I am come that they might have life, and that they might have it more abundantly.

POLYCARP
Bishop of Smyrna, and Martyr
[January 26]

The Collect

ALMIGHTY God, who didst give thy servant Polycarp boldness to confess the Name of our Saviour Jesus Christ before the rulers of this world, and courage to die for this faith: Grant that we likewise may ever be read to give a reason for the hope that is in us, and to suffer gladly for his sake; through the same Jesus Christ our Lord. *Amen.*

The Epistle. Revelation 2:8-11

UNTO the angel of the church in Smyrna write; These things saith the first and the last, which was dead, and is alive; I know thy works, and tribulation, and poverty (but thou art rich) and I know the blasphemy of the which say they are Jews, and are not, but are the synagogue of Satan. Fear none of those things which thou shalt suffer behold, the devil shall cast some of you into prison, that ye may be tried; and ye shall have tribulation ten days: be thou faithful unto death, and I will give thee a crown of life. He that hath an ear, let him hear what the Spirit saith unto the churches; He that overcometh shall not be hurt of the second death.

The Gospel. St. Matthew 20:20-23

THEN came to him the mother of Zebedee's children with her sons, worshipping him, and desiring a certain thing of him. And he said unto her, What wilt thou? She saith unto him, Grant that these my two sons may sit the one on thy right hand, and the other on the left, in thy kingdom. But Jesus answered and said, Ye know not what ye ask. Are ye able to drink of the cup that I shall drink of, and to be baptized with the baptism that I am baptized with? They say unto him, We are able. And he saith unto them, Ye shall drink indeed of my cup, and be baptized with the baptism that I am baptized with: but to sit on my right hand, and on my left, is not mine to give, but it shall be given to them for whom it is prepared of my Father.

JOHN CHRYSOSTOM
Bishop of Constantinople
[January 27.]

The Collect

O GOD, who didst give grace to thy servant John, eloquently to declare thy righteousness in the great congregation, and fearlessly to bear reproach for the honour of thy Name: Mercifully grant unto all bishops and pastors such excellency in preaching, and fidelity in ministering thy Word, that thy people may be partakers with them of the glory that shall be revealed; through Jesus Christ our Lord. *Amen.*

The Epistle. Jeremiah 1:4-9

THE word of the LORD came unto me, saying, Before I formed thee in the belly I knew thee; and before thou camest forth out of the womb I sanctified thee, and I ordained thee a prophet unto the nations. Then said I, Ah, LORD GOD! behold, I cannot speak: for I am a child. But the LORD said unto me, Say not, I am a child: for thou shalt go to all that I shall send thee, and whatsoever I command thee thou shalt speak. Be not afraid of their faces: for I am with thee to deliver thee, saith the LORD. Then the LORD put forth his hand, and touched my mouth. And the LORD said unto me, Behold, I have put my words in thy mouth.

The Gospel. St. Luke 21:12-15

THEY shall lay their hands on you, and persecute you, delivering you up to the synagogues, and into prisons being brought before kings and rulers for my name's sake. And it shall turn to you for a testimony. Settle it therefore in your hearts, not to meditate before what ye shall answer: for I will give you a mouth and wisdom, which all your adversaries shall not be able to gainsay nor resist.

IGNATIUS
Bishop of Antioch, and Martyr
[February 1.]

The Collect

ALMIGHTY God, by whose grace and power thy holy Bishop and martyr Ignatius triumphed over suffering and despised death: Grant, we beseech thee, that enduring hardness, and waxing valiant in fight, we may with the noble army of martyrs receive the crown of everlasting life; through Jesus Christ our Lord. *Amen.*

The Epistle. Romans 8:35-39

WHO shall separate us from the love of Christ? shall tribulation, or distress, or persecution, or famine, or nakedness, or peril, or sword? As it is written,

> For thy sake we are killed all the day long;
> we are accounted as sheep for the slaughter.

Nay, in all these things we are more than conquerors through him that loved us. For I am persuaded, that neither death, nor life, nor angels, nor principalities, nor powers, nor things present, nor things to come, nor height, nor depth, nor any other creature, shall be able to separate us from the love of God, which is in Christ Jesus our Lord.

The Gospel. St. John 12:24-26

VERILY, verily, I say unto you, Except a corn of wheat fall into the ground and die, it abideth alone: but if it die, it bringeth forth much fruit. He that loveth his life shall lose it; and he that hateth his life in this world shall keep it unto life eternal. If any man serve me, let him follow me; and where I am, there shall also my servant be: if any man serve me, him will my Father honour.

ANSGARIUS
Archbishop of Hamburg,
Missionary to Denmark and Sweden
[February 3.]

The Collect

ALMIGHTY and everlasting God, we thank thee for thy servant Ansgarius, whom thou didst call to preach the Gospel to the people of Scandinavia: Raise up, we pray thee, in this and every land, heralds and evangelists of thy kingdom, that thy Church may make known the unsearchable riches of Christ, and may increase with the increase of God; through the same thy son Jesus Christ our Lord. *Amen.*

SAINT CORNELIUS, THE CENTURION
[February 4.]

The Collect

O GOD, who by thy Spirit didst call Cornelius the Centurion to be the first Christian among the Gentiles: Grant to thy Church in every nation a ready mind and will to proclaim thy love to all who turn to thee with unfeigned hope and faith; for the sake of Jesus Christ our Lord, who liveth and reigneth with thee and the same Spirit ever, one God, world without end. *Amen.*

The Epistle. Acts 11:1-18

AND the apostles and brethren that were in Judaea heard that the Gentiles had also received the word of God. And when Peter was come up to Jerusalem, they that were of the circumcision contended with him, saying, Thou wentest in to men uncircumcised, and didst eat with them. But Peter rehearsed the matter from the beginning, and expounded it by order unto them, saying, I was in the city of Joppa praying: and in a trance I saw a vision, A certain vessel descended, as it had been a great sheet, let down from heaven by four corners; and it came even to me: upon the which when I had fastened mine eyes, I considered, and saw fourfooted beasts of the earth, and wild beasts, and creeping things, and fowls of the air. And I heard a voice saying unto me, Arise, Peter; slay and eat. But I said, Not so, Lord: for nothing common or unclean hath at any time entered into my mouth. But the voice answered me again from heaven, What God hath cleansed, that call not thou common. And this was done three times: and all were drawn up again into heaven. And, behold, immediately there were three men already come unto the house where I was, sent from Caesarea unto me. And the Spirit bade me go with them, nothing doubting. Moreover these six brethren accompanied me, and we entered into the man's house: and he shewed us how he had seen an angel in his house which stood and said unto him, Send men to Joppa, and call for Simon, whose surname is Peter; who shall tell the words, whereby thou and all thy house shall be saved. And as I began to speak, the Holy Ghost fell on them, as on us at the beginning. Then remembered I the word of the Lord, how that he said, John indeed baptized with water; but ye shall be baptized with the Holy Ghost. Forasmuch then as God gave them the like gift as he did unto us, who believed on the Lord Jesus Christ; what was I, that I could withstand God? When they heard these things, they held their peace, and glorified God, saying, Then hath God also to the Gentiles granted repentance unto life.

The Gospel. St. John 4:4-14

JESUS must needs go through Samaria. Then cometh he to a city of Samaria, which is called Sychar, near to the parcel of ground that Jacob gave to his son Joseph. Now Jacob's well was there. Jesus therefore, being wearied with his journey, sat thus on the well: and it was about the sixth hour. There cometh a woman of Samaria to draw water: Jesus saith unto her, Give me to drink. (For his disciples were gone away unto the city to buy meat.) Then saith the woman of Samaria unto him, How is it that thou, being a Jew, askest drink of me, which am a woman of Samaria? for the Jews have no dealings with the Samaritans. Jesus answered and said unto her, If thou knewest the gift of God, and who it is that saith to thee, Give me to drink; thou wouldest have asked of him, and he would have given thee living water. The woman saith unto him, Sir, thou hast nothing to draw with, and the well is deep: from whence then hast thou that living water? Art thou greater than our father Jacob, which gave us the well, and drank thereof himself, and his children, and his cattle? Jesus answered and said unto her, Whosoever drinketh of this water shall thirst again: but whosoever drinketh of the water that I shall give him shall never thirst; but the water that I shall give him shall be in him a well of water springing up into everlasting life.

THE MARTYRS OF JAPAN
[February 5.]

The Collect

ALMIGHTY God, by whose grace and power thy holy martyrs in Japan triumphed over suffering and despised death: Grant, we beseech thee, that enduring hardness, and waxing valiant in fight, we may with the noble army of martyrs receive the crown of everlasting life; through Jesus Christ our Lord. *Amen.*

SAINT TITUS
[February 6.]

The Collect

BLESSED Lord, who didst charge Saint Titus to speak the things that accord with sound doctrine and to offer himself a pattern of good works: Grant to all thy people to live soberly, righteously, and godly in this present age, that they may with sure confidence look for the blessed hope and glorious appearing of our great God and Saviour Jesus Christ, who liveth and reigneth with thee and the Holy Spirit ever, one God, world without end. *Amen.*

The Epistle. Titus 1:1-5

PAUL, a servant of God, and an apostle of Jesus Christ according to the faith of God's elect, and the acknowledging of the truth which is after godliness; in hope of eternal life, which God, that cannot lie, promised before the world began; but hath in due times manifested his word through preaching, which is committed unto me according to the commandment of God our Saviour; To Titus mine own son after the common faith: Grace, mercy, and peace, from God the Father and the Lord Jesus Christ our Saviour. For this cause left I thee in Crete, that thou shouldest set in order the things that are wanting, and ordain elder in every city, as I had appointed thee.

The Gospel. St. John 10:1-5

VERILY, verily, I say unto you, He that entereth not by the door into the sheepfold, but climbeth up some other way, the same is a thief and a robber. But he that entereth in by the door is the shepherd of the sheep. To him the porter openeth; and the sheep hear his voice: and he calleth his own sheep by name, and leadeth them out. And when he putteth forth his own sheep, he goeth before them, and the sheep follow him: for they know his voice. And a stranger will they not follow, but will flee from him: for they know not the voice of strangers. This parable spake Jesus unto them: but they understood not what things they were which he spake unto them.

THOMAS BRAY
Priest and Missionary
[February 15.]

The Collect

O GOD, who dost ever hallow and protect thy Church: Raise up therein through thy Spirit good and faithful stewards of the mysteries of Christ, as thou didst in thy servant Thomas Bray; that by their ministry and example thy people may abide in thy favour and walk in the way of truth; through Jesus Christ our Lord, who liveth and reigneth with thee in the unity of the same Spirit ever, one God, world without end. *Amen.*

GEORGE HERBERT
Priest
[February 27.]

The Collect

O ETERNAL Lord God, who holdest all souls in life: We beseech thee to shed forth upon thy whole Church in paradise and on earth the bright beams of thy light and thy peace; and grant that we, following the good examples of thy servant George Herbert, and of all those who loved and served thee here, may at the last enter with them into thine unending joy; through Jesus Christ our Lord. *Amen.*

DAVID
Bishop of Menevia
[March 1.]

The Collect

O ALMIGHTY God, who in thy providence didst choose thy servant David to be an apostle to the people of Wales, to bring those who were wandering darkness and error to the true light and knowledge of thee: Grant us so to walk in that light, that we may come at last to the light of everlasting life; through the merits of Jesus Christ thy Son our Lord. *Amen.*

The Epistle. Ephesians 2:4-10

GOD, who is rich in mercy, for his great love wherewith he loved us, even when we were dead in sin hath quickened us together with Christ, (by grace ye are saved;) and hath raised us up together, and made us sit together in heavenly places in Christ Jesus: that in the age to come he might shew the exceeding riches of his grace his kindness toward us through Christ Jesus. For by grace are ye saved through faith; and that not of yourselves: it is the gift of God: not of works, lest any man should boast. For we are his workmanship, created in Christ Jesus unto good works, which God hath before ordained that we should walk in them.

The Gospel. St. Mark 4:26-29

JESUS said, So is the kingdom of God, as if a man should cast seed into the ground; and should sleep, and rise night and day, and the seed should spring and grow up, knoweth not how. For the earth bringeth forth fruit of herself; first the blade, then the ear, after that the full corn in the ear. But when the fruit is brought forth, immediately he putteth in the sickle, because the harvest is come.

CHAD
Bishop of Lichfield
[March 2.]

The Collect

ALMIGHTY and everlasting God, who didst enkindle the flame of thy love in the heart of thy servant Chad: Grant to us, thy humble servants, the same faith and power of love; that, as we rejoice in his triumph, we may profit by his example; through Jesus Christ our Lord. *Amen.*

JOHN AND CHARLES WESLEY
Priests
[March 3.]

O GOD of mercy, enlighten the hearts of thy faithful people, and grant us after the example of thy servants, John and Charles Wesley, not to mind earthly things, but to love things heavenly; through Jesus Christ our Lord. *Amen.*

PERPETUA AND HER COMPANIONS
Martyrs of Carthage
[March 7.]

The Collect

ALMIGHTY and everlasting God, with whom thy meek ones go forth as the mighty: Grant us so to cherish the memory of thy blessed martyrs Perpetua and her companions, that we may share their pure and steadfast faith in thee; through Jesus Christ our Lord. *Amen.*

The Epistle. Hebrews 10:32-39

BUT call to remembrance the former days, in which, after ye were illuminated, ye endured a great fight of afflictions; partly, whilst ye were made a gazingstock both by reproaches and afflictions; and partly, whilst ye became companions of them that were so used. For ye had compassion of me in my bonds, and took joyfully the spoiling of your goods, knowing in yourselves that ye have in heaven a better and an enduring substance. Cast not away therefore your confidence, which hath great recompence of reward. For ye have need of patience, that, after ye have done the will of God, ye might receive the promise.

> For yet a little while,
> and he that shall come will come, and will not tarry.
> Now the just shall live by faith:
> but if any man draw back, my soul shall have no pleasure in him.

But we are not of them who draw back unto perdition; of them that believe to the saving of the soul.

The Gospel. St. Matthew 24:9-14

THEY shall deliver you up to be afflicted, and shall kill you: and ye shall be hated of all nations for my name's sake. And then shall many be offended, and shall betray one another, and shall hate one another. And many false prophets shall rise, and shall deceive many. And because iniquity shall abound, the love of many shall wax cold. But he that shall endure unto the end, the same shall be saved. And this gospel of the kingdom shall be preached in all the world for a witness unto all nations.

THOMAS AQUINAS
Friar
[March 8.]

The Collect

ALMIGHTY God, who hast enriched thy Church the singular learning and holiness of thy servant Thomas: Grant us to hold fast the true doctrine of thy Son our Saviour Jesus Christ, and to fashion our lives according to the same, to the glory of thy great Name and the benefit of thy holy Church; through the same Jesus Christ our Lord. *Amen.*

GREGORY
Bishop of Nyssa
[March 9.]

The Collect

ALMIGHTY and everlasting God, whose servant Gregory steadfastly confessed thy Son our Saviour Jesus Christ to be Very God and Very Man: Grant that we may hold fast to this faith, and evermore magnify his holy Name; through the same thy Son Jesus Christ our Lord, who liveth and reigneth with thee and the Holy Spirit ever, one God, world without end. *Amen.*

The Epistle. Wisdom 7:22-28

FOR wisdom, which is the worker of all things, taught me: for in her is an understanding spirit, holy, one only, manifold, subtil, lively, clear, undefiled, plain, not subject to hurt, loving the thing that is good, quick, irresistible, ready to do good, kind to man, stedfast, sure, free from care, having all power, overseeing all things, and going through all understanding, pure, and most subtil, spirits. For wisdom is more moving than any motion: she passeth and goeth through all things by reason of her pureness. For she is the breath of the power of God, and a pure influence flowing from the glory of the Almighty: therefore can no defiled thing fall into her. For she is the brightness of the everlasting light, the unspotted mirror of the power of God, and the image of his goodness. And being but one, she can do all things: and remaining in herself, she maketh all things new: and in all ages entering into holy souls, she maketh them friends of God, and prophets. For God loveth none but him that dwelleth with wisdom.

The Gospel. St. John 5:19-24

JESUS said unto them, Verily, verily, I say unto you, The Son can do nothing of himself, but what he seeth the Father do: for what things soever he doeth, these also doeth the Son likewise. For the Father loveth the Son, and sheweth him all things that himself doeth: and he will shew him greater works than these, that ye may marvel. For as the Father raiseth up the dead, and quickeneth them; even so the Son quickeneth whom he will. For the Father judgeth no man, but hath committed all judgment unto the Son: that all men should honour the Son, even as they honour the Father. He that honoureth not the Son honoureth not the Father which hath sent him. Verily, verily, I say unto you He that heareth my word, and believeth on him that send me, hath everlasting life, and shall not come into condemnation; but is passed from death unto life.

GREGORY THE GREAT
Bishop of Rome
[March 12.]

The Collect

ALMIGHTY and merciful God, who didst raise up Gregory a servant of the servants of God, by whose labour the English people were brought into the knowledge of the Catholic and Apostolic faith: Preserve in thy Church evermore a thankful remembrance of his zeal and devotion that thy people, being fruitful in every good work, may receive with him and thy servants everywhere the crown of glory that fadeth not away; through Jesus Christ our Lord. *Amen.*

The Epistle. Ecclesiasticus 47:8-11

IN all his works he praised the Holy One most high with words of glory; with his whole heart he sung songs, and loved him that made him. He set singers also before the altar, that by their voices they might make sweet melody, and daily sing praises in their songs. He beautified their feasts, and set in order the solemn times until the end, that they might praise his holy name, and that the temple might sound from morning. The Lord took away his sins, and exalted his horn for ever: he gave him a covenant of kings, and a throne of glory in Israel.

The Gospel. St. Mark 10:42-45

JESUS called them to him, and saith unto them, Ye know that they which are accounted to rule over the Gentiles exercise lordship over them; and their great ones exercise authority upon them. But so shall it not be among you: but whosoever will be great among you, shall be your minister: and whosoever of you will be the chiefest, shall be servant of all. For even the Son of man came not to be ministered unto, but to minister, and to give his life a ransom for many.

PATRICK
Bishop and Missionary of Ireland
[March 17.]

The Collect

O ALMIGHTY God, who in thy providence didst choose thy servant Patrick to be an apostle to the people of Ireland, to bring those who were wandering in darkness and error to the true light and knowledge of thee: Grant us so to walk in that light, that we may come at last to the light of everlasting life; through the merits of Jesus Christ thy Son our Lord. *Amen.*

The Epistle. 1 Thessalonians 2:2-12

WE were bold in our God to speak unto you the gospel of God with much contention. For our exhortation was not of deceit, nor of uncleanness, nor in guile: but as we were allowed of God to be put in trust with the gospel, even so we speak; not as pleasing men, but God, which trieth our hearts. For neither at any time used we flattering words, as ye know, nor a cloke of covetousness; God is witness: nor of men sought we glory, neither of you, nor yet of others, when we might have been burdensome, as the apostles of Christ. But we were gentle among you, even as a nurse cherisheth her children: so being affectionately desirous of you, we were willing to have imparted unto you, not the gospel of God only, but also our own souls, because ye were dear unto us. For ye remember, brethren, our labour and travail: for labouring night and day, because we would not be chargeable unto any of you, we preached unto you the gospel of God. Ye are witnesses, and God also, how holily and justly and unblameably we behaved ourselves among you that believe: as ye know how we exhorted and comforted and charged every one of you, as a father doth his children, that ye would walk worthy of God, who hath called you unto his kingdom and glory.

The Gospel. St. Matthew 5:43-48

YE have heard that it hath been said, Thou shalt love thy neighbour, and hate thine enemy. But I say unto you, Love your enemies, bless them that curse you, do good to them that hate you, and pray for them which despitefully use you, and persecute you; that ye may be the children of your Father which is in heaven: for he maketh his sun to rise on the evil and on the good, and sendeth rain on the just and on the unjust. For if ye love them which love you what reward have ye? do not even the publicans the same? And if ye salute your brethren only, what do ye more than others? do not even the publicans so? Be ye therefore perfect, even as your Father which is in heaven is perfect.

CYRIL
Bishop of Jerusalem
[March 18.]

The Collect

ALMIGHTY God, who hast enriched thy Church with the singular learning and holiness of thy servant Cyril: Grant us to hold fast the true doctrine of thy Son our Saviour Jesus Christ, and to fashion our lives according to the same, to the glory of thy great Name and the benefit of thy holy Church; through the same Jesus Christ our Lord. *Amen.*

SAINT JOSEPH
[March 19.]

The Collect

O GOD, who didst call blessed Joseph to be the faithful guardian of thine only-begotten Son, and the spouse of his virgin Mother: Give us grace to follow his example in constant worship of thee and obedience to thy commands, that our homes may be sanctified by thy presence, and our children nurtured in thy fear and love; through the same Jesus Christ our Lord. *Amen.*

The Epistle. Isaiah 63:7-9, 16

I WILL mention the lovingkindnesses of the LORD, and the praises of the LORD, according to all that the LORD hath bestowed on us, and the great goodness toward the house of Israel, which he hath bestowed on them according to his mercies, and according to the multitude of his loving-kindnesses. For he said, Surely they are my people, children that will not lie: so he was their Saviour. In all their affliction he was afflicted, and the angel of his presence saved them: in his love and in his pity he redeemed them; and he bare them, and carried them all the days of old. Doubtless thou art our father, though Abraham be ignorant of us, and Israel acknowledge us not: thou, O LORD, art our father, our redeemer; thy name is from everlasting.

The Gospel. St. Matthew 1:18-25

NOW the birth of Jesus Christ was on this wise: When as his mother Mary was espoused to Joseph, before they came together, she was found with child of the Holy Ghost. Then Joseph her husband, being a just man, and not willing to make her a publick example, was minded to put her away privily. But while he thought on these things, behold, the angel of the Lord appeared unto him in a dream, saying, Joseph, thou son of David, fear not to take unto thee Mary thy wife: for that which is conceived in her is of the Holy Ghost. And she shall bring forth a son, and thou shalt call his name JESUS: for he shall save his people from their sins. Now all this was done, that it might be fulfilled which was spoken of the Lord by the prophet, saying,

> Behold, a virgin shall be with child, and shall bring forth a son,
> and they shall call his name Emmanuel,

which being interpreted is, God with us. Then Joseph being raised from sleep did as the angel of the Lord had bidden him, and took unto him his wife: and knew her not till she had brought forth her firstborn son: and he called his name JESUS.

CUTHBERT
Bishop of Lindisfarne
[March 20.]

The Collect

ALMIGHTY and everlasting God, who didst enkindle the flame of thy love in the heart of thy servant Cuthbert: Grant to us, thy humble servants, the same faith and power of love; that, as we rejoice in his triumph, we may profit by his example; through Jesus Christ our Lord. *Amen.*

THOMAS KEN
Bishop of Bath and Wells
[March 21.]

The Collect

ALMIGHTY and everlasting God, we give thee thanks for the purity and strength with which thou didst endow thy servant Thomas Ken; and we pray that by thy grace we may have a like power to hallow and conform our souls and bodies, to the purpose of thy most holy will; through Jesus Christ our Lord. *Amen.*

JAMES DE KOVEN
Priest
[March 22.]

The Collect

ALMIGHTY God, who hast enriched thy Church with the singular learning and holiness of thy servant James De Koven: Grant us to hold fast the true doctrine of thy Son our Saviour Jesus Christ, and to fashion our lives according to the same, to the glory of thy great Name and the benefit of thy holy Church; through the same Jesus Christ our Lord. *Amen.*

GREGORY THE ILLUMINATOR
Bishop and Missionary of Armenia
[March 23.]

The Collect

ALMIGHTY and everlasting God, we thank thee for thy servant Gregory, whom thou didst call to preach the Gospel to the people of Armenia: Raise up, we pray thee, in this and every land, heralds and evangelists of thy kingdom, that thy Church may make known the unsearchable riches of Christ, and may increase with the increase of God through the same thy Son Jesus Christ our Lord. *Amen.*

JOHN KEBLE
Priest
[March 29.]

The Collect

O ETERNAL Lord God, who holdest all souls in life. We beseech thee to shed forth upon thy whole Church in paradise and on earth the bright beams of thy light and thy peace; and grant that we, following the good examples of thy servant John Keble, and of all those who loved and served thee here, may at the last enter with them into thine unending joy; through Jesus Christ our Lord. *Amen.*

JOHN DONNE
Priest
[March 31.]

The Collect

ALMIGHTY God, who in this wondrous world dost manifest thy power and beauty: Open the eyes of all men to see, as did thy servant John Donne, that whatsoever, has any being is a mirror wherein we may behold thee, the root and fountain of all being; through Jesus Christ, thy Son our Lord. *Amen.*

JOHN FREDERICK DENISON MAURICE
Priest
[April 1.]

The Collect

LET thy continual mercy, O Lord, enkindle in thy Church the never-failing gift of charity, that, following the example of thy servant John Frederick Denison Maurice, we may have grace to defend the children of the poor, and maintain the cause of them that have no helper; for the sake of him who gave his life for us, thy Son our Saviour Jesus Christ. *Amen.*

RICHARD
Bishop of Chichester
[April 3.]

The Collect

O GOD, the light of the faithful and shepherds of souls, who didst call thy servant Richard to feed thy sheep by his word, and guide them by his example: Grant us, we pray thee, to keep the faith which he taught, and to follow in his footsteps; through Jesus Christ our Lord. *Amen.*

AMBROSE
Bishop of Milan
[April 4.]

The Collect

O GOD, who didst give grace to thy servant Ambrose, eloquently to declare thy righteousness in the great congregation, and fearlessly to bear reproach for the honour of thy Name: Mercifully grant unto all bishops and pastors such excellency in preaching, and fidelity in ministering thy Word, that thy people may be partakers with them of the glory that shall be revealed; through Jesus Christ our Lord. *Amen.*

The Epistle. Ecclesiasticus 2:7-11,16-18

YE that fear the Lord, wait for his mercy; and go no aside, lest ye fall. Ye that fear the Lord, believe him; and your reward shall not fail. Ye that fear the Lord, hope for good, and for everlasting joy and mercy. Look at the generations of old, and see; did ever any trust in the Lord, and was confounded? or did any abide in his fear, and was forsaken? or whom did he ever despise, that called upon him? For the Lord is full of compassion and mercy, long-suffering, and very pitiful, and forgiveth sins, and saveth time of affliction.

They that fear the Lord will seek that which is well pleasing unto him; and they that love him shall be filled with the law. They that fear the Lord will prepare their hearts and humble their souls in his sight, saying, We will fall into the hands of the Lord, and not into the hands of men: for as his majesty is, so is his mercy.

The Gospel. St. Luke 12:42-44

JESUS said, Who then is that faithful and wise steward whom his lord shall make ruler over his household, to give them their portion of meat in due season? Blessed is that servant, whom his lord when he cometh shall find so doing. Of a truth I say unto you, that he will make him ruler over all that he hath.

WILLIAM AUGUSTUS MUHLENBERG
Priest
[April 8.]

The Collect

ALMIGHTY and everlasting God, who didst enkindle the flame of thy love in the heart of thy servant William Augustus Muhlenberg: Grant to us, thy humble servants, the same faith and power of love; that, as we rejoice in his triumph, we may profit by his example; through Jesus Christ our Lord. *Amen.*

WILLIAM LAW
Priest
[April 9.]

The Collect

ALMIGHTY and everlasting God, we give thee thanks for the purity and strength with which thou didst endow thy servant William Law; and we pray that by thy grace we may have a like power to hallow and conform our souls and bodies, to the purpose of thy most holy will; through Jesus Christ our Lord. *Amen.*

LEO THE GREAT
Bishop of Rome
[April 11.]

The Collect

ALMIGHTY, everlasting God, whose servant Leo steadfastly confessed thy Son our Saviour Jesus Christ to be Very God and Very Man: Grant that we may hold fast to this faith, and evermore magnify his holy Name; through the same thy Son Jesus Christ our Lord, who liveth and reigneth with thee and the Holy Spirit ever, one God, world without end. *Amen.*

The Epistle. 2 Timothy 1:12-14

FOR I know whom I have believed, and am persuaded that he is able to keep that which I have committed unto him against that day. Hold fast the form of sound words, which thou hast heard of me, in faith and love which is in Christ Jesus. That good thing which was committed unto thee keep by the Holy Ghost which dwelleth in us.

The Gospel. St. Matthew 5:13-19

YE are the salt of the earth: but if the salt have lost his savour, wherewith shall it be salted? it is thenceforth good for nothing, but to be cast out, and to be trodden under foot of men. Ye are the light of the world. A city that is set on an hill cannot be hid. Neither do men light a candle, and put it under a bushel, but on a candlestick; and it giveth light unto all that are in the house. Let your light so shine before men, that they may see your good works, and glorify your Father which is in heaven. Think not that I am come to destroy the law, or the prophets: I am not come to destroy, but to fulfil. For verily I say unto you, Till heaven and earth pass, one jot or one tittle shall in no wise pass from the law, till all be fulfilled. Whosoever therefore shall break one of these least commandments, and shall teach men so, he shall be called the least in the kingdom of heaven: but whosoever shall do and teach them, the same shall be called great in the kingdom of heaven.

GEORGE AUGUSTUS SELWYN
Bishop of New Zealand
[April 12.]

The Collect

ALMIGHTY and everlasting God, we thank thee for thy servant George Augustus Selwyn, whom thou didst call to preach the Gospel to the people of New Zealand: Raise up, we pray thee, in this and every land, heralds and evangelists of thy kingdom, that thy Church may make known the unsearchable riches of Christ, and may increase with the increase of God; through the same thy Son Jesus Christ our Lord. *Amen.*

JUSTIN
Martyr at Rome
[April 14.]

The Collect

ALMIGHTY God, who didst give thy servant Justin boldness to confess the Name of our Saviour Jesus Christ before the rulers of this world, and courage to die for this faith: Grant that we likewise may ever be ready to give a reason for the hope that is in us, and to suffer gladly for his sake; through the same Jesus Christ our Lord. *Amen.*

The Epistle. 1 Peter 3:14-18, 22

IF ye suffer for righteousness' sake, happy are ye: and be not afraid of their terror, neither be troubled; but sanctify the Lord God in your hearts: and be ready always to give an answer to every man that asketh you a reason of the hope that is in you with meekness and fear: having a good conscience; that, whereas they speak evil of you, as of evildoers, they may be ashamed that falsely accuse your good conversation in Christ. For it is better, if the will of God be so, that ye suffer for well doing, than for evil doing. For Christ also hath once suffered for sins, the just for the unjust, that he might bring us to God, being put to death in the flesh, but quickened by the Spirit: who is gone into heaven, and is on the right hand of God; angels and authorities and powers being made subject unto him.

The Gospel. St. John 12:44-50

JESUS cried and said, He that believeth on me, believeth not on me, but on him that sent me. And he that seeth me seeth him that sent me. I am come a light into the world, that whosoever believeth on me should not abide in darkness And if any man hear my words, and believe not, I judge him not: for I came not to judge the world, but to save the world. He that rejecteth me, and receiveth not my words, hath one that judgeth him: the word that I have spoken, the same shall judge him in the last day. For I have not spoken of myself; but the Father which sent me, he gave me a commandment, what I should say, and what I should speak. And I know that his commandment is life everlasting: whatsoever I speak therefore, even as the Father said unto me, so I speak.

ALPHEGE
Archbishop of Canterbury, and Martyr
[April 19.]

The Collect

O GOD, who dost support and defend us with the glorious witness of thy blessed martyr Alphege: Grant us to go forward in his footsteps, and ever to rejoice in fellowship with him; through Jesus Christ our Lord. *Amen.*

ANSELM
Archbishop of Canterbury
[April 21.]

The Collect

O GOD, who hast enlightened thy Church by the teaching of thy servant Anselm: Enrich us evermore, we beseech thee, with thy heavenly grace, and raise up faithful witnesses who by their life and doctrine will set forth the truth of thy salvation; through Jesus Christ our Lord. *Amen.*

The Epistle. Romans 1:16-20

FOR I am not ashamed of the gospel of Christ: for it is the power of God unto salvation to every one that believeth; to the Jew first, and also to the Greek. For therein is the righteousness of God revealed from faith to faith: as it is written, The just shall live by faith. For the wrath of God is revealed from heaven against all ungodliness and unrighteousness of men, who hold the truth in unrighteousness; because that which may be known of God is manifest in them; for God hath shewed it unto them. For the invisible things of him from the creation of the world are clearly seen, being understood by the things that are made, even his eternal power and Godhead.

The Gospel. St. John 7:16-18; 8:12

JESUS answered them, and said, My doctrine is not mine, but his that sent me. If any man will do his will, he shall know of the doctrine, whether it be of God, or whether I speak of myself. He that speaketh of himself seeketh his own glory: but he that seeketh his glory that sent him, the same is true, and no unrighteousness is in him. Then spake Jesus again unto them, saying, I am the light of the world: he that followeth me shall not walk in darkness, but shall have the light of life.

CATHERINE OF SIENA
[April 30.]

The Collect

ALMIGHTY and everlasting God, who didst enkindle the flame of thy love in the heart of thy servant Catherine: Grant to us thy humble servants, the same faith and power of love; that, as we rejoice in her triumph, we may profit by her example; through Jesus Christ our Lord. *Amen.*

ATHANASIUS
Bishop of Alexandria
[May 2.]

The Collect

ALMIGHTY, everlasting God, whose servant Athanasius steadfastly confessed thy Son our Saviour Jesus Christ to be Very God and Very Man: Grant that we may hold fast to this faith, and evermore magnify his holy Name; through the same thy Son Jesus Christ our Lord, who liveth and reigneth with thee and the Holy Spirit ever, one God, world without end. *Amen.*

The Epistle. 2 Corinthians 4:5-14

WE preach not ourselves, but Christ Jesus the Lord; and ourselves your servants for Jesus' sake. For God, who commanded the light to shine out of darkness, hath shined in our hearts, to give the light of the knowledge of the glory of God in the face of Jesus Christ. But we have this treasure in earthen vessels, that the excellency of the power may be of God, and not of us. We are troubled on every side, yet not distressed; we are perplexed, but not in despair; persecuted, but not forsaken; cast down, but not destroyed; always bearing about in the body the dying of the Lord Jesus, that the life also of Jesus might be made manifest in our body. For we which live are always delivered unto death for Jesus' sake, that the life also of Jesus might be made manifest in our mortal flesh. So then death worketh in us, but life in you. We having the same spirit of faith, according as it is written, I believed, and therefore have I spoken; we also believe, and therefore speak; knowing that he which raised up the Lord Jesus shall raise up us also by Jesus, and shall present us with you.

The Gospel. St. Matthew 10:23-32

WHEN they persecute you in this city, flee ye into another: for verily I say unto you, Ye shall not have gone over the cities of Israel, till the Son of man be come. The disciple is not above his master, nor the servant above his lord.

It is enough for the disciple that he be as his master, and the servant as his lord. If they have called the master of the house Beelzebub, how much more shall they call them of his household? Fear them not therefore: for there is nothing covered, that shall not be revealed; and hid, that shall not be known. What I tell you in darkness, that speak ye in light: and what ye hear in the ear, that preach ye upon the housetops. And fear not them which kill the body, but are not able to kill the soul: but rather fear him which is able to destroy both soul and body in hell. Are not two sparrows sold for a farthing? and one of them shall not fall on the ground without your Father. But the very hairs of your head are all numbered. Fear ye not therefore, ye are of more value than many sparrows. Whosoever therefore shall confess me before men, him will I confess also before my Father which is in heaven.

MONNICA
Mother of Augustine of Hippo
[May 4.]

The Collect

ALMIGHTY and everlasting God, who didst enkindle the flame of thy love in the heart of thy servant Monnica: Grant to us, thy humble servants, the same faith and power of love; that, as we rejoice in her triumph, we may profit by her example; through Jesus Christ our Lord. *Amen.*

GREGORY OF NAZIANZUS
Bishop of Constantinople
[May 9.]

The Collect

ALMIGHTY, everlasting God, whose servant Gregory steadfastly confessed thy Son our Saviour Jesus Christ to be Very God and Very Man: Grant that we may hold fast to this faith, and evermore magnify his holy Name through the same thy Son Jesus Christ our Lord, who liveth and reigneth with thee and the Holy Spirit ever, one God, world without end. *Amen.*

The Epistle. Wisdom 7:7-14

I CALLED upon God, and the spirit of wisdom came to me. I preferred her before sceptres and thrones, and esteemed riches nothing in comparison of her. Neither compared I unto her any precious stone, because all gold in respect of her is as a little sand, and silver shall be counted as clay before her. I loved her above health and beauty, and chose to have her instead of light: for the light that cometh from her never goeth out. All good things together came to me with her, and innumerable riches in her hands. And I rejoiced in them all, because wisdom goeth before them: and I knew not that she was the mother of them. I learned diligently, and do communicate her liberally: I do not hide her riches. For she is a treasure unto men that never faileth: which they that use become the friends of God, being commended for the gifts that come from learning.

The Gospel. St. John 8:25-32

THEN said they unto him, Who art thou? And Jesus saith unto them, Even the same that I said unto you from the beginning. I have many things to say and to judge of you: but he that sent me is true; and I speak to the world those things which I have heard of him. They understood not that he spake to them of the Father. Then said Jesus unto them, When ye have lifted up the Son of man, then shall ye know that I am he, and that I do nothing of myself; but as my Father hath taught me, I speak these things. And he that sent me is with me: the Father hath not left me alone; for I do always those things that please him. As he spake these words, many believed on him. Then said Jesus to those Jews which believed on him, If ye continue in my word, then are ye my disciples indeed; and ye shall know the truth, and the truth shall make you free.

CYRIL AND METHODIUS
Missionary Bishops to the Slavs
[May 11.]

The Collect

ALMIGHTY and everlasting God, we thank thee for thy servants Cyril and Methodius, whom thou didst call to preach the Gospel to the Slavic People. Raise up, we pray thee, in this and every land, heralds and evangelists of thy kingdom, that thy Church may make known the unsearchable riches of Christ, and may increase with the increase of God; through the same thy Son Jesus Christ our Lord. *Amen.*

DUNSTAN
Archbishop of Canterbury
[May 19.]

The Collect

O GOD, who dost ever hallow and protect thy Church: Raise up therein through thy Spirit good and faithful stewards of the mysteries of Christ, as thou didst in thy servant Dunstan; that by their ministry and example thy people may abide in thy favour and walk in the way of truth; through Jesus Christ our

Lord, who liveth and reigneth with thee in the unity of the same Spirit ever, one God, world without end. *Amen.*

ALCUIN
Deacon, and Abbot of Tours
[May 20.]

The Collect

ETERNAL Lord God, who holdest all souls in life: We beseech thee to shed forth upon thy whole Church in paradise and on earth the bright beams of thy light and thy peace; and grant that we, following the good examples of thy servant Alcuin, and of all those who loved and served thee here, may at the last enter with them into thine unending joy; through Jesus Christ our Lord. *Amen.*

JACKSON KEMPER
First Missionary Bishop in the United States
[May 24.]

The Collect

ALMIGHTY and everlasting God, we thank thee for thy servant Jackson Kemper, whom thou didst call to preach the Gospel in this our land. Raise up, we pray thee, in every land, heralds and evangelists of thy kingdom that thy Church may make known the unsearchable riches of Christ, and may increase with the increase of God; through the same thy Son Jesus Christ our Lord. *Amen.*

AUGUSTINE
First Archbishop of Canterbury
[May 26.]

The Collect

ALMIGHTY God, who in thy providence didst choose thy servant Augustine to be an apostle to the people of England, to bring those who were wandering in darkness and error to the true light and knowledge of thee: Grant us so to walk in that light, that we may come at last to the light of everlasting life; through the merits of Jesus Christ thy Son our Lord. *Amen.*

The Epistle. 2 Corinthians 5:17-20

IF any man be in Christ, he is a new creature: old things are passed away; behold, all things are become new. And all things are of God, who hath reconciled us to himself by Jesus Christ, and hath given to us the ministry of reconciliation; to wit, that God was in Christ, reconciling the world unto himself, not imputing their trespasses unto them; and hath committed unto us the word of reconciliation. Now then we are ambassadors for Christ, as though God did beseech you by us: we pray you in Christ's stead, be ye reconciled to God.

The Gospel. St. Matthew 23:31-33

ANOTHER parable put Jesus forth unto them, saying, The kingdom of heaven is like to a grain of mustard seed, which a man took, and sowed in his field: which indeed is the least of all seeds: but when it is grown, it is the greatest among herbs, and becometh a tree, so that the birds of the air come and lodge in the branches thereof. Another parable spake he unto them; The kingdom of heaven is like unto leaven, which a woman took, and hid in three measure of meal, till the whole was leavened. All these things spake Jesus unto the multitude in parables.

BEDE THE VENERABLE
Priest and Monk of Jarrow
[May 27.]

The Collect

ALMIGHTY God, who hast enriched thy Church with the singular learning and holiness of thy servant Bede: Grant us to hold fast the true doctrine of thy Son our Saviour Jesus Christ, and to fashion our lives according to the same, to the glory of thy great Name and the benefit of thy holy Church; through the same Jesus Christ our Lord. *Amen.*

The Epistle. Malachi 3:16-18

THEN they that feared the LORD spake one to another: and the LORD hearkened, and heard it, and a book of remembrance was written before him for them that feared the LORD, and that thought upon his name. And they shall be mine, saith the LORD of hosts, in that day when I make up my jewels; and I will spare them, as a man spareth his own son that serveth him. Then once more shall ye discern between the righteous and the wicked, between him that serveth God and him that serveth him not.

The Gospel. St. Matthew 13:47-52

JESUS said, The kingdom of heaven is like unto a net, that was cast into the sea, and gathered of every kind: which, when it was full, they drew to shore, and sat down, and gathered the good into vessels, but cast the bad away. So shall it be at the end of the world: the angels shall come forth, and sever the wicked from among the just, and shall cast them into the furnace of fire: there shall be wailing and gnashing of teeth. Jesus saith unto them, Have ye understood all these things? They say unto him, Yea, Lord. Then said he unto them, Therefore every scribe which is instructed unto the kingdom of heaven is like unto a man that is an householder, which bringeth forth out of his treasure things new and old.

THE MARTYRS OF LYONS
[June 2.]

The Collect

ALMIGHTY and everlasting God, with whom thy meek ones go forth as the mighty: Grant us so to cherish the memory of thy blessed martyrs Blandina and her companions, that we may share their pure and steadfast faith in thee; through Jesus Christ our Lord. *Amen.*

The Epistle. 1 Peter 1:3-9

BLESSED be the God and Father of our Lord Jesus Christ, which according to his abundant mercy hath begotten us again unto a lively hope by the resurrection of Jesus Christ from the dead, to an inheritance incorruptible, and undefiled, and that fadeth not away, reserved in heaven for you, who are kept by the power of God through faith unto salvation ready to be revealed in the last time. Wherein ye greatly rejoice, though now for a season, if need be, ye are in heaviness through manifold temptations: that the trial of your faith, being much more precious than of gold that perisheth, though it be tried with fire, might be found unto praise and honour and glory at the appearing of Jesus Christ: whom having not seen, ye love; in whom, though now ye see him not, yet believing, ye rejoice with joy unspeakable and full of glory: receiving the end of your faith, even the salvation of your souls.

The Gospel. St. Matthew 16:24-27

THEN said Jesus unto his disciples, If any man will come after me, let him deny himself, and take up his cross, and follow me. For whosoever will save his life shall lose it: and whosoever will lose his life for my sake shall find it. For what is a man profited, if he shall gain the whole world, and lose his own soul? or what shall a man give in exchange for his soul? For the Son of man shall come in the glory of his Father with his angels; and then he shall reward every man according to his works.

BONIFACE
*Archbishop of Mainz,
Missionary to Germany and Martyr*
[June 5.]

The Collect

ALMIGHTY God, who didst call thy faithful servant Boniface to be a witness and martyr in the land of Germany, and by his labours and suffering didst raise up a people for thine own possession: Shed forth, we beseech thee, thy Holy Spirit upon thy Church in all lands, that by the sacrifice and service of many, thy holy Name may be glorified and thy blessed kingdom enlarged; through Jesus Christ our Lord, who liveth and reigneth with thee in the unity of the same Spirit ever, one God, world without end. *Amen.*

The Epistle. Acts 20:18-27

YE know, from the first day that I came into Asia, after what manner I have been with you at all seasons, serving the Lord with all humility of mind, and with many tears, and temptations, which befell me by the lying in wait of the Jews: and how I kept back nothing that was profitable unto you, but have shewed you, and have taught you publickly, and from house to house, testifying both to the Jews, and also to the Greeks, repentance toward God, and faith toward our Lord Jesus Christ. And now, behold, I go bound in the spirit unto Jerusalem, not knowing the things that shall befall me there: save that the Holy Ghost witnesseth in every city, saying that bonds and afflictions abide me. But none of these things move me, neither count I my life dear unto myself, so that I might finish my course with joy, and the ministry, which I have received of the Lord Jesus, to testify the gospel of the grace of God. And now, behold, I know that ye all, among whom I have gone preaching the kingdom of God, shall see my face no more. Wherefore I take you to record this day, that I am pure from the blood of all men. For I have not shunned to declare unto you all the counsel of God.

The Gospel. St. Matthew 28:16-20

THEN the eleven disciples went away into Galilee, into a mountain where Jesus had appointed them. And when they saw him, they worshipped him: but some doubted. And Jesus came and spake unto them saying, All power is given unto me in heaven and in earth. Go ye therefore, and teach all nations, baptizing them in the name of the Father, and of the Son, and of the Holy Ghost: teaching them to observe all things whatsoever I have commanded you: and, lo, I am with you alway, even unto the end of the world. *Amen.*

COLUMBA
Abbot of Iona
[June 9.]

The Collect

O GOD, who by the preaching of thy blessed servant Columba didst cause the light of the Gospel to shine in the land of Scotland: Grant, we beseech thee, that having his life and labours in remembrance, we may show forth our thankfulness unto thee for the same by following the example of his zeal and patience; through Jesus Christ our Lord. *Amen.*

THE FIRST BOOK OF COMMON PRAYER
[June 10.]

The Collect

ALMIGHTY and everliving God, who didst guide thy servant Thomas Cranmer, with others, to render the worship of thy Church in a language understanded of the people: Make us ever thankful for this our heritage, and help us so to pray in the Spirit and with the understanding also, that we may worthily magnify thy holy Name; through Jesus Christ our Lord, who liveth and reigneth with thee and the same Holy Spirit ever, one God, world without end. *Amen.*

The Epistle. Acts 2:38-42

THEN Peter said unto them, Repent, and be baptized every one of you in the name of Jesus Christ for the remission of sins, and ye shall receive the gift of the Holy Ghost. For the promise is unto you, and to your children, and to all that are afar off, even as many as the Lord our God shall call. And with many other words did he testify and exhort, saying, Save yourselves from this untoward generation. Then they that gladly received his word were baptized: and the same day there were added unto them about three thousand souls. And they continued stedfastly in the apostles' doctrine and fellowship, and in breaking of bread, and in prayers.

The Gospel. St. Matthew 6:5-15

WHEN thou prayest, thou shalt not be as the hypocrites are: for they love to pray standing in the synagogues and in the corners of the streets, that they may be seen of men. Verily I say unto you, They have their reward. But thou, when thou prayest, enter into thy closet, and when thou hast shut thy door, pray to thy Father which is in secret; and thy Father which seeth in secret shall reward thee openly. But when ye pray, use not vain repetitions, as the heathen do: for they think that they shall be heard for their much speaking. Be not ye therefore like unto them: for your Father knoweth what things ye have need of, before ye ask them. After this manner therefore pray ye: Our Father which art in heaven, Hallowed be thy name. Thy kingdom come. Thy will be done in earth, as it is in heaven. Give us this day our daily bread. And forgive us our debts, as we forgive our debtors. And lead us not into temptation, but deliver us from evil: For thine is the kingdom, and the power, and the glory, for ever. Amen. For if ye forgive men their trespasses, your heavenly Father will also forgive you: but if ye forgive not men their trespasses, neither will your Father forgive your trespasses.

BASIL THE GREAT
Bishop of Caesarea
[June 14.]

The Collect

ALMIGHTY, everlasting God, whose servant Basil steadfastly confessed thy Son our Saviour Jesus Christ to be Very God and Very Man: Grant that we may hold fast to this faith, and evermore magnify his holy Name; through the same thy Son Jesus Christ our Lord, who liveth and reigneth with thee and the Holy Spirit ever, one God, world without end. *Amen.*

The Epistle. 1 Corinthians 2:6-13

HOWBEIT we speak wisdom among them that are perfect: yet not the wisdom of this world, nor of the princes of this world, that come to nought: but we speak the wisdom of God in a mystery, even the hidden wisdom, which God ordained before the world unto our glory: which none of the princes of this world knew: for had they known it, they would not have crucified the Lord of glory. But as it is written,

> Eye hath not seen, nor ear heard,
> Neither have entered into the heart of man,
> The things which God hath prepared for them that love him.

But God hath revealed them unto us by his Spirit: for the Spirit searcheth all things, yea, the deep things of God. For what man knoweth the things of a man, save the spirit of man which is in him? even so the things of God knoweth no man, but the Spirit of God. Now we have received, not the spirit of the world, but the spirit which is of God; that we might know the things that are freely given to us of God. Which things also we speak, not in the words which man's wisdom teacheth, but which the Holy Ghost teacheth; comparing spiritual things with spiritual.

The Gospel. St. Luke 10:22-24

JESUS said, All things are delivered to me of my Father and no man knoweth who the Son is, but the Father and who the Father is, but the Son, and he to whom the Son will reveal him. And he turned him unto his disciples, and said privately, Blessed are the eyes which see the things that ye see: for I tell you, that many prophets and kings have desired to see those things which ye see, and have not seen them; and to hear those things which ye hear, and have heard them.

JOSEPH BUTLER
Bishop of Durham
[June 16.]

The Collect

O GOD, who hast enlightened thy Church by the teaching of thy servant Joseph Butler: Enrich us evermore, we beseech thee, with thy heavenly grace, and raise up faithful witnesses who by their life and doctrine will set forth the truth of thy salvation; through Jesus Christ our Lord. *Amen.*

EPHREM OF EDESSA
Deacon
[June 18.]

The Collect

ALMIGHTY God, who hast enriched thy Church with the singular learning and holiness of thy Deacon Ephrem: Grant us to hold fast the true doctrine of thy Son our Saviour Jesus Christ, and to fashion our lives according to the same, to the glory of thy great Name and the benefit of thy holy Church; through the same Jesus Christ our Lord. *Amen.*

ALBAN
First Martyr of Britain
[June 22.]

The Collect

ALMIGHTY God, by whose grace and power thy holy martyr Alban triumphed over suffering, and despised death: Grant, we beseech thee, that enduring hardness, and waxing valiant in fight, we may with the noble army of martyrs receive the crown of everlasting life; through Jesus Christ our Lord. *Amen.*

The Epistle. 1 John 3:13-16

MARVEL not, my brethren, if the world hate you. We know that we have passed from death unto life, because we love the brethren. He that loveth not his brother abideth in death. Whosoever hateth his brother is a murderer: and ye know that no murderer hath eternal life abiding in him. Hereby perceive we the love of God, because he laid down his life for us: and we ought to lay down our lives for the brethren.

The Gospel. St. Matthew 10:34-42

THINK not that I am come to send peace on earth: I came not to send peace, but a sword. For I am come to set a man at variance against his father, and the daughter against her mother, and the daughter in law against her mother in law. And a man's foes shall be they of his own household. He that loveth father or mother more than me is not worthy of me: and he that loveth son or daughter more than me is not worthy of me. And he that taketh not his cross, and followeth after me, is not worthy of me. He that findeth his life shall lose it: and he that loseth his life for my sake shall find it. He that receiveth you receiveth me, and he that receiveth me receiveth him that sent me. He that receiveth a prophet in the name of a prophet shall receive a prophet's reward; and he that receiveth a righteous man in the name of a righteous man shall receive a righteous man's reward. And whosoever shall give to drink unto one of these little ones a cup of cold water only in the name of a disciple, verily I say unto you, he shall in no wise lose his reward.

IRENAEUS
Bishop of Lyons
[June 28.]

ALMIGHTY God, who didst uphold thy servant Irenaeus with strength to maintain the truth against every wind of vain doctrine: We beseech thee to keep us steadfast in thy true religion, that we may walk in constancy and in peace the way that leadeth to eternal life; through Jesus Christ our Lord. *Amen.*

The Epistle. Malachi 2:5-7

MY covenant was with him of life and peace; and I gave them to him for the fear wherewith he feared me, and was afraid before my name. The law of truth was in his mouth, and iniquity was not found in his lips: he walked with me in peace and equity, and did turn many away from iniquity. For the priest's lips should keep knowledge, and they should seek the law at his mouth: for he is the messenger of the LORD of hosts.

The Gospel. St. Luke 11 :33-36

NO man, when he hath lighted a candle, putteth it in a secret place, neither under a bushel, but on a candlestick, that they which come in may see the light. The light of the body is the eye: therefore when thine eye is single, thy whole body also is full of light; but when thine eye is evil, thy body also is full of darkness. Take heed therefore that the light which is in thee be not darkness. If thy whole body therefore be full of light, having no part dark, the whole shall be full of light, as when the bright shining of a candle doth give thee light.

THE VISITATION OF THE BLESSED VIRGIN MARY
[July 2.]

The Collect

O CHRIST, our God Incarnate, whose virgin Mother was blessed in bearing thee, but still more blessed in keeping thy word: Grant us, who honour the exaltation of her lowliness, to follow the example of her devotion to thy will; who livest and reignest with the Father and the He Ghost ever, one God, world without end. *Amen.*

The Epistle. Zechariah 2:10-13

SING and rejoice, O daughter of Zion: for, lo, I come, and I will dwell in the midst of thee, saith the LORD. And many nations shall be joined to the LORD in that day and shall be my people: and I will dwell in the midst of thee and thou shalt know that the LORD of hosts hath sent me unto thee. And the LORD shall inherit Judah his portion in the holy land, and shall choose Jerusalem again. Be silent, O all flesh, before the LORD: for he is raised up out of his holy habitation.

The Gospel. St. Luke 1:39-45

AND Mary arose in those days, and went into the hill country with haste, into a city of Judah; and entered into the house of Zacharias, and saluted Elisabeth. And came to pass, that, when Elisabeth heard the salutation of Mary, the babe leaped in her womb; and Elisabeth was filled with the Holy Ghost: and she spake out with a loud voice and said, Blessed art thou among women, and blessed is the fruit of thy womb. And whence is this to me, that the mother of my Lord should come to me? For, lo, as soon as the voice of thy salutation sounded in mine ears, the babe leaped in my womb for joy. And blessed is she that believed: for there shall be a performance of those things which were told her from the Lord.

BENEDICT OF NURSIA
Abbot of Monte Cassino
[July 11.]

The Collect

ALMIGHTY and everlasting God, we give thee thanks for the purity and strength with which thou didst endow thy servant Benedict; and we pray that by thy grace we may have a like power to hallow and conform our souls and bodies to the purpose of thy most holy will; through Jesus Christ our Lord. *Amen.*

The Epistle. Acts 2:44-47

AND all that believed were together, and had all things common; and sold their possessions and goods, and parted them to all men, as every man had need. And they, continuing daily with one accord in the temple, and breaking bread from house to house, did eat their meat with gladness and singleness of heart, praising God, and having favour with all the people.

The Gospel. St. Luke 14:26-33

IF any man come to me, and hate not his father, and mother, and wife, and children, and brethren, and sisters, yea, and his own life also, he cannot be my disciple. And whosoever doth not bear his cross, and come after me, cannot be my disciple. For which of you, intending to build a tower, sitteth not down first, and counteth the cost, whether he have sufficient to finish it? Lest haply, after he hath laid the foundation, and is not able to finish it, all that behold it begin to mock him, saying, This man began to build, and was not able to finish. Or what king, going to make war against another king, sitteth not down first, and consulted whether he be able with ten thousand to meet him that cometh against him with twenty thousand? Or else, while the other is yet a great way off, he sendeth an ambassage and desireth conditions of peace. So likewise, whosoever he be of you that forsaketh not all that he hath, he cannot be my disciple.

WILLIAM WHITE
Bishop of Pennsylvania
[July 17.]

The Collect

O GOD, who dost ever hallow and protect thy Church: Raise up therein through thy Spirit good and faithful stewards of the mysteries of Christ, as thou didst in thy servant William White; that by their ministry and example thy people may abide in thy favour and walk in the way of truth; through Jesus Christ our Lord, who liveth and reigneth with thee in the unity of the same Spirit ever, one God, world without end. *Amen.*

SAINT MARY MAGDALENE
[July 22.]

The Collect

O ALMIGHTY God, whose blessed Son did sanctify Mary Magdalene, and call her to be a witness to his Resurrection: Mercifully grant that by thy grace we may be healed of all our infirmities, and serve thee in the power of his endless life; who with thee and the Holy Ghost liveth and reigneth, one God, world without end. *Amen.*

The Epistle. 2 Corinthians 5:14-18

FOR the love of Christ constraineth us; because we thus judge, that if one died for all, then were all dead: and that he died for all, that they which live should not henceforth live unto themselves, but unto him which died for them, and rose again. Wherefore henceforth know we no man after the flesh: yea, though we have known Christ after the flesh, yet now henceforth know we him no more. Therefore if any man be in Christ, he is a new creature: old things are passed away; behold, all things are become new. And all things are of God, who hath reconciled us to himself by Jesus Christ.

The Gospel. St. John 20:1, 11-18

THE first day of the week cometh Mary Magdalene early, when it was yet dark, unto the sepulchre, and seeth the stone taken away from the sepulchre. But Mary stood without at the sepulchre weeping: and as she wept, she stooped down, and looked into the sepulchre, and seeth two angels in white sitting, the one at the head, and the other at the feet, where the body of Jesus had lain. And they say unto her, Woman, why weepest thou? She saith unto them, Because they have taken away my Lord, and I know not where they have laid him. And when she had thus said, she turned herself back, and saw Jesus standing, and knew not that it was Jesus. Jesus saith unto her, Woman, why weepest thou? whom seekest thou? She, supposing him to be the gardener, saith unto him, Sir, if thou have borne him hence, tell me where thou hast laid him, and I will take him away. Jesus saith unto her, Mary. She turned herself, and saith unto him, Rabboni; which is to say, Master. Jesus saith unto her, Touch me not; for I am not yet ascended to my Father: but go to my brethren, and say unto them, I ascend unto my Father, and your Father; and to my God, and your God. Mary Magdalene came and told the disciples that she had seen the Lord, and that he had spoken these things unto her.

THOMAS A KEMPIS
Priest
[July 24.]

The Collect

O ETERNAL Lord God, who holdest all souls in life: We beseech thee to shed forth upon thy whole Church in paradise and on earth the bright beams of thy light and thy peace; and grant that we, following the good examples of thy servant Thomas, and of all those who love and served thee here, may at the last enter with them into thine unending joy; through Jesus Christ our Lord. *Amen.*

THE PARENTS OF THE BLESSED VIRGIN MARY
[July 26.]

The Collect

ALMIGHTY God, heavenly Father, who settest the solitary in families: We thankfully remember before thee this day the parents of the Blessed Virgin Mary; and we humbly entrust to thy never-failing care the homes in which thy people dwell; that we may be made very members of the heavenly family of thy Son Jesus Christ, who liveth and reigneth with thee and the Holy Spirit, one God, world without end. *Amen.*

WILLIAM REED HUNTINGTON
Priest
[July 27.]

The Collect

ALMIGHTY and everlasting God, the source and perfection of all virtues, who didst inspire thy servant William Reed Huntington both to do what is right and to preach what is true: Grant that all ministers and stewards of thy mysteries may afford to thy faithful people, by word and example, the instruction which is of thy grace; through Jesus Christ our Lord. *Amen.*

SAINTS MARY AND MARTHA OF BETHANY
[July 29.]

The Collect

O GOD, who bestowest divers gifts and graces upon thy saints: We give thee humble thanks for the examples of thy servants Mary and Martha, the friends of our Saviour Jesus Christ; and we pray thee to give us grace to love and serve thee and others for his sake, who with thee and the Holy Ghost liveth and reigneth ever, one God, world without end. *Amen.*

The Epistle. Proverbs 31:10, 26-31

WHO can find a virtuous woman?
For her price is far above rubies.
She openeth her mouth with wisdom;
And in her tongue is the law of kindness.
She looketh well to the ways of her household,
And eateth not the bread of idleness.
Her children arise up, and call her blessed;
Her husband also, and he praiseth her.

Many daughters have done virtuously,
But thou excellest them all.
Favour is deceitful, and beauty is vain:
But a woman that feareth the LORD, she shall be praised.
Give her of the fruit of her hands;
And let her own works praise her in the gates.

The Gospel. St. Luke 10:38-42

NOW it came to pass, as they went, that he entered into a certain village: and a certain woman named Martha received him into her house. And she had a sister called Mary, which also sat at Jesus' feet, and heard his word. But Martha was distracted with much serving, and came to him, and said, Lord, dost thou not care that my sister hath left me to serve alone? bid her therefore that she help me. And the Lord answered and said unto her, Martha, Martha, thou art concerned and troubled about many things: but one thing is needful: and Mary hath chosen that good part, which shall not be taken away from her.

WILLIAM WILBERFORCE
[July 30.]

The Collect

LET thy continual mercy, O Lord, enkindle in thy Church the never-failing gift of charity, that following the example of thy servant William Wilberforce, we may have grace to defend the children of the poor, and maintain the cause of them that have no helper; for the sake of him who gave his life for us, thy Son our Saviour Jesus Christ. *Amen.*

SAINT JOSEPH OF ARIMATHAEA
[July 31.]

The Collect

O MERCIFUL God, by whose servant Joseph the body of our Lord and Saviour was committed to the grave with reverence and godly fear: Grant, we beseech thee, to thy faithful people grace and courage to serve and love Jesus with unfeigned devotion all the days of their life; through the same Jesus Christ our Lord. *Amen.*

The Epistle. Proverbs 4:10-18

HEAR, O my son, and receive my sayings;
And the years of thy life shall be many.
I have taught thee in the way of wisdom;
I have led thee in right paths.
When thou goest, thy steps shall not be hampered;
And when thou runnest, thou shalt not stumble.
Take fast hold of instruction: let her not go:
Keep her; for she is thy life.
Enter not into the path of the wicked,
And go not in the way of evil men.
Avoid it, do not go on it,
Turn away from it, and pass on.
For they sleep not, except they have done mischief;
And their sleep is taken away, unless they cause some to fall.
For they eat the bread of wickedness,
And drink the wine of violence.
But the path of the just is as the shining light,
That shineth more and more unto the perfect day.

The Gospel. St. Luke 23:50-56

BEHOLD, there was a man named Joseph, a counsellor; and he was a good man, and a just: (the same had not consented to the counsel and deed of them;) he was of Arimathaea, a city of the Jews: who also himself waited for the kingdom of God. This man went unto Pilate, and begged the body of Jesus. And he took it down, and wrapped it in linen, and laid it in a sepulchre that was hewn in stone, wherein never man before was laid. And that day was the preparation, and the sabbath drew on. And the women also, which came with him from

Galilee, followed after, and beheld the sepulchre, and how his body was laid. And they returned, and prepared spices and ointments; and rested the sabbath day according to the commandment.

DOMINIC
Friar
[August 4.]

The Collect

ALMIGHTY and everlasting God, we give thee thanks for the purity and strength with which thou didst endow thy servant Dominic; and we pray that by thy grace we may have a like power to hallow and conform our souls and bodies to the purpose of thy most holy will; through Jesus Christ our Lord. *Amen.*

LAURENCE
Deacon, and Martyr at Rome
[August 10.]

The Collect

ALMIGHTY God, by whose grace and power thy holy Deacon and martyr Laurence triumphed over suffering, and despised death: Grant, we beseech thee, that enduring hardness, and waxing valiant in fight, we may with the noble army of martyrs receive the crown of everlasting life; through Jesus Christ our Lord. *Amen.*

CLARE OF ASSISI
Abbess
[August 12.]

The Collect

O GOD of mercy, enlighten the hearts of thy faithful people, and grant us after the example of thy servant Clare, not to mind earthly things, but to love things heavenly; through Jesus Christ our Lord. *Amen.*

HIPPOLYTUS
Bishop and Martyr
[August 13.]

The Collect

O GOD, who has enlightened thy Church by the teaching of thy servant Hippolytus: Enrich us evermore, we beseech thee, with thy heavenly grace, and raise up faithful witnesses who by their life and doctrine will set forth the truth of thy salvation; through Jesus Christ our Lord. *Amen.*

JEREMY TAYLOR
Bishop of Down, Connor and Dromore
[August 14.]

The Collect

ALMIGHTY God, who hast enriched thy Church with the singular learning and holiness of thy servant Jeremy Taylor: Grant us to hold fast the true doctrine of thy Son our Saviour Jesus Christ, and to fashion our lives according to the same, to the glory of thy great Name and the benefit of thy holy Church; through the same Jesus Christ our Lord. *Amen.*

SAINT MARY THE VIRGIN
[August 15.]

The Collect

O GOD, who hast taken to thyself the blessed Virgin Mary, mother of thine only Son: Grant that we who have been redeemed by his blood may share with her the glory of thine eternal kingdom; through the same Jesus Christ our Lord, who liveth and reigneth with thee and the Holy Ghost ever, one God, world without end. *Amen.*

The Epistle. Isaiah 61:7-11

THEREFORE in their land they shall possess a double portion: everlasting joy shall be unto them. For I the LORD love justice, I hate robbery and wrong; and I will direct their work in truth, and I will make an everlasting covenant with them. And their seed shall be known among the Gentiles, and their offspring among the people: all that see them shall acknowledge them, that they are the seed which the LORD hath blessed.

I will greatly rejoice in the LORD, my soul shall be joyful in my God; for he hath clothed me with the garments of salvation, he hath covered me with the robe of righteousness, as a bridegroom decketh himself with ornaments, and as a bride adorneth herself with her jewels. For as the earth bringeth forth her bud, and as the garden causeth the things that are sown in it to spring forth; so the Lord GOD will cause righteousness and praise to spring forth before all the nations.

The Gospel. St. Luke 1:46-55

MY soul doth magnify the Lord,
and my spirit hath rejoiced in God my Saviour.
For he hath regarded the low estate of his handmaiden:
for, behold, from henceforth all generations shall call me blessed.
For he that is mighty hath done to me great things;
and holy is his name.
And his mercy is on them that fear him
from generation to generation.
He hath shewed strength with his arm;
he hath scattered the proud in the imagination of their hearts.
He hath put down the mighty from their seats,
and exalted them of low degree.
He hath filled the hungry with good things;
and the rich he hath sent empty away.
He hath holpen his servant Israel,
in remembrance of his mercy;
as he spake to our fathers,
to Abraham, and to his seed for ever.

BERNARD
Abbot of Clairvaux
[August 20.]

The Collect

ALMIGHTY and everlasting God, who didst enkindle the flame of thy love in the heart of thy servant Bernard: Grant to us, thy humble servants, the same faith and power of love; that, as we rejoice in his triumph, we may profit by his example; through Jesus Christ our Lord. *Amen.*

The Epistle. Ecclesiasticus 39:1-10

HE that giveth his mind to the law of the most High, and is occupied in the meditation thereof, will seek out the wisdom of all the ancient, and be occupied in prophecies. He will keep the sayings of the renowned men: and where subtil parables are, he will be there also. He will seek out the secrets of grave sentences, and be conversant in dark parables. He shall serve among great men, and appear before princes: he will travel through strange countries; for he hath tried the good and the evil among men. He will give his heart to resort early to the Lord that made him, and will pray before the most High, and will open his mouth in prayer, and make supplication for his sins. When the great Lord will, he shall be filled with the spirit of understanding: he shall pour out wise sentences, and give thanks unto the Lord in his prayer. He shall direct his counsel and knowledge, and in his secrets shall he meditate. He shall shew forth that which he hath learned, and shall glory in the law of the covenant of the Lord. Many shall commend his understanding; and so long as the world endureth, it shall not be blotted out; his memorial shall not depart away, and his name shall live from generation to generation. Nations shall shew forth his wisdom, and the congregation shall declare his praise.

The Gospel. St. John 15:7-11

IF ye abide in me, and my words abide in you, ye shall ask what ye will, and it shall be done unto you. Herein is my Father glorified, that ye bear much fruit; so shall ye be my disciples. As the Father hath loved me, so have I loved you: continue ye in my love. If ye keep my commandments, ye shall abide in my love; even as I have kept my Father's commandments, and abide in his love. These things have I spoken unto you, that my joy might remain in you, and that your joy might be full.

Louis
King of France
[August 25.]

The Collect

O GOD, who didst call thy servant Louis to an earthly throne that he might advance thy heavenly kingdom, and didst endue him with zeal for thy Church and charity towards thy people: Mercifully grant that we who commemorate his example may be fruitful in good works, and attain to the glorious fellowship of thy saints; through Jesus Christ our Lord. *Amen.*

AUGUSTINE
Bishop of Hippo
[August 28.]

The Collect

O LORD God, who art the light of the minds that know thee, the life of the souls that love thee, and the strength of the hearts that serve thee: Help us, after the example of thy servant Saint Augustine, so to know thee that we may truly love thee, so to love thee that we may fully serve thee, whom to serve is perfect freedom; through Jesus Christ our Lord. *Amen.*

The Epistle. Hebrews 12:22-24, 28-29

BUT ye are come unto mount Sion, and unto the city of the living God, the heavenly Jerusalem, and to an innumerable company of angels, to the general assembly and church of the firstborn, which are written in heaven, and to God the Judge of all, and to the spirits of just men made perfect, and to Jesus the mediator of the new covenant, and to the blood of sprinkling, that speaketh better things than that of Abel. Wherefore we receiving a kingdom which cannot be moved, let us have grace, whereby we may serve God acceptably with reverence and godly fear: for our God is a consuming fire.

The Gospel. St. John 17:1-8

THESE words spake Jesus, and lifted up his eyes to heaven, and said, Father, the hour is come; glorify thy Son, that thy Son also may glorify thee: as thou hast given him power over all flesh, that he should give eternal life to as many as thou hast given him. And this is life eternal, that they might know thee the only true God, and Jesus Christ, whom thou hast sent. I have glorified thee on the earth: I have finished the work which thou gavest me to do. And now, O Father, glorify thou me with thine own self with the glory which I had with thee before the world was. I have manifested thy name unto the men which thou gavest me out of the world: thine they were, and thou gavest them me; and they have kept thy word. Now they have known that all things whatsoever thou hast given me are of thee. For I have given unto them the words which thou gavest me; and they have received them, and have known surely, that I came out from thee, and they have believed that thou didst send me.

AIDAN
Bishop of Lindisfarne
[August 31.]

The Collect

O ALMIGHTY God, who in thy providence didst choose thy servant Aidan to be an apostle to the people of England, to bring those who were wandering in darkness and error to the true light and knowledge of thee: Grant us so to walk in that light, that we may come at last to the light of everlasting life; through the merits of Jesus Christ thy Son our Lord. *Amen.*

The Epistle. 1 Corinthians 9:16-23

FOR though I preach the gospel, I have nothing to glory of: for necessity is laid upon me; yea, woe is unto me, if I preach not the gospel! For if I do this thing willingly, I have a reward: but if against my will, a dispensation of the gospel is committed unto me. What is my reward then? Verily that, when I preach the gospel, I may make the gospel of Christ without charge, that I abuse not my power in the gospel. For though I be free from all men, yet have I made myself servant unto all, that I might gain the more. And unto the Jews I became as a Jew, that I might gain the Jews; to them that are under the law, as under the law (though not being myself under the law), that I might gain them that are under the law; to them that are without law, as without law, (being not without law to God, but under the law to Christ,) that I might gain them that are without law. To the weak became I as weak, that I might gain the weak: I am made all things to all men, that I might by all means save some. And this I do for the gospel's sake, that I might be partaker thereof with you.

The Gospel. St. Matthew 19:27-30

THEN answered Peter and said unto Jesus, Behold, we have forsaken all, and followed thee; what shall we have therefore? And Jesus said unto them, Verily I say unto you, That ye which have followed me, in the regeneration when the Son of man shall sit in the throne of his glory, ye also shall sit upon twelve thrones, judging the twelve tribes of Israel. And every one that hath forsaken houses, or brethren, or sisters, or father, or mother, or wife, or children, or lands, for my name's sake, shall receive an hundredfold, and shall inherit everlasting life. But many that are first shall be last; and the last shall be first.

JOHN HENRY HOBART
Bishop of New York
[September 12]

The Collect

O GOD, who dost ever hallow and protect thy Church: Raise up therein through thy Spirit good and faithful stewards of the mysteries of Christ, as thou didst in thy servant John Henry Hobart; that by their ministry and example thy people may abide in thy favour and walk in the way of truth; through Jesus Christ our Lord who liveth and reigneth with thee in the unity of the same Spirit ever, one God, world without end. *Amen.*

CYPRIAN
Bishop of Carthage and Martyr
[September 13.]

The Collect

ALMIGHTY God, who didst give thy servant Cyprian boldness to confess the Name of our Saviour Jesus Christ before the rulers of this world, and courage to die for this faith: Grant that we likewise may ever be ready to give a reason for the hope that is in us, and to suffer gladly for his sake; through the same Jesus Christ our Lord. *Amen.*

The Epistle. 1 Peter 5:1-4, 10-11

THE elders which are among you I exhort, who am also an elder, and a witness of the sufferings of Christ, and also a partaker of the glory that shall be revealed: feed the flock of God which is among you, taking the oversight thereof, not by constraint, but willingly; not for filthy lucre, but of a ready mind; neither as being lords over God's heritage, but being ensamples to the flock. And when the chief Shepherd shall appear, ye shall receive a crown of glory that fadeth not away. The God of all grace, who hath called us unto his eternal glory by Christ Jesus, after that ye have suffered a while, make you perfect, stablish, strengthen, settle you. To him be glory and dominion for ever and ever. *Amen.*

The Gospel. St. John 10:11-16

I AM the good shepherd: the good shepherd giveth his life for the sheep. But he that is an hireling, and not the shepherd, whose own the sheep are not, seeth the wolf coming, and leaveth the sheep, and fleeth: and the wolf catcheth them, and scattereth the sheep. The hireling fleeth, because he is an hireling, and careth not for the sheep. I am the good shepherd, and know my sheep, and am known of mine. As the Father knoweth me, even so know I the Father: and I lay down my life for the sheep. And other sheep I have, which are not of this fold: them also I must bring, and they shall hear my voice; and there shall be one fold, and one shepherd.

THE EXALTATION OF THE HOLY CROSS
[September 14.]

The Collect

O GOD, who by the passion of thy blessed Son hast made the instrument of shameful death to be unto us the sign of life and peace: Grant us so to glory in the Cross of Christ, that we may gladly suffer shame and loss; for the sake of the same thy Son our Lord. *Amen.*

The Epistle. Philippians 2:5-11

LET this mind be in you, which was also in Christ Jesus: who, being in the form of God, thought it not robbery to be equal with God: but made himself of no reputation, and took upon him the form of a servant, and was made in the likeness of men: and being found in fashion as a man, he humbled himself, and became obedient unto death, even the death of the cross. Wherefore God also hath highly exalted him, and given him a name which is above every name: that at the name of Jesus every knee should bow, of things in heaven, and things in earth, and things under the earth; and that every tongue should confess that Jesus Christ is Lord, to the glory of God the Father.

The Gospel. St. John 2:31-36

NOW is the judgment of this world: now shall the prince of this world be cast out. And I, if I be lifted up from the earth, will draw all men unto me. This he said, signifying what death he should die. The people answered him, We have heard out of the law that Christ abideth for ever: and how sayest thou, The Son of man must be lifted up? who is this Son of man? Then Jesus said unto them, Yet a little while is the light with you. Walk while ye have the light, lest darkness come upon you: for he that walketh in darkness knoweth not whither he goeth. While ye have light, believe in the light, that ye may be the children of light.

NINIAN
Bishop in Galloway
[September 16.]

The Collect

O GOD, who by the preaching of thy blessed servant Ninian didst cause the light of the Gospel to shine in the land of Britain: Grant, we beseech thee, that having his life and labours in remembrance, we may show forth our thankfulness unto thee for the same by following the example of his zeal and patience; through Jesus Christ our Lord. *Amen.*

THEODORE OF TARSUS
Archbishop of Canterbury
[September 19.]

The Collect

O GOD, who dost ever hallow and protect thy Church: Raise up therein through thy Spirit good and faithful stewards of the mysteries of Christ, as thou didst in thy servant Theodore; that by their ministry and example thy people may abide in thy favour and walk in the way of truth; through Jesus Christ our Lord, who liveth and reigneth with thee in the unity of the same Spirit, one God, world without end. *Amen.*

The Epistle. 2 Timothy 2:1-5, 10

THOU therefore, my son, be strong in the grace that is in Christ Jesus. And the things that thou hast heard of me among many witnesses, the same commit thou to faithful men, who shall be able to teach others also. Thou therefore endure hardness, as a good soldier of Jesus Christ. No man that warreth entangleth himself with the affairs of this life; that he may please him who hath chosen him to be a soldier. And if a man also strive for masteries, yet is he not crowned, except he strive lawfully. Therefore I endure all things for the elect's sakes, that they may also obtain the salvation which is in Christ Jesus with eternal glory.

The Gospel. St. Matthew 24:42-47

WATCH therefore: for ye know not what hour your Lord doth come. But know this, that if the goodman of the house had known in what watch the thief would come, he would have watched, and would not have suffered his house to be broken up. Therefore be ye also ready: for in such an hour as ye think not the Son of man cometh. Who then is a faithful and wise servant, whom his lord hath made ruler over his household, to give them meat in due season? Blessed is that servant, whom his lord when he cometh shall find so doing. Verily I say unto you, That he shall make him ruler over all his goods.

JOHN COLERIDGE PATTESON
Bishop of Melanesia and Martyr
[September 20.]

The Collect

ALMIGHTY God, who didst call thy faithful servant John Coleridge Patteson to be a witness and martyr in the isles of Melanesia, and by his labours and suffering didst raise up a people for thine own possession: Shed forth, we beseech thee, thy Holy Spirit upon thy Church in all lands, that by the sacrifice and service of many, thy holy Name may be glorified and thy blessed kingdom enlarged; through Jesus Christ our Lord, who liveth and reigneth with thee and the same Holy Spirit ever, one God, world without end. *Amen.*

SERGIUS
Abbot
[September 25.]

The Collect

ALMIGHTY and everlasting God, we give thee thanks for the purity and strength with which thou didst endow thy servant Sergius; and we pray that by thy grace we may have a like power to hallow and conform our souls and bodies, to the purpose of thy most holy will; through Jesus Christ our Lord. *Amen.*

LANCELOT ANDREWES
Bishop of Winchester
[September 26.]

The Collect

O ETERNAL Lord God, who holdest all souls in life: We beseech thee to shed forth upon thy whole Church in paradise and on earth the bright beams of thy light and thy peace; and grant that we, following the good examples of thy servant Lancelot Andrewes, and of all those who loved and served thee here, may at the last enter with them into thine unending joy; through Jesus Christ our Lord. *Amen.*

JEROME
Priest, and Monk of Bethlehem
[September 30.]

The Collect

GOD, who hast given us the holy Scriptures for a light to shine upon our path: Grant us, after the example of thy servant Jerome, so to learn of thee according to thy holy Word, that we may find in it the light that shineth more and more unto the perfect day; through Jesus Christ our Lord. *Amen.*

The Epistle. Nehemiah 8:1-3, 5-6, 8-9

AND all the people gathered themselves together as one man into the street that was before the water gate; and they spake unto Ezra the scribe to bring the book of the law of Moses, which the LORD had commanded to Israel. And Ezra the priest brought the law before the congregation both of men and women, and all that could hear with understanding, upon the first day of the seventh month. And he read therein before the street that was before the water gate from the morning until midday, before the men and the women, and those that could understand; and the ears of all the people were attentive unto the book of the law. And Ezra opened the book in the sight of all the people; (for he was above all the people;) and when he opened it, all the people stood up: and Ezra blessed the LORD, the great God. And all the people answered, Amen, Amen, with lifting up their hands: and they bowed their heads, and worshiped the LORD with their faces to the ground. So they read in the book in the law of God distinctly, and gave the sense, and caused them to understand the reading. And Nehemiah, who was the governor and Ezra the priest the scribe, and the Levites that taught the people, said unto all the people This day is holy unto the LORD your God; mourn not, nor weep. For all the people wept, when they heard the word of the law.

The Gospel. St. Luke 24:44-48

JESUS said unto them, These are the words which I spake unto you, while I was yet with you, that all things must be fulfilled, which were written in the law of Moses, and in the prophets, and in the psalms, concerning me. Then opened he their understanding, that they might understand the scriptures, and said unto them, Thus it is written, and thus it behoved Christ to suffer, and to rise from the dead the third day: and that repentance and remission of sins should be preached in his name among all nations, beginning at Jerusalem. And ye are witnesses of these things.

REMIGIUS
Bishop of Rheims
[October 1.]

The Collect

O GOD, the light of the faithful and shepherd of so who didst call thy servant Remigius to feed thy sheep by his word, and guide them by his example: Grant us, pray thee, to keep the faith which he taught, and to follow in his footsteps; through Jesus Christ our Lord. *Amen.*

FRANCIS OF ASSISI
Friar
[October 4.]

The Collect

O MOST high, almighty, and good Lord: Grant thy people grace to renounce gladly the vanities of this world, that, after the example of blessed Francis, we may for love of thee delight in all thy creatures, with perfectness of joy; through Jesus Christ our Lord. *Amen.*

The Epistle. Galatians 6:14-18

GOD forbid that I should glory, save in the cross of our Lord Jesus Christ, by whom the world is crucified unto me, and I unto the world. For in Christ Jesus neither circumcision availeth any thing, nor uncircumcision, but a new creature. And as many as walk according to this rule, peace be on them, and mercy, and upon the Israel of God. From henceforth let no man trouble me: for I bear in my body the marks of the Lord Jesus. Brethren, the grace of our Lord Jesus Christ be with your spirit. Amen.

The Gospel. St. Matthew 11:25-30

JESUS said, I thank thee, O Father, Lord of heaven and earth, because thou hast hid these things from the wise and prudent, and hast revealed them unto babes. Even so, Father: for so it seemed good in thy sight. All things are delivered unto me of my Father: and no man knoweth the Son, but the Father; neither knoweth any man the Father, save the Son, and he to whomsoever the Son will reveal him. Come unto me, all ye that labour and are heavy laden, and I will give you rest. Take my yoke upon you, and learn of me; for I am meek and lowly in heart: and ye shall find rest unto your souls. For my yoke is easy, and my burden is light.

WILLIAM TYNDALE
Priest
[October 6.]

The Collect

ACCEPT, O Lord, our thanksgiving this day for thy servant William Tyndale; and grant unto us in like manner such constancy and zeal in thy service, that we may obtain with him and thy servants everywhere a good confession and the crown of everlasting life; through Jesus Christ our Lord. *Amen.*

SAMUEL ISAAC JOSEPH SCHERESCHEWSKY
Bishop of Shanghai
[October 15.]

The Collect

ALMIGHTY God, who hast enriched thy Church with the singular learning and holiness of thy servant Samuel Isaac Joseph Schereschewsky: Grant us to hold fast the true doctrine of thy Son our Saviour Jesus Christ, and to fashion our lives according to the same, to the glory of thy great Name, and the benefit of thy holy Church; through the same Jesus Christ our Lord. *Amen.*

HUGH LATIMER AND NICHOLAS RIDLEY
Bishops
[October 16.]

The Collect

ACCEPT, O Lord, our thanksgiving this day for thy servants Hugh Latimer and Nicholas Ridley; and grant unto us in like manner such constancy and zeal in thy service, that we may obtain with them and thy servant everywhere a good confession and the crown of everlasting life; through Jesus Christ our Lord. *Amen.*

HENRY MARTYN
Priest, and Missionary to India and Persia
[October 17.]

The Collect

ALMIGHTY and everlasting God, we thank thee for thy servant Henry Martyn, whom thou didst call to preach the Gospel to the people of India and Persia: Raise up, we pray thee, in this and every land, heralds and evangelists of thy kingdom, that thy Church may make known the unsearchable riches of Christ, and may increase with the increase of God; through the same thy Son Jesus Christ our Lord. *Amen.*

SAINT JAMES OF JERUSALEM
Brother of Our Lord Jesus Christ, and Martyr
[October 23.]

The Collect

O LORD Jesus Christ, who didst set thy brother James on the throne of thy church in Jerusalem: Grant, we beseech thee, that as he continually made supplication for the sins of thy people, and laboured to reconcile in one body both Jew and Gentile; so thy Church may ever be faithful in prayer and witness for the salvation of all mankind. Grant this, O Son of Man, who art on the right hand of the Father, in the unity of the Spirit, now and ever. *Amen.*

The Epistle. Acts 5:2-22

THEN all the multitude kept silence and gave audience to Barnabas and Paul, declaring what miracles and wonders God had wrought among the Gentiles by them. And after they had held their peace, James answered, saying, Men and brethren, hearken unto me: Simeon hath declared how God at the first did visit the Gentiles, to take out of them a people for his name. And to this agree the words of the prophets; as it is written,

> After this I will return,
> And will build again the tabernacle of David, which is fallen down;
> And I will build again the ruins thereof,
> And I will set it up:
> That the residue of men might seek after the Lord,
> And all the Gentiles, upon whom my name is called,
> Saith the Lord, who hath made these things known from of old.

Wherefore my sentence is, that we trouble not them, which from among the Gentiles are turned to God: but that we write unto them, that they abstain from pollutions of idols, and from fornication, and from things strangled, and from blood. From early times Moses has had in every city them that preach him, being read in the synagogues every sabbath day. Then pleased it the apostles and elders, with the whole church, to send chosen men of their own company to Antioch with Paul and Barnabas; namely, Judas surnamed Barsabas, and Silas, chief men among the brethren.

The Gospel. St. Mark 3:31-35

THERE came then his brethren and his mother, and, standing without, sent unto him, calling him. And the multitude sat about him, and they said unto him, Behold thy mother and thy brethren without seek for thee. An he answered them, saying, Who is my mother, or my brethren? And he looked round about on them which sat about him, and said, Behold my mother and my brethren. For whosoever shall do the will of God, the same is brother, and my sister, and mother.

ALFRED THE GREAT
King of England
[October 26.]

The Collect

O GOD, who didst call thy servant Alfred to an earthly throne that he might advance thy heavenly kingdom, and didst endue him with zeal for thy Church and charity towards thy people: Mercifully grant that we who commemorate his example may be fruitful in good works, and attain to the glorious fellowship of thy saints; through Jesus Christ our Lord. *Amen.*

The Epistle. Wisdom 6:1-3, 9-12, 24-25

HEAR therefore, O ye kings, and understand; learn, ye that be judges of the ends of the earth. Give ear, ye that rule the people, and glory in the multitude of nations. For power is given you of the Lord, and sovereignty from the Highest, who shall try your works, and search out your counsels. Unto you therefore, O kings, do I speak, that ye may learn wisdom, and not fall away. For they that keep holiness holily shall be judged holy: and they that have learned such things shall find what to answer. Wherefore set your affection upon my words; desire them, and ye shall be instructed. Wisdom is glorious, and never fadeth away: yea, she is easily seen of them that love her, and found of such as seek her. But the multitude of the wise is the welfare of the world: and a wise king is the upholding of the people. Receive therefore instruction through my words, and it shall do you good.

The Gospel. St. Luke 6:43-45

A GOOD tree bringeth not forth corrupt fruit; neither doth a corrupt tree bring forth good fruit. For every tree is known by his own fruit. For of thorns men do not gather figs, nor of a bramble bush gather they grapes. A good man out of the good treasure of his heart bringeth forth that which is good; and an evil man out of the evil treasure of his heart bringeth forth that which is evil: for of the abundance of the heart his mouth speaketh.

JAMES HANNINGTON AND HIS COMPANIONS
Bishop and Martyrs of Uganda
[October 29.]

The Collect

ALMIGHTY God, who didst call thy faithful servants James Hannington and his companions to be witnesses and martyrs in the land of Africa, and by their labours and suffering didst raise up a people for thine own possession: Shed forth, we beseech thee, thy Holy Spirit upon thy Church in all lands, that by the sacrifice and service of many, thy holy Name may be glorified and thy blessed kingdom enlarged; through Jesus Christ our Lord, who liveth and reigneth with thee and the Holy Spirit ever, one God, world without end. *Amen.*

RICHARD HOOKER
Priest
[November 3.]

The Collect

O GOD, who hast enlightened thy Church by the teaching of thy servant Richard Hooker: Enrich us evermore, we beseech thee, with thy heavenly grace, and raise up faithful witnesses who by their life and doctrine will set forth the truth of thy salvation; through Jesus Christ our Lord. *Amen.*

WILLIBRORD
Archbishop of Utrecht,
Missionary to Frisia
[November 7.]

The Collect

O ALMIGHTY God, who in thy providence didst choose thy servant Willibrord to be an apostle to the Frisian people, to bring those who were wandering in darkness and error to the true light and knowledge of thee: Grant us so to walk in that light, that we may come at last to the light of everlasting life; through the merits of Jesus Christ thy Son our Lord. *Amen.*

MARTIN
Bishop of Tours
[November 11.]

The Collect

O GOD, who by thy Holy Spirit didst enable thy servant Martin to withstand the temptations of the world, the flesh, and the devil: Grant that we, in the same Spirit, may with pure hearts and minds follow thee, the only God; through Jesus Christ our Lord. *Amen.*

The Epistle. Isaiah 58:10-12

IF thou draw out thy soul to the hungry, and satisfy the afflicted soul; then shall thy light rise in obscurity, and thy darkness be as the noon day: and the LORD shall guide thee continually, and satisfy thy soul in drought, and make fat thy bones: and thou shalt be like a watered garden, and like a spring of water, whose waters fail not. And they that shall be of thee shall build the old waste places: thou shalt raise up the foundations of many generations; and thou shalt be called, The repairer of the breach, The restorer of path to dwell in.

The Gospel. St. Matthew 25:34-40

THEN shall the King say unto them on his right hand, Come, ye blessed of my Father, inherit the kingdom prepared for you from the foundation of the world: for I was an hungred, and ye gave me meat: I was thirsty, and ye gave me drink: I was a stranger, and ye took me in: naked and ye clothed me: I was sick, and ye visited me: I was in prison, and ye came unto me. Then shall the righteous answer him, saying, Lord, when saw we thee an hungred, and fed thee? or thirsty, and gave thee drink? When saw we thee a stranger, and took thee in? or naked, and clothed thee? Or when saw we thee sick, or in prison, and came unto thee? And the King shall answer and say unto them, Verily I say unto you, Inasmuch as ye have done it unto one of the least of these my brethren, ye have done it unto me.

CHARLES SIMEON
Priest
[November 12.]

The Collect

O ETERNAL Lord God, who holdest all souls in life We beseech thee to shed forth upon thy whole Church in paradise and on earth the bright beams of thy light and thy peace; and grant that we, following the good examples of thy servant Charles Simeon, and of all those who loved and served thee here, may at the last enter with them into thine unending joy; through Jesus Christ our Lord. *Amen.*

THE CONSECRATION OF SAMUEL SEABURY
First American Bishop
[November 14.]

The Collect

ALMIGHTY GOD, who by thy divine providence hast appointed divers Orders of Ministers in thy Church, and by thy Son Jesus Christ didst give to thy holy Apostles many excellent gifts: Give grace, we beseech thee, to all Bishops of thy Church, and more especially to those who serve in that branch of the same planted by thee in this land; that, following the example of thy servant Samuel Seabury, they may diligently preach thy Word, and duly administer the godly Discipline thereof, to the glory of thy Name, and the edification of thy Church; through the same Jesus Christ our Lord. *Amen.*

The Epistle. Acts 20:28-32

TAKE heed therefore unto yourselves, and to all the flock, over the which the Holy Ghost hath made you overseers, to feed the church of God, which he hath purchased with his own blood. For I know this, that after my departing shall grievous wolves enter in among you, not sparing the flock. Also of your own selves shall men arise, speaking perverse things, to draw away disciples after them. Therefore watch, and remember, that by the space of three years I ceased not to warn every one night and day with tears. And now, brethren, I commend you to God, and to the word of his grace, which is able to build you up, and to give you an inheritance among all them which are sanctified.

The Gospel. St. Matthew 9:35-38

JESUS went about all the cities and villages, teaching in their synagogues, and preaching the gospel of the kingdom, and healing every sickness and every disease among the people. But when he saw the multitudes, he was moved with compassion on them, because they fainted, and were scattered abroad, as sheep having no shepherd. Then saith he unto his disciples, The harvest truly is plenteous, but the labourers are few; pray ye therefore the Lord of the harvest, that he will send forth labourers into his harvest.

MARGARET
Queen of Scotland
[November 16.]

The Collect

O GOD, who didst call thy servant Margaret to an earthly throne that she might advance thy heavenly kingdom, and didst endue her with zeal for thy Church and charity towards thy people: Mercifully grant that we who commemorate her example may be fruitful in good works, and attain to the glorious fellowship of thy saints; through Jesus Christ our Lord. *Amen.*

HUGH
Bishop of Lincoln
[November 17.]

The Collect

O GOD, the light of the faithful and shepherd of souls, who didst call thy servant Hugh to feed thy sheep by his word, and guide them by his example: Grant us, we pray thee, to keep the faith which he taught, and to follow in his footsteps; through Jesus Christ our Lord. *Amen.*

HILDA
Abbess of Whitby
[November 18.]

The Collect

ALMIGHTY and everlasting God, we give thee thanks for the purity and strength with which thou didst endow thy servant Hilda; and we pray that by thy grace we may have a like power to hallow and conform our souls and bodies, to the purpose of thy most holy will; through Jesus Christ our Lord. *Amen.*

ELIZABETH
Princess of Hungary
[November 19.]

The Collect

ALMIGHTY and everlasting God, who didst enkindle the flame of thy love in the heart of thy servant Elizabeth: Grant to us, thy humble servants, the same faith and power of love; that as we rejoice in her triumph, we may profit by her example; through Jesus Christ our Lord. *Amen.*

CLEMENT
Bishop of Rome
[November 23.]

The Collect

O GOD, who hast enlightened thy Church by the teaching of thy servant Clement: Enrich us evermore, we beseech thee, with thy heavenly grace, and raise up faithful witnesses who by their life and doctrine will set forth the truth of thy salvation; through Jesus Christ our Lord. *Amen.*

The Common of Saints

¶ *One of the following Collects, Epistles, and Gospels may be used for the Patronal festival of a Saint not listed in the Calendar.*

¶ *The following Collects, Epistles, and Gospels may also be used for the commemoration of a Saint (other than a Patron), for which no provision is made in this Book, PROVIDED, that such commemoration is duly authorized by the Ordinary.*

¶ *And NOTE, That no festival of a Saint shall be observed on a Sunday or Greater Holy Day, contrary to the Tables of Precedence as established in The Book of Common Prayer.*

I. OF A MARTYR

The Collect

ALMIGHTY and everlasting God, who didst strengthen thy blessed martyr _____ with the virtue of constancy in faith and truth: Grant us in like manner for love of thee to despise the prosperity of this world, and to fear none of its adversities; through Jesus Christ our Lord. *Amen.*

The Epistle. 2 Esdras 2:42-48

I ESDRAS saw upon the mount Sion a great people, whom I could not number, and they all praised the Lord with songs. And in the midst of them there was a young man of a high stature, taller than all the rest, and upon every one of their heads he set crowns, and was more exalted; which I marvelled at greatly. So I asked the angel, and said, Sir, what are these? He answered and said unto me, These be they that have put off the mortal clothing, and put on the immortal, and have confessed the name of God: now are they crowned, and receive palms. Then said I unto the angel. What young person is it that crowneth them, and giveth them palms in their hands? So he answered and said unto me, It is the Son of God, whom they have confessed in the world. Then began I greatly to commend them that stood so stiffly for the name of the Lord, Then the angel said unto me, Go thy way, and tell my people what manner of things, and how great wonders of the Lord thy God, thou hast seen.

The Gospel. St. Matthew 10:16-22

BEHOLD, I send you forth as sheep in the midst of wolves: be ye therefore wise as serpents, and harmless as doves. But beware of men: for they will deliver you up to the councils, and they will scourge you in their synagogues; and ye shall be brought before governors and kings for my sake, for a witness to them and the Gentiles. But when they deliver you up, be not anxious how or what ye shall speak: for it shall be given you in that same hour what ye shall speak. For it is not ye that speak, but the Spirit of your Father which speaketh in you. And the brother shall deliver up the brother to death, and the father the child: and the children shall rise up against their parents, and cause them to be put to death. And ye shall be hated of all men for my name's sake: but he that endureth to the end shall be saved.

2. OF A MISSIONARY

The Collect

ALMIGHTY and everlasting God, we thank thee for thy servant ____ , whom thou didst call to preach the Gospel to the people of ____: Raise up, we pray thee, in this and every land, heralds and evangelists of thy kingdom, that thy Church may make known the unsearchable riches of Christ, and may increase with the increase of God; through the same thy Son Jesus Christ our Lord. *Amen.*

The Epistle. Acts 1:1-9

THE former treatise have I made, O Theophilus, of all that Jesus began both to do and teach, until the day in which he was taken up, after that he through the Holy Ghost had given commandments unto the apostles whom he had chosen: to whom also he shewed himself alive after his passion by many infallible proofs, being seen of them forty days, and speaking of the things pertaining to the kingdom of God: and, being assembled together with them, commanded them that they should not depart from Jerusalem, but wait for the promise of the Father, which, saith he, ye have heard of me. For John truly baptized with water; but ye shall be baptized with the Holy Ghost not many days hence.

When they therefore were come together, they asked of him, saying, Lord, wilt thou at this time restore again the kingdom to Israel? And he said unto them, It is not for you to know the times or the seasons, which the Father hath put in his own power. But ye shall receive power, after that the Holy Ghost is come upon you: and ye shall be witnesses unto me both in Jerusalem, and in all Judaea, and in Samaria, and unto the uttermost part of the earth. And when he had spoken these things, while they beheld, he was taken up; and a cloud received him out of their sight.

The Gospel. St. Luke 10:1-9

AFTER these things the Lord appointed other seventy also, and sent them two and two before his face into every city and place, whither he himself would come. Therefore said he unto them, The harvest truly is great, but the labourers are few: pray ye therefore the Lord of the harvest, that he would send forth labourers into his harvest. Go your ways: behold, I send you forth as lambs among wolves. Carry neither purse, nor pack, nor shoes: and salute no man by the way. And into whatsoever house ye enter, first say, Peace be to this house. And if the son of peace be there, your peace shall rest upon it: if not, it shall turn to you again. And in the same house remain, eating and drinking such things as they give: for the labourer is worth of his hire. Go not from house to house. And into whatsoever city ye enter, and they receive you, eat such things as are set before you: and heal the sick that are therein, and say unto them, The kingdom of God is come nigh unto you.

3. OF A THEOLOGIAN OR TEACHER

The Collect

O GOD, who hast endowed thy servant ____ with clarity of faith and holiness of life: Grant us to keep with steadfast minds the faith which he taught, and in his fellowship to be made partakers of eternal glory; through Jesus Christ our Lord. *Amen.*

The Epistle. Wisdom 7:7-14

I CALLED upon God, and the spirit of wisdom came to me. I preferred her before sceptres and thrones, and esteemed riches nothing in comparison of her.

Neither compared I unto her any precious stone, because all gold in respect of her is as a little sand, and silver shall be counted as clay before her. I loved her above health and beauty, and chose to have her instead of light: for the light that cometh from her never goeth out. All good things together came to me with her, and innumerable riches in her hands. And I rejoiced in them all, because wisdom goeth before them: and I knew not that she was the mother of them. I learned diligently, and do communicate her liberally: I do not hide her riches. For she is a treasure unto men that never faileth: which they that use become the friends of God, being commended for the gifts that come from learning.

The Gospel. St. John 17:18-23

AS thou hast sent me into the world, even so have I also sent them into the world. And for their sakes I sanctify myself, that they also might be sanctified through the truth. Neither pray I for these alone, but for them also which shall believe on me through their word; that they all may be one; as thou, Father, art in me, and I in thee, that they also may be one in us: that the world may believe that thou hast sent me. And the glory which thou gavest me I have given them; that they may be one, even as we are one: I in them, and thou in me, that they may be made perfect in one; and that the world may know that thou hast sent me, and hast loved them, as thou hast loved me.

4. OF A MONASTIC

The Collect

O GOD, by whose grace the blessed (abbot) _____ enkindled with the fire of thy love, became a burning and a shining light in thy Church: Grant that we may be inflamed with the same spirit of discipline and love, and ever walk before thee as children of light; through Jesus Christ our Lord. *Amen.*

The Epistle. Philippians 3:7-15

HOWBEIT what things were gain to me, these have I counted loss for Christ. Yea verily, and I count all things to be loss for the excellency of the knowledge of Christ Jesus my Lord: for whom I suffer the loss of all things, and do count them but dung, that I may gain Christ, and be found in him, not having a righteousness of mine own, even that which is of the law, but that which is through faith in Christ, the righteousness which is of God by faith: that I may know him, and the power of his resurrection, and the fellowship of his sufferings, becoming conformed unto his death; if by any means I may attain unto the resurrection of the dead. Not that I have already obtained, or am already made perfect: but I press on, if so be that I may apprehend that for which also I was apprehended by Christ Jesus. Brethren, I count not myself yet to have apprehended:

but one thing I do, forgetting the things which are behind, and stretching forward to the things which are before, I press on toward the goal unto the prize of the high calling of God in Christ Jesus. Let us therefore, as many as be perfect, be thus minded: and if in anything ye are otherwise minded, even this shall God reveal unto you.

The Gospel. St. Luke 2:22-37

JESUS said unto his disciples, Therefore I say unto you, Be not anxious for your life, what ye shall eat; neither for the body, what ye shall put on. The life is more than meat, and the body is more than raiment. Consider the ravens: for they neither sow nor reap; which neither have storehouse nor barn; and God feedeth them: how much more are ye better than the fowls? And which of you by being anxious can add a cubit to his span of life? If ye then be not able to do that which is least, why are ye anxious for the rest? Consider the lilies how they grow: they toil not, they spin not; and yet I say unto you, that Solomon in all his glory was not arrayed like one of these. If then God so clothe the grass, which is to day in the field, and to morrow is cast into the oven; how much more will he clothe you, O ye of little faith? And seek not ye what ye shall eat, or what ye shall drink, neither be ye of anxious mind. For all these things do the nations of the world seek after: and your Father knoweth that ye have need of these things. But rather seek ye the kingdom of God; and all these things shall be added unto you.

Fear not, little flock; for it is your Father's good pleasure to give you the kingdom. Sell that ye have, and give alms; provide yourselves bags which wax not old, a treasure in the heavens that faileth not, where no thief approacheth, neither moth corrupteth. For where your treasure is, there will your heart be also. Let your loins be girded about, and your lamps burning; and ye yourselves like unto men that wait for their lord, when he will return from the wedding; that when he cometh and knocketh, they may open unto him immediately. Blessed are those servants, whom the lord when he cometh shall find watching: verily I say unto you, that he shall gird himself, and make them to sit down to meat, and will come forth and serve them.

5. OF A DEACONESS

The Collect

O GOD, who hast bestowed upon thy Church divers gifts and graces of Ministry: We give thee humble thanks for thy servant _____ whom we commemorate this day; and we beseech thee to help us follow in her steps, and fill our hearts with love of thee, and of others for thy sake; through Jesus Christ our Lord. *Amen.*

The Epistle. Romans 15:30-16:2

NOW I beseech you, brethren, for the Lord Jesus Christ's sake, and for the love of the Spirit, that ye strive together with me in your prayers to God for me; that I may be delivered from them that do not believe in Judaea; and that my service which I have for Jerusalem may be accepted of the saints; that I may come unto you with joy by the will of God, and may with you be refreshed. Now the God of peace be with you all. Amen.

I commend unto you Phebe our sister, which is a deaconess of the church which is at Cenchrea: that ye receive her in the Lord, as becometh saints, and that ye assist her in whatsoever business she hath need of you: for she hath been a succourer of many, and of myself also.

The Gospel. St. Matthew 9:35-38

JESUS went about all the cities and villages, teaching in their synagogues, and preaching the gospel of the kingdom, and healing every sickness and every disease among the people. But when he saw the multitudes, he was moved with compassion on them, because they fainted, and were scattered abroad, as sheep having no shepherd. Then saith he unto his disciples, The harvest truly is plenteous, but the labourers are few; Pray ye therefore the Lord of the harvest, that he will send forth labourers into his harvest.

6. OF A SAINT

The Collect

O ALMIGHTY God, who hast called us to faith in thee, and hast compassed us about with so great a cloud of witnesses: Grant that we, encouraged by the good examples of thy Saints, and especially of thy servant _____ may persevere in running the race that is set before us, until at length, through thy mercy, we with them attain to thine eternal joy; through him who is the author and finisher of our faith, thy Son Jesus Christ our Lord. *Amen.*

The Epistle. Hebrews 12:1-2

SEEING we also are compassed about with so great a cloud of witnesses, let us lay aside every weight, and the sin which doth so easily beset us, and let us run with patience the race that is set before us, looking unto Jesus the author and finisher of our faith; who for the joy that was set before him endured the cross, despising the shame, and is set down at the right hand of the throne of God.

The Gospel. St. Matthew 25:31-40

WHEN the Son of man shall come in his glory, and all the holy angels with him, then shall he sit upon the throne of his glory: and before him shall be gathered all nations: and he shall separate them one from another, as a shepherd divideth his sheep from the goats: and he shall set the sheep on his right hand, but the goats on the left. Then shall the King say unto them on his right hand, Come, ye blessed of my Father, inherit the kingdom prepared for you from the foundation of the world: for I was an hungred, and ye gave me meat: I was thirsty, and ye gave me drink: I was a stranger, and ye took me in: naked, and ye clothed me: I was sick, and ye visited me: I was in prison, and ye came unto me. Then shall the righteous answer him, saying, Lord, when saw we thee an hungred, and fed thee? or thirsty, and gave thee drink? When saw we thee a stranger, and took thee in? or naked, and clothed thee? Or when saw we thee sick, or in prison, and came unto thee? And the King shall answer and say unto them, Verily I say unto you, Inasmuch as ye have done it unto one of the least of these my brethren, ye have done it unto me.

¶ *Or this,*

The Collect

O GOD, who hast brought us near to an innumerable company of Angels, and to the spirits of just men made perfect: Grant us during our pilgrimage to abide in their fellowship, and in our Country to become partakers of their joy; through Jesus Christ our Lord. *Amen.*

The Epistle. Philippians 4:4-9

REJOICE in the Lord alway: and again I say, Rejoice, Let your moderation be known unto all men. The Lord is at hand. Be anxious for nothing; but in every thing by prayer and supplication with thanksgiving let your requests be made known unto God. And the peace of God, which passeth all understanding, shall keep your hearts and minds through Christ Jesus.

Finally, brethren, whatsoever things are true, whatsoever things are honest, whatsoever things are just, whatsoever things are pure, whatsoever things are lovely, whatsoever things are of good report; if there be any virtue, and if there be any praise, think on these things. Those things, which ye have both learned, and received, and heard, and seen in me, do: and the God of peace shall be with you.

The Gospel. St. Luke 6:17-23

JESUS came down and stood in the plain, with the company of his disciples, and a great multitude of people out of all Judaea and Jerusalem, and from the sea coasts of Tyre and Sidon, which came to hear him, and to be healed of their diseases; and they that were vexed with unclean spirits: and they were healed. And the whole multitude sought to touch him: for there went virtue out of him, and healed them all. And he lifted up his eyes on his disciples, and said, Blessed be ye poor: for yours is the kingdom of God. Blessed are ye that hunger now: for ye shall be filled. Blessed are ye that weep now: for ye shall laugh. Blessed are ye, when men shall hate you, and when they shall separate you from their company, and shall reproach you, and cast out your name as evil, for the Son of man's sake. Rejoice ye in that day, and leap for joy: for, behold, your reward is great in heaven.

For Special Occasions

¶ The following Collects, Epistles, and Gospels may be used at special celebrations of the Holy Eucharist on any weekday for which The Book of Common Prayer does not provide an appointed set of propers.

I. OF THE HOLY TRINITY

The Collect

ALMIGHTY and everlasting God, who hast given unto us thy servants grace, by the confession of a true faith, to acknowledge the glory of the eternal Trinity, and in the power of the Divine Majesty to worship the Unity: We beseech thee that thou wouldest keep us stedfast in this faith, and evermore defend us from all adversities, who livest and reignest, one God, world without end. *Amen.*

The Epistle. Romans 11:33-36

THE depth of the riches both of the wisdom and knowledge of God! how unsearchable are his judgments, and his ways past finding out! For who hath known the mind of the Lord? or who hath been his counsellor? Or who hath first given to him, and it shall be recompensed unto him again? For of him, and through him, and to him, are all things: to whom be glory for ever. Amen.

The Gospel. St. Matthew 28:18-20

JESUS came and spake unto them, saying, All power is given unto me in heaven and in earth. Go ye therefore, and make disciples of all nations, baptizing them in the name of the Father, and of the Son, and of the Holy Ghost: teaching them to observe all things whatsoever I have commanded you: and, lo, I am with you alway, even unto the end of the world.

2. OF THE HOLY SPIRIT

The Collect

ALMIGHTY and most merciful God, grant, we beseech thee, that by the indwelling of thy Holy Spirit, we may be enlightened and strengthened for thy service; through Jesus Christ our Lord, who liveth and reigneth with thee in the unity of the same Spirit ever, one God, world without end. Amen.

The Epistle. 1 Corinthians 12:4-14

NOW there are diversities of gifts, but the same Spirit. And there are differences of administrations, but the same Lord. And there are diversities of operations, but it is the same God which worketh all in all. But the manifestation of the Spirit is given to every man to profit withal. For to one is given by the Spirit the word of wisdom; to another the word of knowledge by the same Spirit; to another faith by the same Spirit; to another the gifts of healing by the same Spirit; to another the working of miracles; to another prophecy; to another discerning of spirits; to another divers kinds of tongues; to another the interpretation of tongues: but all these worketh that one and the selfsame Spirit, dividing to every man severally as he will. For as the body is one, and hath many members, and all the members of that one body, being many, are one body: so also is Christ. For by one Spirit are we all baptized into one body, whether we be Jews or Gentiles, whether we be bond or free; and have been all made to drink into one Spirit. For the body is not one member, but many.

The Gospel. St. Luke 11:9-13

JESUS said to his disciples, Ask, and it shall be given you; seek, and ye shall find; knock, and it shall be opened unto you. For every one that asketh receiveth; and he that seeketh findeth; and to him that knocketh it shall be opened. If a son shall ask bread of any of you that is a father, will he give him a stone? or if he ask a fish, will he for a fish give him a serpent? or if he shall ask an egg, will he offer him a scorpion? If ye then, being evil, know how to give good gifts unto your children: how much more shall your heavenly Father give the Holy Spirit to them that ask him?

3. OF THE HOLY ANGELS

The Collect

O EVERLASTING God, who hast ordained and constituted the services of Angels and men in a wonderful order: Mercifully grant that, as thy holy Angels always do thee service in heaven, so, by thy appointment, they may succour and defend us on earth; through Jesus Christ our Lord. *Amen.*

The Epistle. Revelation 5:11-14

I BEHELD, and I heard the voice of many angels round about the throne and the beasts and the elders: and the number of them was ten thousand times ten thousand, and thousands of thousands; saying with a loud voice, Worthy is the Lamb that was slain to receive power, and riches, and wisdom, and strength, and honour, and glory, and blessing. And every creature which is in heaven, and on the earth, and under the earth, and such as are in the sea, and all that are in them, heard I saying, Blessing, and honour, and glory, and power, be unto him that sitteth upon the throne, and unto the Lamb for ever and ever. And the four beasts said, Amen. And the elders fell down and worshipped him.

The Gospel. St. John 1:47-51

JESUS saw Nathanael coming to him, and saith of him, Behold an Israelite indeed, in whom is no guile! Nathanael saith unto him, Whence knowest thou me? Jesus answered and said unto him, Before that Philip called thee, when thou wast under the fig tree, I saw thee. Nathanael answered and saith unto him, Rabbi, thou art the Son of God; thou art the King of Israel. Jesus answered and said unto him, Because I said unto thee, I saw thee under the fig tree, believest thou? thou shalt see greater things than these. And he saith unto him, Verily, verily, I say unto you, Hereafter ye shall see heaven open, and the angels of God ascending and descending upon the Son of man.

4. OF THE INCARNATION

The Collect

WE beseech thee, O Lord, pour thy grace into our hearts; that, as we have known the incarnation of thy Son Jesus Christ by the message of an angel, so by his cross and passion we may be brought unto the glory of his resurrection; through the same Jesus Christ our Lord. Amen.

The Epistle. 1 John 4:1-11

BELOVED, believe not every spirit, but try the spirits whether they are of God: because many false prophets are gone out into the world. Hereby know ye the Spirit of God: Every spirit that confesseth that Jesus Christ is come in the flesh is of God: and every spirit that confesseth not that Jesus Christ is come in the flesh is not of God: and this is that spirit of antichrist, whereof ye have heard that it should come; and even now already is it in the world.

Ye are of God, little children, and have overcome them: because greater is he that is in you, than he that is in the world. They are of the world: therefore speak they of the world, and the world heareth them. We are of God: he that knoweth

God heareth us; he that is not of God heareth not us. Hereby know we the spirit of truth, and the spirit of error.

Beloved, let us love one another: for love is of God; and every one that loveth is born of God, and knoweth God. He that loveth not knoweth not God; for God is love. In this was manifested the love of God toward us, because that God sent his only begotten Son into the world, that we might live through him. Herein is love, not that we loved God, but that he loved us, and sent his Son to be the expiation for our sins. Beloved, if God so loved us, we ought also to love one another.

The Gospel. St. Luke 1:26-38

AND in the sixth month the angel Gabriel was sent from God unto a city of Galilee, named Nazareth, to a virgin espoused to a man whose name was Joseph, of the house of David; and the virgin's name was Mary. And the angel came in unto her, and said, Hail, thou that art highly favoured, the Lord is with thee: blessed art thou among women. And when she saw him, she was troubled at his saying, and cast in her mind what manner of salutation this should be. And the angel said unto her, Fear not, Mary: for thou hast found favour with God. And, behold, thou shalt conceive in thy womb, and bring forth a son, and shalt call his name JESUS. He shall be great, and shall be called the Son of the Highest: and the Lord God shall give unto him the throne of his father David: and he shall reign over the house of Jacob for ever; and of his kingdom there shall be no end. Then said Mary unto the angel, How shall this be, seeing I know not a man? And the angel answered and said unto her, The Holy Ghost shall come upon thee, and the power of the Highest shall overshadow thee: therefore also that holy thing which shall be born of thee shall be called the Son of God. And, behold, thy cousin Elisabeth, she hath also conceived a son in her old age: and this is the sixth month with her, who was called barren. For with God nothing shall be impossible. And Mary said, Behold the handmaid of the Lord; be it unto me according to thy word. And the angel departed from her.

5. OF THE HOLY EUCHARIST

¶ *Especially suitable for Thursdays.*

The Collect

O LORD Jesus Christ, who in a wonderful Sacrament hast left unto us the memorial of thy Passion: Grant us, we beseech thee, so to reverence the sacred mysteries of thy Body and Blood, that we may always perceive within ourselves the fruit of thy redeeming work; who livest and reignest with the Father, in the unity of the Holy Spirit ever, one God, world without end. Amen.

The Epistle. Revelation 19:1-9

AND after these things I heard a great voice of much people in heaven, saying, Alleluia; Salvation, and glory, and honour, and power, unto the Lord our God: for true and righteous are his judgments: for he hath judged the great whore, which did corrupt the earth with her fornication, and hath avenged the blood of his servants at her hand. And again they said, Alleluia. And her smoke rose up for ever and ever. And the four and twenty elders and the four beasts fell down and worshipped God that sat on the throne, saying, Amen; Alleluia. And a voice came out of the throne, saying, Praise our God, all ye his servants, and ye that fear him, both small and great. And I heard as it were the voice of a great multitude, and as the voice of many waters, and as the voice of mighty thunderings, saying, Alleluia: for the Lord God omnipotent reigneth. Let us be glad and rejoice, and give honour to him: for the marriage of the Lamb is come, and his bride hath made herself ready. And to her was granted that she should be arrayed in fine linen, clean and white: for the fine linen is the righteousness of saints. And he saith unto me, Write, Blessed are they which are called unto the marriage supper of the Lamb. And he saith unto me, These are the true sayings of God.

The Gospel. St. John 6:47-59

VERILY, verily, I say unto you, He that believeth on me hath everlasting life. I am that bread of life. Your fathers did eat manna in the wilderness, and are dead. This is the bread which cometh down from heaven, that a man may eat thereof, and not die. I am the living bread which came down from heaven: if any man eat of this bread, he shall live for ever: and the bread that I will give is my flesh, which I will give for the life of the world.

The Jews therefore strove among themselves, saying, How can this man give us his flesh to eat? Then Jesus said unto them, Verily, verily, I say unto you, Except ye eat the flesh of the Son of man, and drink his blood, ye have no life in you. Whoso eateth my flesh, and drinketh my blood, hath eternal life; and I will raise him up at the last day. For my flesh is meat indeed, and my blood is drink indeed. He that eateth my flesh, and drinketh my blood, dwelleth in me, and I in him. As the living Father hath sent me, and I live by the Father: so he that eateth me, even he shall live by me. This is that bread which came down from heaven: not as your fathers did eat manna, and are dead: he that eateth of this bread shall live for ever. These things said he in the synagogue, as he taught in Capernaum.

6. OF THE HOLY CROSS

¶ *Especially suitable for Fridays.*

The Collect

ALMIGHTY God, whose beloved Son for our sake willingly offered himself to endure the agony and shame of the Cross: Remove from us all cowardice of heart, and give us courage to take up our cross and bear it patiently in his service; through the same thy Son Jesus Christ our Lord who liveth and reigneth with thee and the Holy Ghost ever one God, world without end. Amen.

The Epistle. 1 Corinthians 1:18-24

FOR the preaching of the cross is to them that perish foolishness; but unto us which are saved it is the power of God. For it is written,

> I will destroy the wisdom of the wise,
> And will bring to nothing the understanding of the prudent.

Where is the wise? where is the scribe? where is the disputer of this world? hath not God made foolish the wisdom of this world? For after that in the wisdom of God the world by wisdom knew not God, it pleased God by the foolishness of preaching to save them that believe. For the Jews require a sign, and the Greeks seek after wisdom: but we preach Christ crucified, unto the Jews a stumbling-block, and unto the Greeks foolishness; but unto them which are called, both Jews and Greeks, Christ the power of God, and the wisdom of God.

The Gospel. St. John 12:23-33

JESUS answered them, saying, The hour is come, that the Son of man should be glorified. Verily, verily, I say unto you, Except a seed of wheat fall into the ground and die, it abideth alone: but if it die, it bringeth forth much fruit. He that loveth his life shall lose it; and he that hateth his life in this world shall keep it unto life eternal. If any man serve me, let him follow me; and where I am, there shall also my servant be: if any man serve me, him will my Father honour.

Now is my soul troubled; and what shall I say? Father, save me from this hour: but for this cause came I unto this hour. Father, glorify thy name. Then came there a voice from heaven, saying, I have both glorified it, and will glorify it again. The people therefore, that stood by, and heard it, said that it thundered: others said, An angel spake to him. Jesus answered and said, This voice came not because of me, but for your sakes. Now is the judgment of this world: now shall the prince of this world be cast out. And I, if I be lifted up from the earth, will draw all men unto me. This he said, signifying what death he should die.

7. FOR ALL BAPTIZED CHRISTIANS

¶ *Especially suitable for Saturdays.*

The Collect

GRANT, O Lord, that as we are baptized into the death of thy blessed Son, our Saviour Jesus Christ, so by continual mortifying our corrupt affections we may be buried with him; and that through the grave, and gate of death, we may pass to our joyful resurrection; for his merits, who died, and was buried, and rose again for us, the same thy Son Jesus Christ our Lord. Amen.

The Epistle. Romans 6:3-11

DO you not know that all of us who have been baptized into Christ Jesus were baptized into his death? We were buried therefore with him by baptism into death, so that as Christ was raised from the dead by the glory of the Father, we too might walk in newness of life. For if we have been united with him in a death like his, we shall certainly be united with him in a resurrection like his. This we know, that our old self was crucified with him so that the sinful body might be destroyed, and we might no longer be enslaved to sin. For he who has died is set free from sin. But if we have died with Christ, we believe that we shall also live with him. For we know that Christ being raised from the dead will never die again; death no longer has dominion over him. The death he died he died to sin, once for all, but the life he lives he lives to God. So you also must consider yourselves dead to sin and alive to God in Christ Jesus.

The Gospel. St. Mark 10:35-45

JAMES and John, the sons of Zebedee, come unto him, saying, Master, we would that thou shouldest do for us whatsoever we shall desire. And he said unto them, What would ye that I should do for you? They said unto him, Grant unto us that we may sit, one on thy right hand, and the other on thy left hand, in thy glory. But Jesus said unto them, Ye know not what ye ask: can ye drink of the cup that I drink of? and be baptized with the baptism that I am baptized with? And they said unto him, We can. And Jesus said unto them, Ye shall indeed drink of the cup that I drink of; and with the baptism that I am baptized withal shall ye be baptized: but to sit on my right hand and on my left hand is not mine to give; but it shall be given to them for whom it is prepared. And when the ten heard it, they began to be much displeased with James and John. But Jesus called them to him, and saith unto them, Ye know that they which are accounted to rule over the Gentiles exercise lordship over them; and their great ones exercise authority upon them. But so shall it not be among you: but whosoever will be great among you, shall be your minister: and whosoever of you will be the chiefest, shall be servant of all. For even the Son of man came not to be ministered unto, but to minister, and to give his life a ransom for many.

8. OF THE REIGN OF CHRIST

The Collect

ALMIGHTY and everlasting God, who didst will to restore all things in thy well-beloved Son, the King of kings and Lord of lords: Mercifully grant that all the kindreds of the earth, set free from the captivity of sin, may be brought under his most gracious dominion; who liveth and reigneth with thee and the Holy Spirit ever, one God, world without end. *Amen.*

The Epistle. Colossians 1:12-20

WE give thanks to the Father, who has qualified us to share in the inheritance of the saints in light. He has delivered us from the dominion of darkness and transferred us to the kingdom of his beloved Son, in whom we have redemption, the forgiveness of sins. He is the image of the invisible God, the first-born of all creation; for in him all things were created, in heaven and on earth, visible and invisible, whether thrones or dominions or principalities or authorities — all things were created through him and for him. He is before all things, and in him all things hold together. He is the head of the body, the church; he is the beginning, the first-born from the dead, that in everything he might be preeminent. For in him all the fullness of God was pleased to dwell, and through him to reconcile all things to himself, whether things on earth or things in heaven, having made peace by the blood of his cross.

The Gospel. St. John 18:33-37

THEN Pilate entered into the judgment hall again, and called Jesus, and said unto him, Art thou the King of the Jews? Jesus answered him, Sayest thou this thing of thyself, or did others tell it thee of me? Pilate answered, Am I a Jew? Thine own nation and the chief priests have delivered thee unto me: what hast thou done? Jesus answered, My kingdom is not of this world: if my kingdom were of this world, then would my servants fight, that I should not be delivered to the Jews: but now is my kingdom not from hence. Pilate therefore said unto him, Art thou a king then? Jesus answered, Thou sayest that I am a king. To this end was I born, and for this cause came I into the world, that I should bear witness unto the truth. Everyone that is of the truth heareth my voice.

9. FOR A CHURCH CONVENTION

The Collect

ALMIGHTY and everlasting Father, who hast given us the Holy Spirit to abide with us for ever: Bless, we beseech thee, with his grace and presence the Bishops, Clergy, and Laity here assembled in thy Name; that thy Church, being preserved in true faith and godly discipline, may fulfill all the mind of him who loved it, and gave himself for it, thy Son our Saviour Jesus Christ. Amen.

The Epistle. 2 Corinthians 4:1-10

THEREFORE seeing we have this ministry, as we have received mercy, we faint not; but have renounced the hidden things of dishonesty, not walking in craftiness, nor handling the word of God deceitfully; but by manifestation of the truth commending ourselves to every man's conscience in the sight of God. But if our gospel be hid, it is hid to them that are lost: in whom the god of this world hath blinded the minds of them which believe not, lest the light of the glorious gospel of Christ, who is the image of God, should shine unto them. For we preach not ourselves, but Christ Jesus the Lord; and ourselves your servants for Jesus' sake. For God, who commanded the light to shine out of darkness, hath shined in our hearts, to give the light of the knowledge of the glory of God in the face of Jesus Christ.

But we have this treasure in earthen vessels, that the excellency of the power may be of God, and not of us. We are troubled on every side, yet not distressed; we are perplexed, but not in despair; persecuted, but not forsaken; cast down, but not destroyed; always bearing about in the body the dying of the Lord Jesus, that the life also of Jesus might be made manifest in our body.

The Gospel. St. John 15:1-8

I AM the true vine, and my Father is the husbandman. Every branch in me that beareth not fruit he taketh away: and every branch that beareth fruit, he pruneth it, that it may bring forth more fruit. Now ye are clean through the word which I have spoken unto you. Abide in me, and I in you. As the branch cannot bear fruit of itself, except it abide in the vine; no more can ye, except ye abide in me. I am the vine, ye are the branches: He that abideth in me, and I in him, the same bringeth forth much fruit: for without me ye can do nothing. If a man abide not in me, he is cast forth as a branch, and is withered; and men gather them, and cast them into the fire, and they are burned. If ye abide in me, and my words abide in you, ye shall ask what ye will, and it shall be done unto you. Herein is my Father glorified, that ye bear much fruit; so shall ye be my disciples.

10. FOR EDUCATION

The Collect

ALMIGHTY God, our heavenly Father, who hast committed to thy holy Church the care and nurture of thy children: Enlighten with thy wisdom those who teach and those who learn, that, rejoicing in the knowledge of thy truth, we may worship thee and serve thee from generation to generation; through Jesus Christ our Lord. *Amen.*

The Epistle. 2 Timothy 3:14-4:7

CONTINUE thou in the things which thou hast learned and hast been assured of, knowing of whom thou halt learned them; and that from a child thou hast known the holy scriptures, which are able to make thee wise unto salvation through faith which is in Christ Jesus. All scripture is given by inspiration of God, and is profitable for doctrine, for reproof, for correction, for instruction in righteousness: that the man of God may be perfect, throughly furnished unto all good works. I charge thee therefore before God, and the Lord Jesus Christ, who shall judge the quick and the dead at his appearing and his kingdom; preach the word; be instant in season, out of season; reprove, rebuke, exhort with all long-suffering and doctrine. For the time will come when they will not endure sound doctrine; but after their own lusts shall they heap to themselves teachers, having itching ears; and they shall turn away their ears from the truth, and shall be turned unto fables. But watch thou in all things, endure afflictions, do the work of an evangelist, make full proof of thy ministry. For I am now ready to be offered, and the time of my departure is at hand. I have fought a good fight, I have finished my course, I have kept the faith.

The Gospel. St. Matthew 11:25-30

AT that time Jesus answered and said, I thank thee, O Father, Lord of heaven and earth, because thou hast hid these things from the wise and prudent, and hast revealed them unto babes. Even so, Father: for so it seemed good in thy sight. All things are delivered unto me of my Father: and no man knoweth the Son, but the Father; neither knoweth any man the Father, save the Son, and he to whomsoever the Son will reveal him.

Come unto me, all ye that labour and are heavy laden, and I will give you rest. Take my yoke upon you, and learn of me; for I am meek and lowly in heart: and ye shall find rest unto your souls. For my yoke is easy, and my burden is light.

11. FOR THE MINISTRY

The Collect

ALMIGHTY God, the giver of all good gifts, who of thy divine providence hast appointed divers Orders in thy Church: Give thy grace, we humbly beseech thee, to all those who are called to any office and administration in the same; and so replenish them with the truth of thy doctrine, and endue them with innocency of life, that they may faithfully serve before thee, to the glory of thy great Name, and the benefit of thy holy Church; through Jesus Christ our Lord. *Amen.*

The Epistle. 1 Corinthians 3:5-11

WHO then is Paul, and who is Apollos, but ministers by whom ye believed, even as the Lord gave to every man? I have planted, Apollos watered; but God gave the increase. So then neither is he that planteth any thing, neither he that watereth; but God that giveth the increase. Now he that planteth and he that watereth are equal: and every man shall receive his own reward according to his own labour. For we are labourers together with God: ye are God's husbandry, ye are God's building. According to the grace of God which is given unto me, as a wise master-builder, I have laid the foundation, and another buildeth thereon. But let every man take heed how he buildeth thereupon. For other foundation can no man lay than that is laid, which is Jesus Christ.

The Gospel. St. John 4:31-38

IN the mean while his disciples prayed him, saying, Master, eat. But he said unto them, I have meat to eat that ye know not of. Therefore said the disciples one to another, Hath any man brought him ought to eat? Jesus saith unto them, My meat is to do the will of him that sent me, and to finish his work. Say not ye, There are yet four months, and then cometh harvest? behold, I say unto you, Lift up your eyes, and look on the fields; for they are white already to harvest. And he that reapeth receiveth wages, and gathereth fruit unto life eternal: that both he that soweth and he that reapeth may rejoice together. And herein is that saying true, One soweth, and another reapeth. I sent you to reap that whereon ye bestowed no labour: other men laboured, and ye are entered into their labours.

12. FOR THE MISSION OF THE CHURCH

The Collect

O GOD, who hast made of one blood all nations of men for to dwell on the face of the whole earth, and didst send thy blessed Son to preach peace to them that are far off and to them that are nigh: Grant that all men everywhere may seek after thee and find thee. Bring the nations into thy fold, pour out thy Spirit upon all flesh, and hasten thy kingdom; through the same thy Son Jesus Christ our Lord. *Amen.*

The Epistle. Isaiah 2:2-4

AND it shall come to pass in the last days, that the mountain of the Lord's house shall be established in the top of the mountains, and shall be exalted above the hills; and all nations shall flow unto it. And many people shall go and say, Come ye, and let us go up to the mountain of the Lord, to the house of the God of Jacob; and he will teach us of his ways, and we will walk in his paths: for out of Zion shall go forth the law, and the word of the Lord from Jerusalem. And he shall judge among the nations, and shall rebuke many people: and they shall beat their swords into plowshares, and their spears into pruninghooks: nation shall not lift up sword against nation, neither shall they learn war any more.

¶ *Or this,*

The Epistle. Isaiah 49:5-13

NOW saith the Lord that formed me from the womb to be his servant, to bring Jacob again to him, and that Israel be gathered unto him: (for I am honourable in the eyes of the Lord, and my God is become my strength:) yea, he saith, It is too light a thing that thou shouldest be my servant to raise up the tribes of Jacob, and to restore the preserved of Israel: I will also give thee for a light to the Gentiles, that thou mayest be my salvation unto the end of the earth.

Thus saith the Lord, the redeemer of Israel, and his Holy One, to him whom man despiseth, to him whom the nation abhorreth, to a servant of rulers: Kings shall see and arise; princes, and they shall worship; because of the Lord that is faithful, even the Holy One of Israel, who hath chosen thee.

Thus saith the Lord, In an acceptable time have I answered thee, and in a day of salvation have I helped thee: and I will preserve thee, and give thee for a covenant of the people, to raise up the land, to make them inherit the desolate heritages; saying to them that are bound, Go forth; to them that are in darkness, Shew yourselves. They shall feed in the ways, and on all bare heights shall be their pasture. They shall not hunger nor thirst; neither shall the heat nor sun smite them: for he that hath mercy on them shall lead them, even by the springs of water shall he guide them. And I will make all my mountains a way, and my high ways shall be exalted. Lo, these shall come from far: and lo, these from the north and from the west; and these from the land of Sinim. Sing, O heavens; and be joyful, O earth; and break forth into singing, O mountains: for the Lord hath comforted his people, and will have compassion upon his afflicted.

The Gospel. St. Luke 10:1-9

AFTER these things the Lord appointed other seventy also, and sent them two and two before his face into every city and place, whither he himself would come. Therefore said he unto them, The harvest truly is great, but the labourers are few: pray ye therefore the Lord of the harvest, that he would send forth labourers into his harvest. Go your ways: behold, I send you forth as lambs among wolves. Carry neither purse, nor pack, nor shoes: and salute no man by the way. And into whatsoever house ye enter, first say, Peace be to this house. And if the son of peace be there, your peace shall rest upon it: if not, it shall turn to you again. And in the same house remain, eating and drinking such things as they give: for the labourer is worthy of his hire. Go not from house to house. And into whatsoever city ye enter, and they receive you, eat such things as are set before you; and heal the sick that are therein, and say unto them, The kingdom of God is come nigh unto you.

¶ *Or this,*

The Gospel. St. Matthew 9:35-38

JESUS went about all the cities and villages, teaching in their synagogues, and preaching the gospel of the kingdom, and healing every sickness and every disease among the people. But when he saw the multitudes, he was moved with compassion on them, because they fainted, and were scattered abroad, as sheep having no shepherd. Then saith he unto his disciples, The harvest truly is plenteous, but the labourers are few; pray ye therefore the Lord of the harvest, that he will send forth labourers into his harvest.

13. FOR THE NATION

The Collect

O ETERNAL God, through whose mighty power our fathers won their liberties of old: Grant, we beseech thee, that we and all the people of this land may have grace to maintain these liberties in righteousness and peace; through Jesus Christ our Lord. *Amen.*

The Epistle. Micah 4:1-5

IN the last days it shall come to pass, that the mountain of the house of the LORD shall be established in the top of the mountains, and it shall be exalted above the hills; and people shall flow unto it. And many nations shall come, and say, Come, and let us go up to the mountain of the LORD, and to the house of the God of Jacob; and he will teach us of his ways, and we will walk in his paths: for the law shall go forth of Zion, and the word of the LORD from Jerusalem. And he shall judge among many people, and rebuke strong nations afar off; and they shall beat their swords into plowshares, and their spears into pruninghooks: nation shall not lift up a sword against nation, neither shall they learn war any more. But they shall sit every man under his vine and under his fig tree; and none shall make them afraid: for the mouth of the LORD of hosts hath spoken it. For all people will walk every one in the name of his god, and we will walk in the name of the LORD our God for ever and ever.

The Gospel. St. Mark 12:13-17

THEY send unto him certain of the Pharisees and of the Herodians, to catch him in his words. And when they were come, they say unto him, Master, we know that thou art true, and carest for no man: for thou regardest not the person of men, but teachest the way of God in truth: Is it lawful to give tribute to Caesar, or not? Shall we give, or shall we not give? But he, knowing their hypocrisy, said unto them, Why tempt ye me? bring me a penny, that I may see it. And they brought it. And he saith unto them, Whose is this image and superscription? And they said unto him, Caesar's. And Jesus answering said unto them. Render to Caesar the things that are Caesar's, and to God the things that are God's. And they marvelled at him.

14. FOR PEACE

The Collect

ALMIGHTY God, from whom all thoughts of truth and peace proceed: Kindle, we pray thee, in the hearts of all men the true love of peace; and guide with thy pure and peaceable wisdom those who take counsel for the nations of the earth; that in tranquillity thy kingdom may go forward, till the earth is filled with the knowledge of thy love; through Jesus Christ our Lord. *Amen.*

The Epistle. Ephesians 2:13-22

NOW in Christ Jesus ye who sometimes were far off are made nigh by the blood of Christ. For he is our peace, who hath made both one, and hath broken down the middle wall of partition between us; having abolished in his flesh the enmity, even the law of commandments contained in ordinances; for to make in himself of twain one new man, so making peace; and that he might reconcile both unto God in one body by the cross, having slain the enmity thereby: and came and preached peace to you which were afar off, and to them that were nigh. For through him we both have access by one Spirit unto the Father. Now therefore ye are no more strangers and foreigners, but fellow citizens with the saints, and of the household of God; and are built upon the foundation of the apostles and prophets, Jesus Christ himself being the chief corner stone; in whom all the building fitly framed together groweth unto an holy temple in the Lord: in whom ye also are builded together for an habitation of God through the Spirit.

The Gospel. St. John 16:23-33

VERILY, verily, I say unto you, Whatsoever ye shall ask the Father in my name, he will give it you. Hitherto have ye asked nothing in my name: ask, and ye shall receive, that your joy may be full. These things have I spoken unto you by means of figures: but the time cometh, when I shall no more speak unto you in figures, but I shall shew you plainly of the Father. At that day ye shall ask in my name: and I say not unto you, that I will pray the Father for you: for the Father himself loveth you, because ye have loved me, and have believed that I came out from God. I came forth from the Father, and am come into the world: again, I leave the world, and go to the Father. His disciples said unto him, Lo, now speakest thou plainly, and not in any figure of speech. Now are we sure that thou knowest all things, and needest not that any man should ask thee: by this we believe that thou camest forth from God. Jesus answered them, Do ye now believe? Behold, the hour cometh, yea, is now come, that ye shall be scattered, every man to his own, and shall leave me alone: and yet I am not alone, because the Father is with me. These things I have spoken unto you, that in me ye might have peace. In the world ye shall have tribulation: but be of good cheer; I have overcome the world.

15. FOR THE SICK

The Collect

O HEAVENLY Father, watch with us, we pray thee, over thy sick servants for whom our prayers are offered, and grant that they may be restored to that perfect health which it is thine alone to give; through Jesus Christ our Lord. Amen.

The Epistle. James 5:13-16

IS any among you afflicted? let him pray. Is any merry? let him sing psalms. Is any sick among you? let him call for the elders of the church; and let them pray over him, anointing him with oil in the name of the Lord: and the prayer of faith shall save the sick, and the Lord shall raise him up; and if he have committed sins, they shall be forgiven him. Confess your faults one to another, and pray one for another, that ye may be healed. The effectual fervent prayer of a righteous man availeth much.

The Gospel. St. Mark 2:1-12

AGAIN he entered into Capernaum after some days; and it was noised that he was in the house. And straightway many were gathered together, insomuch that there was no room to receive them, no, not so much as about the door: and he preached the word unto them. And they come unto him, bringing one sick of the palsy, which was borne of four. And when they could not come nigh unto him for the press, they uncovered the roof where he was: and when they had broken it up, they let down the bed wherein the sick of the palsy lay. When Jesus saw their faith, he said unto the sick of the palsy, Son, thy sins be forgiven thee. But there were certain of the scribes sitting there, and reasoning in their hearts, Why doth this man thus speak blasphemies? who can forgive sins but God only? And immediately when Jesus perceived in his spirit that they so reasoned within themselves, he said unto them, Why reason ye these things in your hearts? Whether is it easier to say to the sick of the palsy, Thy sins be forgiven thee; or to say, Arise, and take up thy bed, and walk? But that ye may know that the Son of man hath power on earth to forgive (he saith to the sick of the palsy,) I say unto thee, Arise, and take up thy bed, and go thy way into thine house. And immediately he arose, took up the bed, and went forth before them all; insomuch that they were all amazed, and glorified God, saying, We never saw it on this fashion.

16. FOR SOCIAL JUSTICE

The Collect

ALMIGHTY God, who hast created man in thine own image: Grant us grace fearlessly to contend against evil, and to make no peace with oppression; and, that we may reverently use our freedom, help us to employ it in the maintenance of justice among men and nations, to the glory of thy holy Name; through Jesus Christ our Lord. Amen.

The Epistle. Isaiah 42:1-8

BEHOLD my servant, whom I uphold; mine elect, in whom my soul delighteth; I have put my spirit upon him: he shall bring forth judgment to the Gentiles. He shall not cry, nor lift up, nor cause his voice to be heard in the street. A bruised reed shall he not break, and the smoking flax shall he not quench: he shall bring forth judgment unto truth. He shall not fail nor be discouraged, till he have set judgment in the earth: and the isles shall wait for his law. Thus saith God the LORD, he that created the heavens, and stretched them out; he that spread forth the earth, and that which cometh out of it; he that giveth breath unto the people upon it, and spirit to them that walk therein: I the LORD have called thee in righteousness, and will hold thine hand, and will keep thee, and give thee for a covenant of the people, for a light of the Gentiles; to open the blind eyes, to bring out the prisoners from the prison, and them that sit in darkness out of the prison house. I am the LORD: that is my name: and my glory will I not give to another.

The Gospel. St. Matthew 10:32-42

WHOSOEVER therefore shall confess me before men, him will I confess also before my Father which is in heaven. But whosoever shall deny me before men, him will I also deny before my Father which is in heaven. Think not that I am come to send peace on earth: I came not to send peace, but a sword. For

I am come to set a man at variance against his father, and the daughter against her mother, and the daughter in law against her mother in law. And a man's foes shall be they of his own household. He that loveth father or mother more than me is not worthy of me: and he that loveth son or daughter more than me is not worthy of me. And he that taketh not his cross, and followeth after me, is not worthy of me. He that findeth his life shall lose it: and he that loseth his life for my sake shall find it. He that receiveth you receiveth me, and he that receiveth me receiveth him that sent me. He that receiveth a prophet in the name of a prophet shall receive a prophet's reward; and he that receiveth a righteous man in the name of a righteous man shall receive a righteous man's reward. And whosoever shall give to drink unto one of these little ones a cup of cold water only in the name of a disciple, verily I say unto you, he shall in no wise lose his reward.

17. FOR SOCIAL SERVICE

The Collect

O LORD, our heavenly Father, whose blessed Son came not to be ministered unto, but to minister: We beseech thee to bless all who, following in his steps, give themselves to the service of their fellow men. Endue them with wisdom, patience, and courage to strengthen the weak and raise up those who fall; that, being inspired by thy love, they may worthily minister in thy Name to the suffering, the friendless, and the needy; for the sake of him who laid down his life for us, the same thy Son, our Saviour Jesus Christ. *Amen.*

The Epistle. 1 Peter 4:7-11

THE end of all things is at hand: be ye therefore sober, and watch unto prayer. And above all things have fervent charity among yourselves: for charity shall cover the multitude of sins. Use hospitality one to another without grudging. As every man hath received the gift, even so minister the same one to another, as good stewards of the manifold grace of God. If any man speak, let him speak as the oracles of God, if any man minister, let him do it as of the ability which God giveth: that God in all things may be glorified through Jesus Christ to whom be praise and dominion for ever and ever. Amen.

The Gospel. St. Mark 10:42-52

JESUS called them to him, and saith unto them, Ye know that they which are accounted to rule over the Gentiles exercise lordship over them; and their great ones exercise authority upon them. But so shall it not be among you: but whosoever will be great among you shall be your minister: and whosoever of you will be chiefest, shall be servant of all. For even the Son of man came not to be ministered unto, but to minister, and to give his life a ransom for many. And they came to Jericho: and as he went out of Jericho with his disciples and a great number of people, blind Bartimæus, the son of Timæus, sat by the highway side begging. And when he heard that it was Jesus of Nazareth, he began to cry out, and say, Jesus, thou son of David, have mercy on me. And many charged him that he should hold his peace: but he cried the more a great deal, Thou son of David, have mercy on me. And Jesus stood still, and commanded him to be called. And they call the blind man, saying unto him, Be of good comfort, rise; he calleth thee. And he, casting away his garment, rose, and came to Jesus. And Jesus answered and said unto him, What wilt thou that I should do unto thee? The blind man said unto him, Lord, that I might receive my sight. And Jesus said unto him, Go thy way; thy faith hath made thee whole. And immediately he received his sight, and followed Jesus in the way.

18. FOR THE UNITY OF THE CHURCH

The Collect

O LORD Jesus Christ, who saidst unto thine Apostles, Peace I leave with you, my peace I give unto you: Regard not our sins, but the faith of thy Church; and grant to it that peace and unity which is according to thy will, who livest and reignest with the Father and the Holy Ghost, one God, world without end. *Amen.*

The Epistle. Ephesians 4:1-13

I THEREFORE, the prisoner of the Lord, beseech you that ye walk worthy of the vocation wherewith ye are called, with all lowliness and meekness, with longsuffering, forbearing one another in love; endeavouring to keep the unity of the Spirit in the bond of peace. There is one body, and one Spirit, even as ye are called in one hope of your calling; one Lord, one faith, one baptism, one God and Father of all, who is above all, and through all, and in you all. But unto every one of us is given grace according to the measure of the gift of Christ. Wherefore he saith, When he ascended up on high, he led captivity captive, And gave gifts unto men. (Now that he ascended, what is it but that he also descended first into the lower parts of the earth? He that descended is the same also that ascended up far above all heavens, that he might fill all things.) And he gave some, apostles; and some, prophets; and some, evangelists; and some, pastors and teachers; for the perfecting of the saints, for the work of the ministry, for the edifying of the body of Christ: till we all come in the unity of the faith, and of the knowledge of the Son of God, unto a perfect man, unto the measure of the stature of the fulness of Christ.

The Gospel. St. John 17:15-23

JESUS said, I pray not that thou shouldest take them out of the world, but that thou shouldest keep them from the evil. They are not of the world, even as

I am not of the world. Sanctify them through thy truth: thy word is truth. As thou hast sent me into the world, even so have I also sent them into the world. And for their sakes I sanctify myself, that they also might be sanctified through the truth. Neither pray I for these alone, but for them also which shall believe on me through their word; that they all may be one; as thou, Father, art in me, and I in thee, that they also may be one in us: that the world may believe that thou hast sent me. And the glory which thou gavest me I have given them; that they may be one, even as we are one: I in them, and thou in me, that they may be made perfect in one; and that the world may know that thou hast sent me, and hast loved them, as thou hast loved me.

19. FOR VOCATION IN DAILY WORK

The Collect

ALMIGHTY God, our heavenly Father, who declarest thy glory and showest forth thy handiwork in the heavens and in the earth: Deliver us, we beseech thee, in our several callings, from the service of mammon, that we may do the work which thou givest us to do, in truth, in beauty, and in righteousness, with singleness of heart as thy servants, and to the benefit of our fellow men; for the sake of him who came among us as one that serveth, thy Son Jesus Christ our Lord. *Amen.*

The Epistle. Ecclesiastes 3:1, 9-13

TO every thing there is a season, and a time to every purpose under the heaven. What profit hath he that worketh in that wherein he laboureth? I have seen the travail, which God hath given to the sons of men to be exercised in it. He hath made every thing beautiful in his time: also he hath set the world in their heart, so that no man can find out the work that God maketh from the beginning to the end. I know that there is nothing better for them, but for a man to rejoice, and to do good in his life. And also that every man should eat and drink, and enjoy the good of all his labour, it is the gift of God.

The Gospel. St. Luke 12:13-21

ONE of the company said unto him, Master, speak to my brother, that he divide the inheritance with me. And he said unto him, Man, who made me a judge or a divider over you? And he said unto them, Take heed, and beware of covetousness: for a man's life consisteth not in the abundance of the things which he possesseth. And he spake a parable unto them, saying, The ground of a certain rich man brought forth plentifully; and he thought within himself, saying, What shall I do, because I have no room where to bestow my fruits? And he said, This will I do: I will pull down my barns, and build greater; and there will I bestow all my fruits and my goods. And I will say to my soul, Soul, thou hast much goods laid up for many years; take thine ease, eat, drink, and be merry. But God said unto him, Thou fool, this night thy soul shall be required of thee: then whose shall those things be, which thou hast provided? So is he that layeth up treasure for himself, and is not rich toward God.

Indices

Alterations in Scripture Lessons

(From the Authorized Version)

AV Authorized Version (King James)
RV Revised Version
RSV Revised Standard Version

NUMBERS 20:13 (Friday in the Second Week of Lent)
For "was sanctified in them," read "showed himself holy among them" (RSV)

1 KINGS 19:4, 5 (Ember Friday in the First Week of Lent)
For "juniper tree," read "broom tree" (RSV)

NEHEMIAH 8:9 (Jerome, September 30)
For "which is the Tirshatha," read "who was the governor" (RSV)

PROVERBS 4:12, 15 (Saint Joseph of Arimathaea, July 31)
For "straitened," read "hampered" (RSV)
For "avoid it, pass not by it, turn from it, and pass away," read "avoid it, do not go on it; turn away from it, and pass on" (RSV)

ECCLESIASTES 3:12 (Vocation in Daily Work)
For "no good in them," read "nothing better for them" (RV and RSV)

ISAIAH 49:2 (Wednesday in the Fifth Week of Lent)
For "shaft," read "arrow" (RSV)

ISAIAH 49:5-13 (Mission)
Substitution for entire lesson of the RV for the AV

ISAIAH 52:13, 15; 53:2, 9 (Friday in the Fifth Week of Lent)
For "deal prudently," read "prosper" (RSV)
For "astonied," read "astonished" (RSV)
For "sprinkle," read "startle" (RSV)
For "shall grow," read "grew" (RSV)

For "and when we shall see him, there is," read "that we should look at him, and" (RSV)
For "because," read "although" (RSV)

ISAIAH 58:8 (Friday after Ash Wednesday)
For "rereward," read "rear guard" (RSV)

ISAIAH 61:7-8 (Saint Mary the Virgin, August 15)
For "the double," read "a double portion" (RSV)
For "judgment," read "justice" (RSV)
For "for burnt offering," read "and wrong" (RSV)

JEREMIAH 2:8 (Wednesday in the Second Week of Lent)
For "pastors," read "shepherds" (RSV alternate reading)

EZEKIEL 34:16 (Friday in the Fourth Week of Lent)
For "destroy," read "watch over" (RSV)

JOEL 2:23 (Rogation Tuesday)
For "in the first month," read "as before" (RSV)

MALACHI 3:18 (Bede, May 27)
For "Then shall ye return, and," read "Then once more shall ye" (RSV)

WISDOM 7:22 (Gregory of Nyssa, March 9)
For "which cannot be letted," read "irresistible" (RSV)

MATTHEW 10:18, 19 (Of a Martyr)
For "a testimony against them," read "a witness to them"
For "take no thought," read "be not anxious" (RSV)

LUKE 10:4 (Of a Missionary; Mission)
For "scrip," read "pack" (The New English Bible)

LUKE 10:40, 41 (Saints Mary and Martha of Bethany, July 29)
For "cumbered about," read "distracted with" (RSV)
For "Jesus," read "the Lord" (RSV)
For "careful," read "concerned "

LUKE 12:11 (Hilary, January 14)
For "take ye no thought," read "do not be anxious" (RSV)

LUKE 12:22-37, or 25-44 (Of a Monastic; Advent Ember Friday)
For "take no thought" or "take ye thought," read (consistently) "be not anxious" or "are ye anxious" (RSV)
For "to his stature one cubit," read "a cubit to his span of life" (RSV)

For "doubtful," read "anxious" (RSV)
For "lights," read "lamps" (RSV)

JOHN 5:3, 7 (Friday in the Second Week of Lent)
For "impotent," read "crippled"

JOHN 9:35 (Wednesday in the Fourth Week of Lent)
For "Son of God," read "Son of man" (RSV)

JOHN 12:24 (Of the Holy Cross)
For "corn," read "seed"

JOHN 15:2 (Autumn Ember Wednesday; Church Convention)
For "purgeth," read "pruneth" (RSV: "prunes")

JOHN 16:25, 29 (Peace)
For "proverbs," read "by means of figures" (RSV altered)
For "no proverb," read "not in any figure of speech" (RSV altered; cf. The New English Bible)

ACTS 3:17 (Wednesday in Easter Week)
For "wot," read "know" (RSV)

ACTS 15:18, 21 (Saint James of Jerusalem, October z3)
For "saith the Lord, who doeth all these things. Known unto God are all his works from the beginning of the world," read "saith the Lord, who hath made these things known from of old" (RSV)
For "Moses of old time hath," read "from early times Moses has had"

ROMANS 6:3-11 (All Baptized Christians)
Substitution for the entire lesson of RSV for AV (except in vs. 6 read "This we know" for "we know"; in vs. 7 read "set free" for "freed")

ROMANS 16:1 (Of a Deaconess)
For "servant," read "deaconess" (RSV)

1 CORINTHIANS 3:8 (Ember Wednesday in Advent; The Ministry)
For "one," read "equal" (RSV)

1 CORINTHIANS 9:20 (Aidan, August 31)
Insert parenthesis lacking in AV: "(though not being myself under the law)" (RSV)

2 CORINTHIANS 3:4-18 (Lenten Ember Saturday)
Substitution for the entire lesson of RV for AV (except in vs. 8 read "Spirit" for "spirit"; in vs. 16 read "a man" for "it" - RSV)

PHILIPPIANS 3:7-14 (Antony, January 17)
Substitution for the entire lesson of RV for AV

PHILIPPIANS 4:6 (Of a Saint)
For "careful," read "anxious" (RSV altered)

COLOSSIANS 1:12-20 (The Reign of Christ)
Begin lesson "We give thanks," etc.
Substitution for the entire lesson of RSV for AV (with slight alteration in vs. 20)

2 TIMOTHY 1:7 (Timothy, January 24)
For "a sound mind," read "self-control" (RSV)

1 JOHN 4:10 (Of the Incarnation)
For "propitiation," read "expiation" (RSV)

REVELATION 5:14 (Of the Holy Angels)
Deletion of "four and twenty" and "that liveth for ever and ever" from the AV, as not in the original text (RSV)

REVELATION 19:7 (Of the Holy Eucharist)
For "wife," read "bride" (RSV: "Bride")

Index of Scripture Lessons

(In Canonical Order)

Exodus 24:12-18	Lent: Ember Wednesday
Numbers 20:1-13	Lent II: Friday
2 Samuel 12:1-15	Lent III: Wednesday
1 Kings 19:1-8	Lent: Ember Friday
21:1-20	Lent III: Friday
Nehemiah 8:1-3, 5-6, 8-9	Jerome
Proverbs 4:10-18	Saint Joseph of Arimathaea
31:10, 26-31	Saints Mary and Martha
Ecclesiastes 3:1, 9-13	Vocation in Daily Work
Isaiah 2:2-4	Mission of the Church
42:1-8a	Social Justice
49:1-6	Lent V: Wednesday
49:5-13	Mission of the Church

52:13-53:12	Lent V: Friday
58:1-12	Friday after Ash Wednesday
58:10-12	Martin
61:7-11	Saint Mary the Virgin
63:7-9, 16	Saint Joseph
Jeremiah 1:4-9	John Chrysostom
2:4-13	Lent II: Wednesday
31:31-34	Lent IV: Wednesday
Ezekiel 34:11-16	Lent IV: Friday
34: 25-31	Rogation Monday
Joel 2:21-27	Rogation Tuesday
Micah 4:1-5	The Nation
6:6-8	Rogation Wednesday
Zechariah 2:10-13	Visitation of the Blessed Virgin Mary
Malachi 2:5-7	Irenaeus
3:16-18	Bede the Venerable
2 Esdras 2:42-48	Of a Martyr
Wisdom 6:1-3, 9-12, 24-25	Alfred the Great
7:7-14	Gregory of Nazianzus; Of a Theologian or Teacher
7:22-28	Gregory of Nyssa
Ecclesiasticus 2:7-11, 16-18	Ambrose
39:1-10	Bernard
47:8-11	Gregory the Great
St. Matthew 1:18-25	Saint Joseph
5:13-19	Leo the Great
5:43-48	Patrick
5:43-6:8	Friday after Ash Wednesday
6:5-8	Rogation Wednesday
6:5-15	First Book of Common Prayer
9:35-38	Consecration of Samuel Seabury; Of a Deaconess; Mission of the Church
10:16-22	Of a Martyr
10:23-32	Athanasius

10:24-32	Autumn Ember Friday
10:32-42	Social Justice
10:34-42	Alban
11:25-30	Francis of Assisi; Education
13:31-34a	Augustine of Canterbury
13:47-52	Bede the Venerable
16:24-27	Advent Ember Saturday; Martyrs of Lyons
19:27-30	Aidan
20:17-28	Lent: Ember Wednesday
20:20-23	Polycarp
21:33-44	Lent: Ember Friday
24:9-14	Perpetua and her Companions
24:42-47	Theodore of Tarsus
25:31-40	Of a Saint
25:34-40	Martin
28:1-10	Easter Friday
28:16-20	Whitsun Ember Friday; Boniface
28:18-20	Of the Holy Trinity
St. Mark 2:1-12	The Sick
3:31-35	Saint James of Jerusalem
4:26-29	David
10:35-45	All Baptized Christians
10:42-45	Gregory the Great
10:42-52	Social Service
11:22-26	Rogation Tuesday
12:13-17	The Nation
St. Luke 1:26-38	Of the Incarnation
1:39-45	Visitation of the Blessed Virgin Mary
1:46-55	Saint Mary the Virgin
4:16-21	Whitsun Ember Wednesday
6:17-23	Of a Saint
6:43-45	Alfred the Great
9:28-36	Lent: Ember Saturday

10:1-9	Of a Missionary; Mission of the Church
10:22-24	Basil the Great
10:38-42	Saints Mary and Martha
11:5-13	Rogation Monday
11:9-13	Of the Holy Spirit
11:33-36	Irenaeus
12:8-12	Hilary
12:13-21	Vocation in Daily Work
12:22-37	Of a Monastic
12:25-44	Advent: Ember Friday
12:32-34	Antony
12:42-44	Ambrose
14:26-33	Benedict
21:12-15	John Chrysostom
23:50-56	Saint Joseph of Arimathaea
24:1-12	Easter Thursday
24:44-48	Jerome
St. John 1:47-51	Of the Holy Angels
4:4-14	Saint Cornelius the Centurion
4:5-26	Lent II: Wednesday
4:31-38	Advent: Ember Wednesday; The Ministry
5:1-16	Lent II: Friday
5:19-24	Gregory of Nyssa
6:47-59	Of the Holy Eucharist
6:57-63	Clement of Alexandria
7:14-18, 25-30	Lent III: Friday
7:16-18; 8:12	Anselm
8:12, 28-36	Lent III: Wednesday
8:25-32	Gregory of Nazianzus
9:1-38	Lent IV: Wednesday
10:1-5	Saint Titus
10:1-10	Autumn Ember Saturday
10:7-10	Saint Timothy

10:11-16	Cyprian
10:17-31	Lent IV: Friday
11:1-46	Lent V: Wednesday
12:23-32	Lent V: Friday
12:23-33	Of the Holy Cross
12:24-26	Ignatius
12:31-36	Exaltation of the Holy Cross
12:44-50	Justin Martyr
15:1-8	Autumn Ember Wednesday; Church Convention
15:7-11	Bernard
16:12-15	Whitsun Thursday
16:23b-33	Peace
17:1-8	Augustine of Hippo
17:15-23	Unity of the Church
17:18-23	Of a Theologian or Teacher
18:33-37	Of the Reign of Christ
20:1,11-18	Saint Mary Magdalene
20:11-18	Easter Saturday
20:19-23	Whitsun Ember Saturday
21:1-14	Easter Wednesday
Acts 1:1-9	Of a Missionary
2:38-42	First Book of Common Prayer
2:44-47	Benedict
3:13-15, 17-19, 26	Easter Wednesday
11:1-18	Saint Cornelius the Centurion
13:44-49	Autumn Ember Friday
15:12-22	Saint James of Jerusalem
20:18-27	Boniface
20:28-32	Autumn Ember Saturday; Consecration of Samuel Seabury
Romans 1:16-20	Anselm
6:3-11	All Baptized Christians
8:1-11	Whitsun Thursday

8:35-39	Ignatius
11:33-36	Of the Holy Trinity
15:30-16:2	Of a Deaconess
1 Corinthians 1:18-24	Of the Holy Cross
2:6-13a	Basil the Great
3:5-11	Advent: Ember Wednesday; The Ministry
9:16-23	Aidan
12:4-14	Of the Holy Spirit
2 Corinthians 3:4-18	Lent: Ember Saturday
3:17-4:6	Whitsun Ember Wednesday
4:1-10	Church Convention
4:5-14	Athanasius
5:14-18	Saint Mary Magdalene
5:17-20	Augustine of Canterbury
Galatians 6:14-18	Francis of Assisi
Ephesians 2:4-10	David
2:13-22	Whitsun Ember Saturday; Peace
4:1-13	Unity of the Church
4:11-16	Autumn Ember Wednesday
Philippians 2:5-11	Exaltation of the Holy Cross
3:7-14	Antony
3:7-15	Of a Monastic
4:4-9	Of a Saint
Colossians 1:12-20	Of the Reign of Christ
1:18-23	Easter Thursday
2:10-15	Easter Friday
1 Thessalonians 2:2-12	Patrick
1 Timothy 1:12-17	Advent: Ember Saturday
2 Timothy 1:1-7	Saint Timothy
1:12-14	Leo the Great
2:1-5, 10	Theodore of Tarsus
3:14-4:7	Education
4:1-8	Hilary
Titus 1:1-5	Saint Titus

3:4-8	Whitsun Ember Friday
Hebrews 10:32-39	Perpetua and her Companions
12:1-2	Of a Saint
12:22-24, 28-29	Augustine of Hippo
James 5:13-16	The Sick
1 Peter 1:3-5, 13-21	Easter Saturday
1:3-9	Martyrs of Lyons
3:14-18, 22	Justin Martyr
4:7-11	Advent: Ember Friday; Social Service
5:1-4, 10-11	Cyprian
2 Peter 1:2-8	Clement of Alexandria
1 John 3:13-16	Alban
4:1-11	Of the Incarnation
Revelation 2:8-11	Polycarp
5:11-14	Of the Holy Angels
19:1-9	Of the Holy Eucharist

Movable Days and Seasons

(In Calendar Order)

ADVENT III
Ember Wednesday
Ember Friday
Ember Saturday
LENT
Friday after Ash Wednesday
LENT I
Ember Wednesday
Ember Friday
Ember Saturday
LENT II
Wednesday
Friday
LENT III
Wednesday

Friday
LENT IV
Wednesday
Friday
LENT V
Wednesday
Friday
EASTER WEEK
Wednesday
Thursday
Friday
Saturday
ROGATION DAYS
Monday
Tuesday
Wednesday
WHITSUN WEEK
Ember Wednesday
Thursday
Ember Friday
Ember Saturday
AUTUMN EMBER DAYS
Wednesday
Friday
Saturday

Immovable Days

(In Alphabetical Order)

Agnes (January 21)
Aidan (August 31)
Alban (June 22)
Alcuin (May 20)
Alfred the Great (October 26)
Alphege (April 19)

Ambrose (April 4)
Andrewes, Lancelot (September 26)
Anselm (April 21)
Ansgarius (February 3)
Antony (January 17)
Athanasius (May 2)
Augustine of Canterbury (May 26)
Augustine of Hippo (August 28)
Basil the Great (June 14)
Bede the Venerable (May 27)
Benedict (July 11)
Bernard (August 20)
Boniface (June 5)
Book of Common Prayer, First (June 10)
Bray, Thomas (February 15)
Brooks, Phillips (January 23)
Butler, Joseph (June 16)
Catherine of Siena (April 30)
Chad (March 2)
Clare of Assisi (August 12)
Clement of Alexandria (December 4)
Clement of Rome (November 23)
Columba (June 9)
Cornelius the Centurion, Saint (February 4)
Cuthbert (March 20)
Cyprian (September 13)
Cyril and Methodius (May 11)
Cyril of Jerusalem (March 18)
David (March 1)
De Koven, James (March 22)
Dominic (August 4)
Donne, John (March 31)
Dunstan (May 19)
Elizabeth of Hungary (November 19)
Ephrem (June 18)

Fabian (January 20)
Francis of Assisi (October 4)
Gregory of Nazianzus (May 9)
Gregory of Nyssa (March 9)
Gregory the Great (March 12)
Gregory the Illuminator (March 23)
Hannington, James, and Companions (October 29)
Herbert, George (February 27)
Hilary (January 14)
Hilda (November 18)
Hippolytus (August 13)
Hobart, John Henry (September 12)
Holy Cross, Exaltation of (September 14)
Hooker, Richard (November 3)
Hugh of Lincoln (November 17)
Huntington, William Reed (July 27)
Ignatius (February 1)
Irenaeus (June 28)
James of Jerusalem, Saint (October 23)
Jerome (September 30)
John Chrysostom (January 27)
John of Damascus (December 5)
Joseph, Saint (March 19)
Joseph of Arimathaea, Saint (July 31)
Justin Martyr (April 13)
Keble, John (March 29)
Kemper, Jackson (May 24)
Ken, Thomas (March 21)
Latimer, Hugh (October 16)
Laud, William (January 10)
Laurence (August 10)
Law, William (April 9)
Leo the Great (April 11)
Louis (August 25)
Margaret (November 16)

Martin (November 11)
Martyn, Henry (October 17)
Martyrs of Japan (February 5)
Martyrs of Lyons (June 2)
Mary and Martha, Saints (July 29)
Mary the Virgin, Saint (August 15; see also Visitation)
Mary Magdalene, Saint (July 22)
Maurice, John Frederick Denison (April 1)
Methodius (see Cyril and Methodius)
Monnica (May 4)
Muhlenberg, William Augustus (April 8)
Nicholas (December 6)
Ninian (September 16)
Parents of the Blessed Virgin Mary (July 26)
Patrick (March 17)
Patteson, John Coleridge (September 20)
Perpetua and her Companions (March 7)
Polycarp (January 26)
Remigius (October 1)
Richard of Chichester (April 3)
Ridley, Nicholas (October 16)
Schereschewsky, Samuel Isaac Joseph (October 15)
Seabury, Consecration of (November 14)
Selwyn, George Augustus (April 12)
Sergius (September 25)
Simeon, Charles (November 12)
Taylor, Jeremy (August 14)
Theodore of Tarsus (September 19)
Thomas a Kempis (July 24)
Thomas Aquinas (March 8)
Timothy, Saint (January 24)
Titus, Saint (February 6)
Tyndale, William (October 6)
Vincent (January 22)
Visitation of the Blessed Virgin Mary (July 2)

Wesley, John and Charles (March 3)
White, William (July 17)
Wilberforce, William (July 30)
Williams, Channing Moore (December 2)
Willibrord (November 7)
Wulfstan (January 19)

Common of Saints and Special Occasions

Angels, Holy
Baptized Christians, All
Convention, Church
Cross, Holy
Deaconess
Education
Eucharist, Holy
Holy Spirit
Incarnation
Martyr
Ministry
Mission of the Church
Missionary
Monastic
Nation
Peace
Reign of Christ
Saint
Sick
Social Justice
Social Service
Teacher (see Theologian)
Theologian
Trinity, Holy
Unity of the Church
Vocation in Daily Work

PRAYER BOOK STUDIES XVII: THE LITURGY OF THE LORD'S SUPPER

A Revision of Prayer Book Studies IV

The Standing Liturgical Commission
of the Protestant Episcopal Church in the
United States of America

1966

PREFACE

In 1953 the Standing Liturgical Commission issued in *Prayer Book Studies* IV a detailed and comprehensive review of the Eucharistic rite. Extensive comment and criticism of this Study were received from all sections of the Church. This was expected, in view of the primary importance of the subject, since the shape and character of the Eucharistic celebration are fundamental to any major liturgical revision. Over 150 communications were sent to the Commission, almost equally from clergymen and laymen. This material was carefully collated for the use of the Commission, and the findings have been invaluable in the preparation of this new Study. A copy of our collation, and the documents supporting it, may be consulted in the archives of the Commission, which are regularly deposited in the library of The Church Historical Society in Austin, Texas.

The present Study is thus, in the first instance, a report to the Church, in accordance with our canonical obligations, of the analysis of reaction to *Prayer Book Studies* IV. Though the general tenor of comment was favorable with respect to the principal directions of the changes proposed, there was not a sufficient consensus, except for a few details of formulary and ceremony, to suggest that the proposed draft of Study IV would receive a widespread and enthusiastic acceptance. Meanwhile an extensive interest in experimental forms of Eucharistic worship has developed during the past decade in all traditions of Christendom, Catholic and Protestant.

In view of all these currents of concern the Commission felt it unwise to engage in a mere revision of its revision in Study IV. A fresh start on the subject seemed to be needed. The present project was initiated in 1960, under the chairmanship of the late Bishop Goodrich Fenner. All former and present members of the Commission since that time have been involved in its preparation. We have sought constantly to keep abreast of the new currents of experiment in Eucharistic rites in all the Churches; and we have taken counsel with many knowledgeable and experienced liturgical scholars of other Anglican Churches in Europe, Asia, and Africa. At each meeting of the Commission we have tested the forms in private celebrations. These have invariably suggested further improvements. In the later stages of our work, we have had the helpful assistance and advice of the Joint Commission on Church Music, which has kindly prepared the settings of the Proper Prefaces.

We would be the last to say that we have achieved a definitive, ideal liturgy. But we believe that what is offered is a significant improvement on the proposals of Study IV—a rite that may well have a contribution to make in the larger, ecumenical ferment of our time. We look forward to many constructive criticisms—indeed we request them urgently—from all sectors of the Church. Only out of such exchanges may we hope for forward steps in shaping a liturgy that is both an inspiration and a satisfaction to the Church as a whole.

It must be emphasized that this Study is not authorized for trial use until, and unless, the General Convention sees fit to do so. That decision may be determined in large measure by the reaction of the Church to these proposals, after a period of examination and study. The Commission is not committed, by this publication, to ask permissive use of the proposed rite from the General Convention. It may do so, if the response from the Church appears to be overwhelmingly favorable to the experiment.

THE STANDING LITURGICAL COMMISSION:[1]

W. R. CHILTON POWELL, *Chairman*
JONATHAN G. SHERMAN
MASSEY H. SHEPHERD, JR., *Vice Chairman*
CHARLES W. F. SMITH
LOUIS B. KEITER
H. BOONE PORTER
CHARLES M. GUILBERT, *Custodian*
BONNELL SPENCER, O.H.C.
FRANK ST. CELLIER, *Secretary*
DUPUY BATEMAN, JR.
ARTHUR C. LICHTENBERGER, *Consultant*
ALBERT R. STUART, *Consultant*

---

1. Editor's Note: It's worth noting that even though this is a re-write of the liturgy from PBS IV, there are several members with ties to the original: Massey Shepherd, Jr was on the SLC for both studies; Bishop Goodrich Fenner who began this re-write was the Chair of the SLC during the drafting of PBS IV; Arthur Lichtenberger was on the SLC during the drafting of PBS IV; Albert Stuart was also a former Chair of the SLC.

Introduction
A Report on *Prayer Book Studies* IV

THE COMMUNICATIONS sent to the Liturgical Commission with regard to *Prayer Book Studies* IV on the Eucharist were almost evenly divided between the comments of single individuals and those of groups—whether of clerical, lay, or mixed character. Among these latter, the size of the group or congregation varied considerably—from five or six persons in intimate discussion, to meetings attended by over 100 people. The length of time spent by these groups in the study of the proposals also varied a great deal. Most of them met for one or two sessions. But one lay group assembled weekly for a period of nine months before preparing a detailed report of its conclusions. Another group made a tape recording of its trial use of the service for reference and use in discussion.

Comments from individuals ranged all the way from brief remarks on a few selected details to lengthy essays or the submission of complete, alternative rites. In addition to the customary book reviews, several critical articles concerning the proposals were published in theological journals and church magazines.[2]

Reports from groups were often a mere consensus of opinion. In other instances, votes had been taken on each specific item, and the tallies *pro* and *con* were submitted. Most of the group reports, as also some of the individual letters, were based on participation in a trial use of the proposed rite, as authorized by resolution of the House of Bishops, meeting at Williamsburg, Virginia, on November 12, 1953. This resolution was neither sought nor requested by the Commission. It read as follows:

> *Be it resolved* that the consensus of the House of Bishops is as stated in the following: No general authorization for continued use may be made of forms of service which are substitutes for those forms of service which are not in the Book of Common Prayer, nor may such substitute forms of service be used at times of regular public worship. However, for the purpose of promoting study and understanding of the forms of service proposed by the official Liturgical Commission of General Convention,

---

2. See, for example:
- C. K. Sansbury, "Revisions of the Eucharistic Rite in the Anglican Communion—II," *Theology* 57 (1954), 163-66.
- E. R. Hardy, "Experiments in Prayer Book Revision," *Church Quarterly Review* 155 (1954), 162-70.
- B. J. Wigan, "The Commissioners' Liturgy," *Episcopal Churchnews* 120, 5 (March 6, 1955), 22-24.
- G. W. Barrett, "Prayer Book Studies IV, The Eucharistic Liturgy," *Anglican Theological Review* 37 (1955), 55-63.
- P. H. Vogel, "The Proposed Liturgy: An Old Catholic Appraisal," *ibid.* 39 (1957), 148-53.
- R. H. Fuller, "The Draft Liturgy of 1953 in Anglican Perspective," *ibid.* 41 (1959), 190-98.

the Bishop of a Diocese or Missionary District may authorize the special use on a particular occasion of any one of the forms of service now proposed by that Commission. . . . Further, it is suggested that opportunity for participation in such special occasions be given to both clerical and lay members of this Church, and that reports on the experience of such occasions be made to the Liturgical Commission of the General Convention.

The Commission was not surprised by the wide divergence of opinion about the proposals, in view of the differences of doctrinal emphasis and ceremonial practice in the Church. Neither in general outline nor in detailed changes did the proposals create a unanimity of opinion, whether favorable or unfavorable. Every item in the proposed Liturgy received both hearty assent and ardent opposition. Relatively few items called forth a preponderant majority for or against them.

For example, most correspondents favored the removal of the *Gloria in excelsis* from its post-communion position; but there was disagreement about the place in the service to which it should be removed. Very few persons or groups were satisfied with the revised draft of the Prayer for the Church. But the criticisms of each and every phrase and paragraph—whether with regard to doctrine or to style—revealed little in the way of a consensus. Most correspondents favored the extension of the use of Proper Prefaces; yet criticisms were offered not only about the new ones proposed, but also with respect to those already in the Prayer Book, which the Commission had retained.

In certain instances there was a notable difference in the reactions of the clergy and the laity, respectively. On the whole, the laity approved most suggestions aimed at clarifying and modernizing the language of the rite, and often suggested further modifications along these lines. The clergy were more conservative about retaining "Cranmer's English," and often assumed that changes in the language were deliberate alterations of doctrine. One interesting result of our collation was the discovery that the laity almost without exception welcomed the restoration of the Fraction to its historic position after the Prayer of Consecration. The clergy, on the other hand, were for the most part opposed to this change on the grounds that such a restoration would be unintelligible to the laity. It should also be recorded that the outstanding theological critique of the proposed Prayer of Consecration was submitted to the Commission by a layman.

It has not always been easy to evaluate objectively much of the material that has been received—to separate the comments based upon careful study and reasoned conviction from those that are due to judgments made either in haste or from long-standing preferences and prejudices. The tallies of group reaction were especially difficult to evaluate. For one thing, the Commission could seldom judge whether the persons who presented the proposals to the group reporting were in sympathy with the changes or not. Many reactions were obviously based upon preconceived, partisan positions. This was especially true of many clergymen who reported, and whose communications too often displayed unnecessary hostility and sarcasm.

In one diocese, for example, a clerical group wrote that "the Commission should be thanked for its conscientious and able effort to improve the Liturgy and embody different viewpoints without sacrificing principles." But a priest of the same diocese wrote, "Were your revision to be adopted it would be a triumph for those forces of magic and superstition fostered by sacerdotalism which have been infiltrating this Church since the nineteenth century." One clerical group, made up of members of two dioceses, stated that the proposed Liturgy was too short to be reverent and that its least satisfactory features were "due to a desire to bring it up to date." They also affirmed that "the Proposed Liturgy makes us too different from the rest of Anglicanism." Yet a clerical gathering in another diocese informed us that the proposal "represents a great step forward and may be the most complete and balanced rite in Anglicanism today."

A single illustration of the tendency to read partisan interpretations into the proposed rite came from the comments on the suggested rewording of the Invocation:

> that they may be unto us the most blessed Body and Blood of thy dearly beloved Son Jesus Christ.

Almost without exception, the clergy of one school of thought accused the Commission of writing into the Liturgy at this point a receptionist doctrine. With equal vehemence, many of the opposite party said the Commission was in this phrase committing the Church to the Roman Catholic dogma of Transubstantiation. The fact is that the wording conforms to that of the First Prayer Book of 1549. On pages 264-265 of the introduction to the Study, the Commission tried to make it perfectly clear that it was not proposing either Receptionism or Transubstantiation.[3]

---

3. Editor's Note--here is the full text of the passage mentioned:

> Among ancient liturgical forms, Hippolytus alone makes no mention of the *res sacramenti*: his Invocation does not pray that the Bread and Wine may be made to be for us the Body and Blood, but goes on immediately to the *virtus* or Benefits. All historic liturgies, however, are at pains to make explicit mention of the *res*, with an antithetical balance of expression of the *sacramentum* of the Bread and Wine and the *res* of the Body and Blood. Yet in all the liturgies, the *virtus* of the Benefits constitutes the goal and objective of the action.
>
> The only liturgies which go to the length of specifying a definite *change* in the Elements are those of 'St. Chrysostom,' and two minor lines which show Byzantine influences, namely the Anaphora of Nestorius, and a few Gallican Invocations. This, incidentally, accounts for a certain recalcitrance on the part of the extremists in the Eastern Orthodox Church, who are disposed to deny that our present American Liturgy has a 'valid *Epiclesis*,' because it does not ask in so many words that the Bread and Wine may be *made* to be the Body and Blood. This may be considered for what it may be worth. It is certainly worth *something*, since obviously clarity and precision of statement is much to be desired at such a vital point of the service. On the other hand, it really might appear to be a bit doctrinaire to deny all efficacy to a form which happens to be a little vague and roundabout in its expressions, as is the case with our present Invocation: especially in view of the fact that

The Problem of Norms

MANY of the contradictions in the criticisms sent to the Commission in regard to Prayer Book Studies IV stem from differences in the Church about the norms by which liturgical revision should be approached.

A small number of correspondents, chiefly lay people, raised the question as to whether any changes in the present rite are needed at all, other than those essential for clarification. Rarely were such essential changes spelled out in detail, other than instances of archaic language no longer intelligible, or rubrical directions designed to sanction customary usages. Beneath these conservative attitudes, no doubt, lies a deep-seated and sincere attachment to a rite that has served us well for many generations.

The Church must respect this conservative concern by the reminder that change for the mere sake of change or novelty is of no value. Alterations in the rite, however radical, must endeavor to conserve all the real values of the old order. At the same time they must so deepen and enrich these values that those who are attached to the familiar ways will find themselves at home in the new usages, and, if possible, enthusiastic about the gains to devotion, by reason of the inherent

---

a rigid application of the Byzantine footrule would completely disallow the Anaphora of Hippolytus, and cast grave doubts upon some other historic forms.

But the really remarkable circumstance is that the Roman Rite is utterly lacking in any language whatsoever as would imply any such physical change 'in the Elements' as is suggested in the Invocation of 'St. Chrysostom.' The Roman expression 'ut *nobis* Corpus et Sanguis fiat,' points directly away from any such an affirmation of Transubstantiation as we should certainly expect if that doctrine had been held in the day/ when the Roman Liturgy was being formulated. Obviously it was not so held then. Explicit expression is given to the subjective reality. The objective factor, which is implied rather than stated, consists at most of a 'mystical' change of values.

All the available evidence concurs in suggesting that the idea of a literal Transubstantiation was unknown to primitive Roman doctrine, as it was no part of the primitive Roman liturgy; but that it originated on Gallican soil, where it did receive liturgical expression, and from thence infected the thinking of the Church of Rome.

Cranmer in the First Prayer Book found the Latin phrase perfectly acceptable, and translated it directly, if none too forcibly, as 'that they *maye be vnto vs* the bodye and bloud.' The English revision of 1928 found it could do no better than to restore this. This English form is followed by Ceylon. India in 1933 rendered it 'become unto us,' — a somewhat stronger, if not necessarily a preferable, rendering of the Latin *fiat*. The Scottish line since 1764 has been ultra-Roman in bluntly saying 'may become the Body and Blood.' It was this excess of zeal which doomed the acceptance of the Scottish phrase in the first American Prayer Book in 1789.

It will be observed that all these revisions which have been named take the obviously necessary step of canceling the interpolated *Anamnesis* of 1552; and then, seeking to retain the inherited tradition of an equipoise of subjective and objective expressions, return to some form of the simple, direct, and balanced language of the Latin original. And the ones which do this best, we consider to be those which do it most absolutely, by restoring the form of the First Prayer Book. After experimenting with a considerable variety of qualifying phrases, substitutions, and paraphrases, the Liturgical Commission has come to the same conclusion.

excellence of the changes. The discovery of these gains can only come by proper testing in actual "live situations" of corporate worship. Hence the Commission reaffirms its strong support for the method of trial use, duly authorized, and now made possible under the amendment to Article X of the Church's Constitution passed at the General Convention in 1964.

An important insight brought into clearer focus by modern liturgical study is the realization that liturgical worship does not remain static so long as the Church is responsive to new cultural situations and new opportunities of mission. Enrichments of text in prayer and hymnody, and alterations of ceremony, are constantly evolving to replace or modify older usages. The pace of change may be gradual or swift, with or without official authorization. Yet few generations worship exactly in the form and manner of their forefathers.

In certain periods in the western tradition of Christendom, the dynamic of change has been sufficiently swift and comprehensive so that it seemed more revolutionary than evolutionary. Such were the liturgical modifications in rite and ceremony in the fourth, the eighth, and the sixteenth centuries. Many believe that our own times show unmistakable indications of similar revisions, which are demanded by the sudden and radical changes in the Church's status and mission in our contemporary world.

If this be the case—and we are convinced that it is—then the task of liturgical revision is the more delicately complex. It demands a just proportion of sensitivity to tradition, acknowledgment of widespread changes already in use, and creative innovation. The problem cannot be solved by simplistic categories of conservative—moderate—radical. The only viable procedure is the attempt to meet all three of these categories at one and the same time.

A common criticism of the Commission's Study IV pointed to the tendency to give weight to historical precedent rather than to present usage and practice. The difficulty here is a proper definition of "present practice," in view of the great diversity of usages in the Church. We do not refer to outright lawlessness and disregard of the Church's canonical and rubrical law, but to experiments and developments that are quite legal and legitimate within the present, flexible limits of the Prayer Book itself.

An eminent liturgiologist of the Church of England accused the draft in *Prayer Book Studies IV* of being too bound to the work of Cranmer and hence to the defects of Cranmer's liturgical knowledge. He was frank enough to say that the Commission had sacrificed "great principles" of what is now commonly accepted by liturgical scholars "in order to produce a rite which seems likely to be readily acceptable to the majority."[4] A well-informed priest of our American Church lamented that the Commission did not produce "the best possible liturgy, incorporating all the fullness that is traditional in the Western and English rites and let this Liturgy compete with the present Prayer Book Order." But, said he,

---

4. See B. J. Wigan, "The Commissioners' Liturgy," *Episcopal Churchnews*, 120, 5 (March 6, 1955), 22-24.

it is apparent that "the Commission wishes to avoid such a situation." A distinguished scholar in one of our seminaries posed the question this way:

> In what spirit should we engage in liturgical revision? Should we be more radical than official advisors are likely to contemplate being? Should we base on Justin Martyr rather than on the use of Sarum? Instead of discussing the position of the General Confession, should we consider whether such a penitential exercise belongs in the common Thanksgiving of the redeemed family of God at all? There is not much value in the kind of revision which these Studies exemplify.

Such comments, though few, carry weight because of the knowledge and perspicacity of their authors. They may well be prophetic voices crying in the wilderness of ignorance, apathy, and prejudice. They have for support the prestige of the Lambeth Conference Report of 1958. The Bishops there assembled admitted that "we have entered upon a period of liturgical change," when the classic Prayer Books of 1549, 1552, and 1662, can no longer be kept "as the basic pattern, and indeed, as a bond of unity in doctrine and in worship for our Communion as a whole."[5]

Startling as it may seem, the statement of the Bishops is in line with what modern liturgical scholarship has brought to light: namely, that Cranmer, in his laudable aim to recover for the Church the character of the worship of the primitive Church, did not have "available in his day the historical material necessary for the full accomplishment of his aim." In the light of evidence now accessible we must be prepared to develop what he began. "Therefore," said the Bishops, "we might ask what elements in the Book of Common Prayer are due to the sixteenth and seventeenth century misunderstanding of what is 'primitive' in public worship, and what elements need to be substituted or added in order to make Prayer Book services truer to the ideal towards which Cranmer was feeling his way."[6]

We may endorse the principal thrust of the Bishops' argument with respect to the normative character of the Reformation settlement of worship, but at the same time question whether they have not implied a historical norm of the "primitive Church" to take its place. No one questions the necessity of our liturgical offices being doctrinally in conformity with the teaching of the New Testament. But the reconstruction of a "primitive" rite as a pattern and basis of contemporary revision is another matter. It could be even more archaic and irrelevant than a norm taken from the sixteenth century. Would it mean, for example, the revival of the so-called "seven-action shape" of the Eucharist, with its accompanying

---

5. *The Lambeth Conference 1958.* The Encyclical Letter from the Bishops together with the Resolutions and Reports. London: S.P.C.K; Greenwich: Seabury Press, 1959, p. 78.

6. *The Lambeth Conference 1958.* The Encyclical Letter from the Bishops together with the Resolutions and Reports. London: S.P.C.K; Greenwich: Seabury Press, 1959, p. 80.

meal, or would it settle for the later development of the "four-action shape" of the patristic liturgies?[7]

If on the other hand we take current usage as a basic norm for revision we face another complication: namely, the flexibility and variety of usages now allowed. In the draft proposal of Study IV there was offered a larger flexibility than what obtains at present with regard to lengthening or shortening the rite, but at the same time a more rigid rubrical direction of ceremonial postures. Judging from the comments received, the Commission found little support in these directions. Our critics by and large dislike flexibility. They want the rules to be definite and clear, with a minimum of variation. This sentiment goes against the trend in the last two revisions of the American Prayer Book in 1892 and 1928 respectively.

No doubt a major factor in this attitude is the confusion of many of our people who find themselves caught up in the mobility of population today. Both clergymen and laymen are much more "on the move" than they were even a generation ago. To their dismay they find a bewildering variety of customs as they go from parish to parish, especially in ceremonial. Frequently what one rector labors to develop, his successor labors within a few years to remove or change. In one place the people stand for the Prayer for the Church; in another they stand at the *Sursum corda*. In one parish the Prayer of Humble Access and the Prayer of Thanksgiving are said by the people with the priest; in another place they are not. In one congregation it is customary to bless unconfirmed children at the altar rail; in another it is forbidden. Some ministers allow intinction; others refuse to permit it.

Any one of these customs by itself is of minor importance. But the accumulation of variation that touches and affects all parts of the rite is undoubtedly disturbing to many people, and especially so when they are taken to imply—whether rightly or wrongly—theological significance. Feelings of partisanship then arise to becloud the differences. In addition to these ceremonial variations, the provision of permissive or alternative formularies provides another cause of distress. To "keep up" with the service the worshipper must resort to his leaflet, with the page numbers, and by the time he has found the place in the Prayer Book, the officiant has passed on to another part of the service.

If there is to be any variation in the rite—even the minimum demanded by a variable lectionary and the use of Proper Prefaces—there is bound to be some difficulty for the untrained worshipper in following the Prayer Book order. And it must be accepted that an increasing number of worshippers in the Episcopal Church have little background or training in its forms of worship. The provision in Study IV of a copious supply of titles and subtitles to the various parts of the rite was generally received with favor, though some felt that it was overly fussy and complicated.

---

7. See, e.g., A. H. Couratin, "The Sacrifice of Praise, The Church's Thanksgiving in New Testament Times," *Theology* 58 (1955), 285-91.

But this does not solve the problem, if, for example, certain parts are allowed to be omitted at weekday celebrations or other occasions that are not major festivals. Certainly one of the most baffling problems is the format and typography of the Prayer Book—whether it assists or hinders the inexpert worshipper in the use of the Prayer Book at common prayers. Yet the question remains: Do we really desire a rigidity and uniformity of usage that rules out reasonable and helpful variation?

Related to the problem of flexibility is the difference over the norm of a sung or said service. Historically, there is no question that the choral service has been the norm. Yet in most parishes the majority of celebrations are said services, with or without the addition of a few hymns. It is also fair to say that most of the trial uses of the proposed liturgy in Study IV were said and not sung.

A simple illustration of the problem concerns the *Kyrie*. Many correspondents desired the removal from the rite of both the Ten Commandments and the Summary of the Law, leaving the *Kyrie* (whether in its Greek or English form) to stand alone in its original hymnodic character as a great acclamation comparable to Hosanna or Alleluia. Such an appraisal of the *Kyrie* is historically and liturgically sound. Its use in this way is very effective at choral celebrations when the *Kyrie* is sung in ninefold form to many of its majestic musical settings, both ancient and modern. But experience in trial use at our Commission meetings, with a said service, was sufficient to convince us that the bare recital of the *Kyrie*, whether in a threefold or a ninefold form, without its being attached as a responsory to anything that precedes it, was not only ineffective: it was in large measure meaningless.

We do not cite this example as a mere justification for retaining the Commandments or Summary. In these problems of order and structure there are many possible solutions. We refer primarily to a principle that must inform any adequate revision: namely, it must be sufficiently imaginative regarding the various ways and the various settings in which the liturgy is celebrated in our congregations. Patterns of order and structure must be found that make the liturgy as effective as possible, whether it be said or sung, whether it be rendered simply or elaborately.

New Perspectives

OUR PROPOSALS in this Study are not a revision of the draft presented in *Prayer Book Studies IV*. They are essentially a fresh and independent approach to the problem of Eucharistic worship. We believe the time is ripe for a more radical searching after the goal of an "ideal" liturgy. The inconclusiveness of the reaction to Study IV indicated that a cautious and diplomatic revision of the present Prayer Book rite fails to arouse the Church with any enthusiasm to undertake the arduous labor of revision. Such an approach also removes us from our rightful place of responsible leadership in liturgical reform, which

Anglicanism considers its peculiar vocation and contribution in the present ecumenical ferment of liturgical interests.

The relatively short period since the publication of Study IV has seen the momentum of liturgical renewal develop rapidly in all sectors of Christendom. A vast, ever-growing literature in the science of liturgics—Biblical, historical, theological—continues to enlarge our understanding of the nature and meaning of Christian worship.[8] A major fruit of such study is the inter-confessional and ecumenical spirit of exchange that informs this concern. At the same time, liturgical renewal in all the Churches shows increasing awareness of the profound relationship that exists between the worship of the Church and its mission in all kinds of societies and cultures of our contemporary world.

The most dramatic, certainly the most publicized, development in liturgical renewal of the past decade has been the reform of worship in the Roman Catholic Church. The long ferment of liturgical revival has at last received official and articulate focus in the promulgation of the Constitution on the Liturgy issued by Pope Paul VI at the conclusion of the second session of Vatican Council II in December 1963.[9] The implementation of this Constitution by practical reforms has been swift and decisive, most notably in the revisions and translation into the vernacular of the liturgy of the Mass. The full ecumenical impact of this reform cannot as yet be evaluated; but it is no exaggeration to say that it gives promise of far-reaching influence on the liturgical developments of all other Christian communions.

An encouraging sign is the widespread effort of Roman Catholic leaders to invite and engage discussion and criticism of the Constitution on the part of "separated brethren." The manner in which this reform is being carried out in the Roman Communion indicates, too, a laudable concern to keep this vast effort open and flexible, so that sufficient experimentation can take place before new structures and vernacular renderings are stabilized in permanent forms.

Protestant traditions have also been active in liturgical renewal and reform. To cite examples only from our own country within the past decade—we may note the Liturgy published in 1958 by a joint liturgical commission of eight Lutheran bodies, after a ten-year period of trial use;[10] the new "Service for the Lord's Day" issued by the United Presbyterian Church in the USA and the Presbyterian Church in the US in 1964—firstfruits of a massive revision of the *Book of Common Worship* that implements principles laid down in the revised Directory

---

8. The extent of publication in liturgics may be reviewed in the bibliographical listings now available in the following scholarly annuals: *Archiv für Liturgiewissenschaft* (Regensburg: Postet, 1950—), sponsored by the Benedictines of Maria Laach; *Jahrbuch für Liturgik and Hymnologie* (Kassel: Johannes Stauda Verlag, 1955—), edited by Lutheran scholars; *Yearbook of Liturgical Studies* (Notre Dame: Fides Publishers, 1960—), edited by John H. Miller and others.

9. See Bibliography, under "Roman Catholic Reforms."

10. See Appendix 2, No. 6.

for Worship, published in 1959;[11] the similar rite (to that of the Presbyterians) of the United Church of Christ;[12] and the revision of its Order for the Lord's Supper by the Methodist Church in 1964.[13]

Two Protestant liturgies of recent date have exercised a large influence ecumenically, and have received favorable comment from Roman Catholic leaders in liturgical renewal. One is the Liturgy of the Church of South India, first issued in 1950, and after several revisions incorporated in its *Book of Common Worship* of 1963.[14] The other is the Eucharistic Liturgy of the Community of Taizé in France, a monastic brotherhood founded in 1948 with special concern for Christian reunion. Their brothers today include members of the Reformed, Lutheran and Anglican traditions.[15]

Mention should be made also of two individual and unofficial Eucharistic liturgies published with the express intention of their use in ecumenical contexts. *An Experimental Liturgy*, produced in England by a group of Anglicans, has received a number of "trial runs" for educational purposes, including a broadcast of it over BBC.[16] The other was prepared by Professor Keith Watkins of the Disciples of Christ in this country, and published with a symposium of comment by several liturgiologists. It is designed for experimental use in Churches of a "free" tradition of worship.[17]

In the Anglican Communion, most of the autonomous Provinces are involved in liturgical revision, at various stages of preparation or completion.[18] The Anglican Church of Canada and the Church of India, Pakistan, Burma, and Ceylon brought to conclusion complete revisions of their Prayer Books in 1959 and 1960 respectively. The Churches of Japan and of the West Indies issued revised Eucharistic liturgies, with other parts of the Prayer Book, in 1959.[19] At the present writing, liturgical commissions are at work on revisions of the Eucharist in the Churches of England,[20] Ireland, Wales, Australia, and New Zealand.[21]

---

11. See Appendix 2, No. 7.

12. *The Lord's Day Service*, With Explanatory Notes. Boston—Philadelphia: The United Church Press, 1964.

13. *The Book of Worship for Church and Home*. New York-Nashville: Abingdon Press, 1964. The Eucharistic rite is basically similar in its Consecration Prayer to that of the English Prayer Book.

14. See Appendix 2, No. 2.

15. See Appendix 2, No. 4.

16. See Appendix 2, No. 11.

17. See Appendix 2, No. 12.

18. See Bernard Wigan, *The Liturgy in English*, Second edition (Oxford, 1964).

19. Bibliographical references for these rites in M. H. Shepherd, Jr., "Another Prayer Book Anniversary," *Historical Magazine of the Protestant Episcopal Church*, 31 (1962), 351-64.

20. See Appendix 2, No. 10.

21. For the newly proposed liturgy in New Zealand, see Appendix 2, No. 13. This is the first Anglican rite to employ contemporary English throughout.

Nor should we overlook the newly revised liturgies of our sister Communions in the Wider Episcopal Fellowship: the Philippine Independent Church,[22] and the Lusitanian Church in Portugal.[23]

One of the most interesting developments in Anglicanism is *A Liturgy for Africa*, sponsored by the Archbishops of the five autonomous Churches of West Africa, Uganda, East Africa, Central Africa, and South Africa.[24] This rite is intended principally for use in the manifold African vernaculars. Leadership in the project was due to the Archbishop of Uganda, the Most Reverend Leslie W. Brown (now Bishop of St. Edmundsbury and Ipswich), who was one of the chief architects of the Liturgy of the Church of South India before his appointment to the see of Uganda (Namirembe). The African Liturgy shows close affinities with the South India rite. One of its notable features is the provision of a form of Ante-Communion that is adequate for Sunday worship in places that do not have the regular weekly ministry of a priest.

The African Liturgy was a principal item on the agenda of the unprecedented Consultation on the Liturgy which met in Toronto for two days following the Anglican Congress of August 1963. By arrangements of Bishop Stephen F. Bayne, then Executive Officer of the Anglican Communion, representatives of almost all the Anglican Churches were brought together for exchange of views on the more pressing problems of Prayer Book revision, and for the development of effective channels of inter-communication among the liturgical commissions of the several Churches.[25] It may be said, in passing, that the discussion of the African Liturgy was the first occasion when an Anglican rite has been subject to review by liturgical leaders of the entire Anglican Communion before its definitive publication.

One of the agreements reached at the Consultation was the appointment of a subcommittee to prepare a basic outline of the structure and contents of the Eucharistic rite, which might serve as a guide for the several Anglican Churches engaged in revision. A report of this committee, under the chairmanship of Archbishop Brown, has been circulated to all the Anglican Provinces, and is published in Appendix I of this Study. One may readily note that the present proposed draft follows the basic recommendations of this committee.

Individual Anglicans have made contributions in recent years by the publication of complete drafts, with commentary, or revised Eucharistic rites. We have

---

22. *The Filipino Missal (Book of Divine Office): The Liturgy for the Holy Mass*, According to the Use of the Iglesia Filipina Independiente, Including the Pontifical, Ordinal and Articles of Religion. Manila: The Supreme Council of Bishops, 1961.

23. See Appendix 2, No. 5.

24. See Appendix 2, No. 8.

25. The Standing Liturgical Commission was able to hold a regular meeting in Toronto at the time of the Consultation, and to participate fully in its discussions.

already mentioned *An Experimental Liturgy*, issued in England in 1958.[26] Two American priests have also suggested revisions which have received wide attention.[27] Many cathedral churches and college chapels in England have developed their own versions of our common tradition. Widely known is the rite celebrated in Clare College, Cambridge, through the full discussion of it in a book by the Bishop of Woolwich.[28]

Another fruitful source of insight has been the various articles and books published in connection with the 300th anniversary of the English Prayer Book of 1661-62.[29] Whether favorably or unfavorably disposed to this standard rite that is still official in many Anglican Churches, these critiques have been of great value in setting our Anglican tradition in a proper historical context and perspective.

This brief survey of liturgical revisions of the Eucharistic liturgy since the publication of *Prayer Book Studies IV* may be ample justification for the conviction of the Standing Liturgical Commission that a new Study of the subject is desirable, and that the Bishops at Lambeth spoke truly when they said, "we have entered upon a period of liturgical change."

Rationale of Proposed Revision

1. The Title

The title of a service is descriptive of its content, but serves also as a sign of its character and emphasis. At the Last Supper, our Lord gave his disciples and us an act of thanksgiving and remembrance that sums up in word and deed our whole life and hope in his redemption of our sins and promise of our glory. The Church has never found, in any language, a simple word or phrase that captures all the meaning of this worship. No title adequately describes it. Each term devised in the long tradition of Christian reflection and participation, invested in this act, must of necessity bear manifold connotations.

In *Prayer Book Studies IV*, the title given to the rite was "The Liturgy for the Celebration of the Holy Eucharist and the Administration of Holy Communion." The caption was inspired chiefly by the title of The Scottish Liturgy,

---

26. Bernard Wigan, *The Liturgy in English*, Second edition (Oxford, 1964).

27. Bonnell Spencer, O.H.C., "A Functional Liturgy," *Anglican Theological Review*, 43 (1961), 333-69; Loren N. Gavitt, "What do Catholics Want in Prayer Book Revision?" *The American Church Quarterly*, 3 (1963), 83-118. See also Fr. Spencer's "What's Wrong with the Rite," ibid., 14-25, and his *Sacrifice of Thanksgiving* (West Park, N.Y.: Holy Cross Publications, 1965), pp. 157-65.

28. J. A. T. Robinson, *Liturgy Coming to Life* (London: Mowbray, 1960).

29. M. H. Shepherd, Jr., "Another Prayer Book Anniversary," *Historical Magazine of the Protestant Episcopal Church*, 31 (1962), 351-64.

a principal parent of our American Prayer Book form. In general, the reaction to this title was most favorable. But two proper objections were made:

a. The omission of the Biblical title, "Lord's Supper" (1 Cor. 11:20), which has been characteristic of all English and American Prayer Books since 1549—and a term that links our rite with both its Latin inheritance (cf. *Coena Domini* in the Maundy Thursday liturgy of the Missal), and our brethren of the Reformation traditions.
b. The absolute use of the term "The Liturgy" for the Eucharistic rite alone—a usage common among the Eastern Orthodox Christians, but one less restricted in reference in the Western Churches, where "liturgy" has been generally understood to embrace the whole complex of corporate rites and ceremonies authorized by the Church.

The reshaping of the title in the present draft attempts to meet both these responses, by phrasing the major title as

The Liturgy of the Lord's Supper

The subtitle carries the two terms most commonly used in the Church: Eucharist and Communion; and emphasizes them by the headings of the alternate pages of the service.

The word "Celebration" is universally employed among us—often in an absolute sense, to describe the whole act. It needs no justification, and has already found its way into the title of the rite in the Scottish and West Indian Prayer Books, and in the *Book of Common Order* of the Church of Scotland. "Ministration" has been substituted for "Administration," the term most commonly used in Anglican liturgies, since it conveys a more pastoral and sacramental meaning. Modern English usage of "administration" has a more officious sound. The two terms together—"celebration . . . and ministration"—suggest the twofold movement of the rite, its God-to-man and man-to-God dimensions, and point up its corporate nature of sharing in manifold ministries.

As it is now devised, the title provides a richly historical and theological reference that should be useful in teaching: Biblical and Patristic; Anglican and Ecumenical; festal and corporate; pastoral and liturgical. Each term is employed in the strict sense of its meaning, yet each is inter-related in a way that brings out the comprehensive character of the rite.

Prayer Book formularies use other traditional phrases, such as "Holy Mysteries" and "Blessed Sacrament." But these have not been employed as titles in any of the Anglican Prayer Books. The simple (and non-theological) word "Mass" from the Latin and Roman tradition is widely used by Anglicans but unfortunately carries with it controversial overtones. It has not appeared in the Prayer Book since the First Book of 1549. It is interesting to note the increasing use of "Eucharist" in modern Roman Catholic documents and writings. In both the Constitution on the Sacred Liturgy of Vatican Council II (1963), and the Instruction based upon it (1964), the caption of the chapter on the Mass is: "Concerning the Most Holy Mystery of the Eucharist."

2. Rubrics: General and Particular

Two of the features of the draft revision in Prayer Book Studies IV that received much comment were:

a. The subtitles given to the several formularies and sections of the service. On the whole, the reaction to these was most favorable, though some considered them overly fussy and unnecessarily detailed.
b. The comprehensive directives to both officiant and people in regard to postures of standing, sitting, and kneeling. Most correspondents favored this ceremonial *Ordo*; but a few strongly objected to its rigorous elimination of choice in such matters.

The Commission has labored long and hard on these questions. There may be no definitive solution to the problems which they raise. The basic consideration is obviously one of devising a service that can be followed easily by the congregation. The people should recognize readily their responses and manners of participation. At the same time, they should be able to comprehend the several parts of the rite and how they fit into its total structure and order. To achieve this end the service must have a format and typography that assist the worshipper in the pew no less than the officiant in the chancel.

In all honesty it must be confessed that the Prayer Book we have inherited is more suitable in these matters for the officiating clergy than it is for the responding laity. Of course, it has been assumed for many generations that communicants would be sufficiently familiar with their Prayer Books so that they would have no difficulties in participation. Hence no attention has been given in past revisions to the problem of format. This is not to say that the typography of the Prayer Book lacks dignity, taste, and its own inherent beauty. But it is true, no less, that more and more people in our congregations today become lost in their effort to follow the rite from the Prayer Book layout. Blocks of fine italic print mix directives to priest and people and obscure references to major divisions of the service. Large, heavy capital letters at the beginning of formularies are not a clear indication of subject matter. Permissive or occasionally used materials stand in the way of a ready following of shortened orders, when omission is made of the Ten Commandments, the Nicene Creed (if Morning Prayer has been said), most of the Offertory Sentences, and the Proper Prefaces.

In most congregations today resort is made to printed or mimeographed leaflets of Orders of Service, with or without the additional oral announcements of Prayer Book page numbers. These leaflets often give valuable teaching regarding the outline and significance of the various parts of the rite. They have become almost essential aids to worship, especially when Prayer Book pages and Hymnal numbers must be coordinated. No one disputes their usefulness. Yet there are pedagogical and psychological values to be gained by having the people familiar with the Prayer Book itself, by receiving the Word through the eye no less than through the ear.

Many suggestions have been offered, as partial solutions to the problem: *e.g.*, the use of bold-face type for the people's parts; the insertion of block-type captions in the margins of the several formularies; better spacing of texts on a single page; a return to the use of color—for example, the restoration of red for rubrics, to distinguish them more clearly from the texts that are recited; indenting of alternatives that are more commonly omitted; the use of poetic form in line arrangement for hymnodic and credal texts, which gives better phrasing than the more complicated punctuation marks of commas, colons, and semicolons. (All these suggestions are pertinent, of course, to all offices of the Prayer Book.)

The Commission has sought in this draft to apply some of these criteria in what may be not a final answer to, but an initial opening of the question. The matter needs more study than we have been able to give; and hence we invite those who are concerned and experienced in the subject to send in their recommendations. Those who are gifted in calligraphy and typography can make a significant contribution to future revision of the Prayer Book. We need not be bound always to patterns of format in our liturgical books that derive in all their particulars from the style of medieval manuscripts, which was simply transcribed and transferred to the earliest printed books. Moreover, medieval liturgical manuscripts were designed for officiants only, and not for the worshipping congregation.

Major captions have been provided for:

- The Ministry of the Word,
- The Offertory,
- The Consecration,
- The Breaking of the Bread.

No caption has been given to what is variously called The Preparation or The Introduction, or sometimes The Entrance. It is variable and flexible in length, and difficult to describe by any significant liturgical term. The title of The Breaking of the Bread seemed to the Commission a fitting way of including both the Fraction and the Communion since the one is so inevitably a ceremonial preparatory to the other. Nor did it appear needful to have another major caption for the brief thanksgiving and dismissal that concludes the Communion.

Titles in smaller type have been given to principal formularies or sections (some of them permissive at certain times), such as the *Gloria in excelsis*, the Lessons and Sermon, the Creed, the Peace, the Prayer of Intercession, and the Presentation. Similar titles are provided for the more occasional sections of the Penitential Order, Offertory Sentences, and Proper Prefaces—the latter two largely the concern of the celebrant.

These captions do not provide a complete outline, in detail, as in *Prayer Book Studies IV*, such as might appear in a parish leaflet. It may be that these additional captions are desirable. Trial use, combined with teaching sessions, should give us a better direction about what is needed. But many felt that the overly elaborate titling in Study IV impeded the flow of response by the people, and made the order of service too complex in appearance.

A Table of Outlines

Longest Form	Shortest Form	Median Form
INTRODUCTION	INTRODUCTION	INTRODUCTION
Hymn		(Hymn)
Doxology	Doxology	Doxology
Collect for Purity	Collect for Purity	Collect for Purity
Summary of Law	Summary of Law	Summary of Law
Kyrie *or* Trisagion	Kyrie *or* Trisagion	Kyrie *or* Trisagion
Gloria *or* Te Deum		
MINISTRY OF THE WORD	MINISTRY OF THE WORD	MINISTRY OF THE WORD
Salutation	Salutation	Salutation
Collect of Day	Collect of Day	Collect of Day
O. T. Lesson		
Hymn		
Epistle	Epistle	Epistle
Hymn		(Hymn)
Gospel	Gospel	Gospel
Sermon		(Sermon)
Creed		(Creed)
Penitential Order		
Peace	Peace	Peace
Prayer of Intercession	Prayer of Intercession	Prayer of Intercession
THE OFFERTORY	THE OFFERTORY	THE OFFERTORY

The Liturgy of the Lord's Supper 235

Longest Form	Shortest Form	Median Form
Hymn		(Hymn)
Procession		Procession
Presentation	Presentation	Presentation
THE CONSECRATION	THE CONSECRATION	THE CONSECRATION
Preface and Sanctus	Preface and Sanctus	Preface and Sanctus
Thanksgiving	Thanksgiving	Thanksgiving
Lord's Prayer	Lord's Prayer	Lord's Prayer
BREAKING OF THE BREAD	BREAKING OF THE BREAD	BREAKING OF THE BREAD
Fraction	Fraction	Fraction
Anthem	Anthem	Anthem
Hymn		(Hymn)
Ministration	Ministration	Ministration
Final Thanksgiving	Final Thanksgiving	Final Thanksgiving
Blessing (Bishop)		
Dismissal	Dismissal	Dismissal
Hymn		(Hymn)

A principal change in format from that obtaining in all previous Prayer Books will be seen in the handling of rubrics. The greater portion of rubrical direction in the liturgy concerns the officiant, not the people. We have attempted therefore to leave in the text of the rite only those directions which are of concern to the whole body of worshippers, and to gather in other places the details of order, alternatives, and regulation that are the responsibility of the celebrant—or "master of ceremonies." This relief of the text from the burden of interruption by detailed rules for the officiant (who does not, in any case, need to be reminded of them while he is celebrating) should assist the congregation in a more ready following of the action. It should also add materially to the attractiveness of the page for the persons following the rite in the pew.

At the conclusion of the rite a general outline or "Order" is provided for the officiating ministers, giving them details of ceremony and usage according to times and seasons, and directions about re-consecration and reservation of the elements as needed. But a general rubric about "The Ministers of the Liturgy" is placed on the page opposite the opening of the service. This clarifies the traditions, customs, and regulations about what ministers are authorized to take the several parts of the liturgy—and indeed suggests the appropriate assignments in the liturgy when a variety of Orders, both of clergy and of laity, are present. It opens the way, without spelling out in detail, for experiment with the ancient custom of con-celebration when more than one Priest is in attendance. Perhaps, more importantly, it reminds the Church of the traditional presidency of the Bishop at the liturgy, and not simply (as in our present Prayer Book) of his precedence of rank in giving Absolution and Blessing.

Prayer Book rubrics have never given a completely detailed guide to ceremonial, such as one finds in the Roman Missal. It has generally been assumed that traditional or customary ceremonial will continue unless the rubrics specifically change it. Only certain ceremonies of standing and kneeling, etc., have been underscored. This permissiveness in ceremonial in our Prayer Book is, of course, the principal reason for the great variety of ceremonial that has developed in our Church, often to the distress of many clergymen and laymen.

The rubrics in *Prayer Book Studies IV* exhibited a very marked trend towards fixing ceremonial, especially that of the postures of celebrant and people. Many welcomed this as a move towards clarifying confusion. Others resented it as an unnecessary intrusion upon and limitation of what should remain free and open to local custom and choice. It is difficult to find a middle way between these opposite opinions, if not convictions, about matters which are in any case not essential to the valid performance of the rite. No one wishes a rigid uniformity; yet all recognize the confusions and irritations that cause frustration to many sincere worshippers in our very mobile church constituency.

The Commission has tried to face the problem objectively and has come to the unanimous conclusion that the Prayer Book tradition of openness with regard to ceremonial should be continued. This opinion is not merely a concession to the difficulty of achieving any basic norm of practice in a Church such as ours, with its deep-seated dislike of authoritarian uniformity in matters that are essentially "indifferent." It stems from our conviction that the present age is one of liturgical change and experiment, which is affecting all of Christendom. Despite the difficulties and inconveniences for many worshippers, we believe that new experiments and trial usages will in the long run help us to establish patterns of worship more meaningful in the modern age, and give us a flexibility in the present ecumenical ferment of liturgical renewal. An attempt to "freeze" ceremonial at the present time might cut us off from valuable insights and possibilities of development, as they are working out within the exchanges of our Anglican tradition and of fellow Christians of other communions.

We have kept, obviously, certain ceremonials that are universally recognized not only as traditional but as fitting—such as sitting for the lessons, standing for the Gospel, and kneeling for formal acts of confession of sin. We have noted certain postures that are appropriate because of the character of the formulary—standing at the great acts of praise and acknowledgment in the *Gloria*, Creed, *Sursum corda*, Preface and *Sanctus*, and during the people's corporate action at the Offertory. But we have left open the postures of the people in most of the prayers (including the Consecration Prayer following the *Sanctus*); and we have not attempted to give specific directions about the exchange of the Peace. In these matters there is no fixed tradition.

In the ancient Church, standing for prayer was customary. In the medieval period, both standing and kneeling were common. Only in recent times has kneeling become a habit for prayer. Yet there are signs of a reaction. In an increasing number of churches, standing instead of kneeling is favored for the more solemn prayers of the liturgy. The ancient custom of standing has generally been kept so far as the celebrant is concerned, and this continues also for the people in some of the occasional rites, such as Baptism and Confirmation and Holy Matrimony. The officiant is not performing for an audience. He is leading a community in a common action. Postures of sitting, kneeling, and standing, come by habit or taste to express attitudes and relationships. They have nothing to do with reverence. It is certainly as reverent to stand in God's presence when we address him in prayer as it is to stand in his presence when we hear his Word.

3. The Introduction

There is no traditional pattern for the opening of the liturgy. The ancient Church was satisfied with a simple greeting of celebrant and people before the reading of the lessons. But later ages felt this beginning too abrupt, and elaborated the opening by a variety of devotional acts, whether of praise or penitence, recollection or petition.

The Anglican tradition, since the Second Prayer Book of 1552, has opted for a somewhat somber beginning based upon a preparatory act of self-examination through recital of the Ten Commandments or Summary of the Law, which replaces the medieval penitential preparation of priest and assistants before the beginning of the Mass. Recent Anglican revisions, especially in Asia and Africa, have tended to balance this dominant note of penitence by restoring the *Gloria in excelsis* to its more ancient position after the Kyrie.[30] The same proposal was made in *Prayer Book Studies IV*, and from the comments received this transposition of the *Gloria* was accepted with an almost unanimous consensus. It is true, that since the Elizabethan Prayer Book, the liturgy has allowed an "introit" psalm or hymn; but the texts chosen exhibit a variety of mood and substance, sometimes addressed to God in acts of praise, sometimes addressed to the self-examination of the congregation meeting in his presence.

---

30. The evidence may be readily found in Wigan, *The Liturgy in English*. The West Indian rite has returned to the 1549 pattern: Collect for Purity, *Kyrie*, and *Gloria*. The new proposal in New Zealand provides on Sundays, holy days, and weekdays of Eastertide for Collect for Purity and *Gloria*; on other occasions, *Kyrie* and penitential devotions may be substituted. The recent alternative draft for the Church of England allows the *Gloria* after the *Kyrie*.

The Commission has had difficulty in resolving the question, not readily or easily answered, "How does one begin an act of corporate worship?" Does one address God, or do the officiant and congregation address one another? Is the dominant attitude of the worshipper who faces God, deliberately and attentively, one of adoration or of unworthiness? Is it more natural to begin with

- *Acclamation*: *Alleluia, Hosanna, Kyrie eleison*;
- *Petition*: Open our lips, Cleanse our hearts, Remember not our offenses;
- *Bidding*: The Lord be with you, Come let us worship?

Experienced worshippers would no doubt affirm that all three approaches are agreeable, that a combination of them in proper proportion is fitting and edifying. The opening acts of any corporate assembly, religious or otherwise, are always crucial—both for the establishing of an *esprit de corps* that may well dominate the rest of the proceedings, and for the definition of the purpose and end of the assembly. The gathering of the scattered Church for "Eucharist" and "Communion" should be marked from its very beginning by the aim of praise and reconciliation.

The present proposal of the Commission—the result of much experimentation—is an attempt to meet the conditions of brevity and flexibility suggested by the inter-Anglican committee on structure and contents of the Eucharistic Liturgy.[31] It is designed to preserve values of long-standing in the tradition of Western and Anglican custom, to provide a just balance in the acknowledgment of God's glory and man's sinfulness and need of mercy, and to give sufficient flexibility in the distinction of festal and non-festal character in the several times and seasons of the year. Inasmuch as this Introduction is the most variable in content of any major section of the proposed rite, we have sought to avoid as much confusion as possible on the part of the worshipper, by printing in full only those formularies which would be more commonly used on Sundays and principal holy days, and by leaving permissible alternatives to these basic norms to the regulation of the rubrics. (The general rubrics on pages 19-20 of the rite provide direction for necessary ceremonial and textual options.)

An Introit Psalm or Hymn is permitted, when desired, which may cover the procession and disposition of the ministers in sanctuary and choir. It has long been provided by the general rubric of the Prayer Book (page viii) on "Hymns and Anthems." The specific notation here simply underscores its appropriateness and the time-honored values of psalmody at the Eucharist.[32]

---

31. See Appendix 1.

32. This draft does not provide for, though it does not exclude, the use of the Litany before the Eucharist, which is customary in many churches on certain occasions, since the liturgy contains a comparable litany form in the Prayers. This circumstance is not intended to prejudge a future over-all

The opening formulary is a doxological greeting of officiant and people, which fulfills both the need of mutual salutation and an immediate direction of the Eucharistic assembly towards God and his Kingdom. The text is based upon the opening doxology of the Eastern liturgies. These liturgies continue to witness to the primary Biblical and Patristic understanding of the Eucharist as foretaste and participation in the here and now of the Messianic banquet in the Kingdom of God.[33] The Eucharist unites heaven and earth in a communion of reconciliation and obedience to the will of God. And where his will is done, the Kingdom is manifest.

Following the doxology, the structure of Collect for Purity, Summary of the Law, and *Kyrie*, follows the pattern familiar in our present rite, with the addition on festal occasions of the *Gloria* or *Te Deum*. These forms, alternating in address to God and to the people, spell out in ways that have long been satisfying, the varied approaches of praise, acknowledgment, petition, and confession, which as we have noted are agreeable to a proper opening of corporate worship.[34] In the forms of both prayer and hymnody, there is combined a dual theme of acclamation of God's sovereign lordship and appeal for his gracious mercy and aid.

A few remarks concerning textual revisions may be noted:

a. Here, and throughout the Liturgy, "Holy Spirit" has been substituted for "Holy Ghost." The reason for this up-dating of the English usage of the rite is obvious.

b. The text of the Summary has been revised, using basically the RSV version, which in turn will be generally followed for all Biblical citations in the Liturgy. The passage in Mark 12:29-31 has been utilized, with some conflation taken from Matthew 22:37-40. The quotation marks make it clear that our Lord is not giving a commandment of his own, but citing the Old Testament—in fact, the fundamental confession of the people of God (the *Shema*, "Hear, O Israel," of Deuteronomy 6:4 ff.).[35]

c. The permission to use *Kyrie eleison* untranslated has been retained from *Prayer Book Studies IV*, despite the objections of some to the use of an "unknown tongue." The *Kyrie* is essentially an acclamation of praise, with much the same overtones of meaning that other ancient and untranslated

---

revision of the Prayer Book, in which the relationships that may obtain among its several offices will find proper adjustment.

33. See the address of Alexander Schmemann at the liturgical conference held in St. Paul's, San Antonio, November 16-18, 1959, in *The Eucharist and Liturgical Renewal*, edited for The Associated Parishes, Inc., by Massey H. Shepherd, Jr., Oxford University Press, 1960, pp. 117-32.

34. The Commission has eliminated the recital of the Decalogue, for the reasons stated in *Prayer Book Studies IV*, Vol. 1, pp. 237-239. Its legalistic form makes it more suitable for a special service of self-examination or of catechesis, where it can be interpreted according to the teaching of our Lord in the gospels.

35. See the perceptive study of the form of the Summary in Anglican liturgies by C. Leo Barry, "'These Two Commandments' in Liturgy and Catechism," *The Modern Churchman*, N.S. 8 (1965), 206-11.

words of the liturgy bear, such as *Alleluia, Hosanna,* and *Amen.* It is part of our heritage of praise from the ancient undivided Church. It is strange to suppose that people cannot understand its force and meaning; for, in fact, we use it as a title in our Hymnal and in our printed or mimeographed service leaflets, and we always refer to this formulary by its Greek, not its English terms. In any case, the English translation is there to use whenever desired.[36]

d. As an alternative to the *Kyrie,* we have provided another ancient acclamation from the Eastern liturgies, the *Trisagion.* It is also a trinitarian doxology, and serves adequately, as does the *Kyrie,* as a sufficient substitute for the *Gloria* on non-festal occasions.[37]

e. The *Gloria in excelsis* is printed as a hymn in three stanzas, the individual lines corresponding to the customary musical phrases when it is sung. A few textual changes have been made, in the interest of greater accuracy, but with the hope that they will not materially disturb the many fine musical settings (other than simple chant forms) that are our inheritance.[38] As in *Prayer Book Studies IV,* we have sought to restore the use of the *Gloria* to festal seasons and occasions. If this should seem burdensome by overmuch repetition, we have allowed the equally ancient and doxological hymn *Te Deum* as a substitute. Our present rite allows a "proper hymn" to be used in place of the *Gloria* at any time. This has been a boon in shortening the post-communion devotions. But the permission has often been abused by the selection of

---

36. See *Prayer Book Studies IV,* pp. 249-251. Though many prefer the shorter, and perhaps more accurate, English translation, "Lord, have mercy," we have retained the longer version so as not to rule out of use so much of our musical heritage.

37. According to some interpreters, "Holy God" refers to the Father, "Holy Mighty" to the Son, and "Holy Immortal" to the Holy Spirit. But the trinitarian interpretation may be as contrived as that given to the threefold *Kyrie.*

38. In *Prayer Book Studies IV,* the text of the second line was changed to read: "and on earth peace to men of good will." This is perhaps a more accurate rendering of the original text of Luke 2:14 than is our present form. But the textual history of this verse is very complicated and much disputed. The RSV reads: "and on earth peace among men with whom he is pleased," with an alternative in the notes: "peace, good will among men." The New English Bible reads: "and on earth his peace for men on whom his favour rests," with an alternative in the notes: "and on earth, his peace, his favour towards men." A recent study prepared for the vernacular use in the Roman Catholic Church has offered two other translations: "Peace on earth and God's good will to men," and "And on earth peace to men through God's good will." (The word "God's" is, of course, an interpretation, not a strict translation.)

In view of these difficulties, we have decided to retain the current version, in the hope that further discussion—preferably on an ecumenical basis—may help resolve the problem. Indeed, the Commission expresses a very fervent hope that within the near future, it may be possible for Roman Catholics, Anglicans, and others to find agreement in the vernacular texts used in common among us in the liturgy.

The current proposal has two textual changes that should be noted: 1) "sin" for "sins" in lines 8 and 10—though ancient liturgical texts offer a choice of singular or plural, the Gospel text cited, John 1:29, is in the singular; and 2) the insertion of "Jesus" in line 16, in accordance with the ancient texts.

hymns that are not proper doxologies or that lack the objective and doctrinal substance of the *Gloria* or the *Te Deum*.

4. The Ministry of the Word

One of the most frequent requests to the Commission has been the proposal to restore to the Liturgy at least the permission for an Old Testament lesson in addition to the Epistle and Gospel. At the present time, the only way this can be done is by way of "Short Morning Prayer" immediately preceding the Eucharist—a device that is very good in theory, but is awkward in practice because of the disjunction created by a double preparation, one of Morning Prayer, the other of the Eucharistic rite.[39] There is certainly ancient precedent for an Old Testament lesson in the Eucharist; and it still survives as a kind of "vestigial remain" in certain masses of the Latin rite. In general, however, both the Eastern and the Western liturgies ultimately settled for two lessons rather than three or more; though in some cases in the Latin Mass an Old Testament lection won out over the Epistle. From this circumstance, there survive in the Prayer Book a few "Old Testament Epistles."[40]

There is certainly a tendency in recent liturgical revisions to provide an Old Testament lection. It is a characteristic feature of the Reformed (Calvinistic) liturgies, including the rite of Taizé, and it is required in the Liturgy of the Church of South India. Among the Anglican liturgies, it is permitted in the Prayer Book of India, in *A Liturgy for Africa*, in the recent *Alternative Services* of the Church of England; and it is required in the latest proposal of the Church of New Zealand. We have accordingly made provision for it in the present proposals.

The question is raised, however, whether three lessons are not too much for one service. It is not so much a matter of lengthening the rite, although on all sides there are voices raised for a shorter rite than what we have at present. It is a problem concerning how much of the Word can be fruitfully received by a congregation in a single service. It is possible that the historic tendency of the liturgies to reduce the lessons to two was responsive to a greater edification. Hence some have proposed a larger number of Old Testament selections to replace some of the New Testament Epistles.

The division of opinion regarding two or three lessons is related to the larger question of a radical reform of the Eucharistic lectionary as a whole, and the increasing tendency to look with favor upon a three-year, or at least two-year, cycle of readings. It is known that the Roman Catholic Church is preparing a

---

39. It should not be forgotten that Cranmer and his fellow reformers intended that Morning Prayer always be said, even when followed by Holy Communion (or Ante-Communion).

40. The Commission has included a number of Old Testament lections in the additional propers for the Lesser Feasts and Fasts (*Prayer Book Studies XVI*).

more extended Eucharistic lectionary, probably on a three-year cycle. The Vatican Council's Constitution on the Liturgy directed a reform in the Mass that would open to use more of the treasures of the Bible, and more varied and extensive reading from it. Should this new lectionary—the first major overhauling of it since the sixth century—prove to be excellent in choices and sequences, there is no valid reason why our own Church should not welcome a testing of it in trial use.[41]

The Sermon has been placed after the Gospel and before the Creed. This position for the Sermon is actually a return to a more ancient structure that is still preserved in the liturgies of the Eastern and Roman Churches. The transposition has also been made in the recent liturgies of South India, Taizé, *A Liturgy for Africa*, the English *Alternative Services*, and in the new rite of the Church of New Zealand. The historical reason for this more ancient structure is simply due to the early Church's sense of appropriateness in placing the Sermon in the "Liturgy of the Catechumens," the Creed in the "Liturgy of the Faithful." But apart from this antiquarian precedent, there is practical value in relating the Sermon more closely to the lessons, and then employing the Creed as a corporate response of the Church to the whole Word of God that has been read and proclaimed.

We have permitted the Creed to be omitted except on Sundays and festivals, for the summary of the Faith is in actuality contained in the whole rite, and more particularly in the Consecration Prayer. Again, in the Western tradition, there is precedent for using the Creed as a festal adornment, in the same way as the *Gloria in excelsis*. We have omitted the provision of the present Prayer Book that allows the Apostles' Creed, except on certain occasions, to be substituted for the Nicene Creed. Our reason may seem artificial to some. But we believe that the Apostles' Creed properly belongs to Baptism, and the daily renewal of our baptismal pledge in the Offices of Morning and Evening Prayer. It is a purely Western creed in liturgical use, and from its origin has been intimately associated with the baptismal professions.

The Nicene Creed is, on the other hand, ecumenical and used by most of the Churches of Christendom. We have therefore restored its text to the original plural form: "We believe." Other alterations in the text as now commonly recited are designed for greater accuracy and clarity and the removal of archaic words. Many of these changes, including some of the new punctuation, were anticipated in *Prayer Book Studies IV*. The dropping of the *filioque* clause in the statement of the "procession of the Holy Spirit" is not done out of scruple or hesitancy, because of the long-standing controversy between the Eastern and Western Churches about the doctrinal validity of the "double procession" from the Father and the Son. It is simply a recognition of the fact that it was not originally in the Creed,

---

41. The Standing Liturgical Commission is on record as favoring, whenever possible or suitable, a concordance of our Eucharistic lectionary with that of the Roman Catholic Church, and in this principle we hope other liturgical Churches will join. Our common Eucharistic lectionary over the centuries has had great value.

and is therefore not truly ecumenical. Though the Creed is not a hymn, it has a hymnodic quality. We have consequently printed it in verse lines, comparable to the Gloria, in the hope that this format will assist the congregation in corporate recitation (or singing) and possibly encourage a readier comprehension.

The general rubrics (pages 19-20) make provision for suitable places for the necessary announcements and special prayers. With the Creed, these form a kind of "Prone" traditionally associated with the Sermon. In addition, we have required on certain occasions, but left permissive for all occasions if desired, The Penitential Order.

The origin and history of the material in The Penitential Order is well-known, and can be found in any handbook on the history of the Prayer Book.[42] It is part of the oldest vernacular used in the Anglican liturgies, stemming from Cranmer's *Order of the Communion* of 1548, and it has been a characteristic feature of them until recent revisions. It was intended to serve as a preparation of communicants, the more appropriate in view of the abandonment of the requirement of the Sacrament of Penance.

In the First Prayer Book of 1549 it was placed, as it still is in the Scottish Liturgy, immediately before Communion. The Second Prayer Book, followed by later Anglican rites, moved it to a position immediately before the Consecration. The Second Prayer Book did not have an Offertory of the elements; hence the offering of alms and Prayer for the Church were accounted part of the Ante-Communion. The penitential devotions were actually the beginning of the second part of the rite, namely that which concerned those who intended to remain for Communion. The introduction into later Anglican liturgies of a proper Eucharistic Offertory thus produced the anomalous situation of lengthy prayers and devotions separating the Offertory actions from the consecratory Giving of Thanks.

Only in recent years have Anglican revisions sought to repair this awkwardly undramatic structure. The Ceylon Liturgy of 1933 placed the penitential devotions at the beginning of the rite. The Japanese Liturgy of 1959 and, most recently, the English *Alternative Services* have removed them to a place immediately before the Offertory. In both the Ceylon and the Japanese rites the text is very much altered, being more closely akin to the forms of Confession and Absolution in the Roman Mass. The Liturgy of the Church of South India also places the material in the introductory portion of the rite, with a major rewriting of the General Confession. Its influence, both in order and text, may now be seen in *A Liturgy for Africa* and the new rite of the Church of New Zealand.

Many of the queries and problems which these formularies have raised were canvassed in *Prayer Book Studies IV*. Principally they concern the subjective,

---

42. The source of these forms is given in F. E. Brightman, *The English Rite* (London: Rivingtons, 1915), I, lxxi-lxxvi.

highly emotional expressions of the General Confession, which make the form less apt for a corporate act, and the attributions of the so-called Comfortable Words. More recently a serious query has been posited regarding the redundancy, and hence the inappropriateness, of an Absolution in a rite that is sealed in Communion.[43] The revisions made by the Commission for this draft have been guided in part by the work done in *Prayer Book Studies IV*; but there are some new suggestions:

a. The Invitation has incorporated the "communal" character of the Confession by the phrase "in the presence of his Church" without sacrificing its direct summons to the individual conscience.

b. The General Confession has been tightened with a more objective and factual manner of expression.

c. The Scriptural Words—placed before the Absolution, as in *Prayer Book Studies IV*—have been spared the misleading and archaic descriptive adjective "comfortable," and stripped of their questionable attributions. They are presented as a single block of the "Word of God" and put into modern English. Except for the first Word, the texts basically conform to the Revised Standard Version. The last Word from 1 John has been extended by the completion of the sentence as it appears in that Epistle, an addition which is a considerable enrichment.

d. In the Absolution, "true repentance and sincere faith" replaces "hearty repentance and true faith." The archaic meaning of "hearty" is lost today; and "true faith" has overtones of "orthodoxy" when the context demands that "faith" be understood as confidence and trust in God.

Lastly, it should be noted that the general rubrics allow those who desire a more penitential introduction to the Liturgy to insert The Penitential Order after the Summary of the Law.

It is only fair to say that some have questioned the propriety of allowing the omission of The Penitential Order, except on a few stated days of the Christian Year. They readily admit that our present rite, with its inheritance of medieval and Reformation piety, has doubtless over-emphasized the mood of penitence, for it carries over from these particular devotions into the Consecration Prayer and the pre-Communion Prayer of Humble Access. And at many celebrations a further accent is given by the texts of certain hymns that are inserted. The result is that for many people the Eucharist lacks a proper emphasis of joy and thanksgiving, and seems more agreeable to a day of fasting than a day of feasting. On the other hand, there can be no argument about the necessity of sincere contrition for sin,

---

43. See, for example, the discussion of J. G. Davies, "The Eucharist and the Remission of Sins," *Church Quarterly Review*, 162 (1961), 50-58.

and acceptance of God's freely given forgiveness to the penitent, as an essential dimension of the Eucharistic liturgy, and indeed of all true Christian worship. The forms which have been inherited have served well in evoking and expressing these responses.

After weighing carefully all these considerations, the Commission has decided that a just balance and proportion of emphasis in the rite can only be resolved by flexible experiment in trial use. The Penitential Order may be used, if desired, more frequently than on the stated days when it is required; and it may be used as part of the Introduction, or after the Creed and before the Prayers. Even when it is omitted, it should be pointed out that The Prayer of Intercession contains a specific penitential petition with an appropriate response. The acknowledgment of our sinfulness is also explicit in the introductory Collect for Purity and the acclamations of *Kyrie, Trisagion,* and *Gloria*. The Consecration Prayer states no less explicitly the unique and crucial significance of our Lord's death and sacrifice, a pledge of our forgiveness, and his eternal mediation through which all our offering and prayer and praise are alone acceptable and pleasing to God. Finally, the Lord's Prayer, which is both climax of Consecration and preparation for Communion, contains the most fundamental petition for forgiveness in all the liturgy. Hence the act of Communion may properly be taken as a seal of acceptance and absolution.

5. The Prayers

Modern liturgical research, with its discovery of more ancient sources of Christian worship than those available to the Reformers, has been able to reconstruct with a fair degree of accuracy the structural pattern of the liturgy of the early Church. After the Ministry of the Word was concluded and the catechumens were dismissed, the congregation of the faithful began its "closed communion" with the exchange of the Kiss of Peace and then engaged themselves to common prayers and intercessions, supplications and thanksgivings "for all men" (cf. 1 Tim. 2:1-4). Then followed the Offertory, Consecration, Fraction, and Communion. The Kiss of Peace was, of course, a familiar ceremony inherited from the Jews—a greeting expressive of the love and unity of God's people in God's peace. It was the first greeting of the risen Lord to his disciples (cf. John 20: 19-2 1); it is the common salutation and bidding of St. Paul at the conclusion of his letters to his churches.

Ceremonially, the "Peace" was exchanged by the embrace of one's nearest neighbor and a light kiss upon the cheek. The gesture may still be seen in the Orthodox Churches or at the Roman High Mass. In other Eastern Churches, it was symbolized by a clasp of hands, with or without a kiss of the fingers, or by a bow. During the late medieval period in the West, it became common to express the Peace by kissing a wooden tablet bearing an image of the crucifixion or of a saint (the *Pax Brede* or "Peace Board"), which was passed around the congregation. The Reformation liturgies gave up the ceremony. But it has been revived in modern times by the Liturgy of the Church of South India, in this form: "When the Peace is given, the giver places his right palm against the right palm of the receiver, and each closes his left hand over the other's right hand.... The presbyter gives the Peace to those ministering with him, and these in turn give it to the congregation. It may be passed through the congregation either along the rows, or from those in front to those behind. It is suggested that each person as he gives the Peace may say in a low voice, 'The peace of God,' or 'The peace of God be with you.'"

The example of South India has been "catching"; and many individual congregations today throughout the world, Catholic and Protestant, are reintroducing the ceremony of the Peace, along with its accompanying words, in some gesture of handclasp. We have not in this draft attempted to describe by rubric any particular ceremony or manner of "exchange." Again, we believe that the latitude of trial use and experiment may produce a commonly agreed upon pattern that is dignified, natural, and effective.

The primitive sequence of Peace-Prayer-Offering was not maintained in many of the liturgies, when they were elaborated in the period after the Constantinian era. The Greek liturgies transferred the Peace to a place after the Offertory and before the Consecration. The Roman rite, at some unknown time, transferred the prayers of intercession to a position within the Canon of Consecration, and the Peace to a place between the Fraction and Communion. This Roman order was followed in the First Prayer Book of 1549. But the Second Prayer Book of 1552 took the intercessions out of the Consecration, and associated them, in a "Prayer for the whole state of Christ's Church," with the offering of alms.[44] Thus was established a sequence found in all later Anglican liturgies of Offertory followed by prayers of intercession—then the Penitential devotion and the Consecration. The Second Prayer Book also eliminated the Peace altogether.[45]

Most of the modern revisions of the Anglican rite have restored the Peace, in its "Roman" position of association with the Fraction. The American liturgy is one of the few exceptions to this restoration. The Liturgy for Africa, the English Alternative Services, and the new rite of New Zealand have followed the example of South India in a sequence of Prayers-Peace-Offertory. In this draft we propose the restoration of the original sequence of Peace-Prayers-Offertory—for two reasons: 1) The Prayers take up the theme of the Peace and develop it in intercession

---

44. It is commonly thought that Cranmer was influenced in this new arrangement of the intercessions by the description of the liturgy in the mid-second century contained in Justin Martyr's first *Apology*, a writing with which he became familiar after the issuance of the First Prayer Book of 1549.

45. It is possible that Cranmer considered the Peace to be adequately expressed in the final Blessing, "The peace of God which passeth understanding, etc." This Blessing, however, as well as the Peace, is contained in the liturgy of the First Prayer Book.

for "all sorts and conditions of men"; and 2) there is no interruption of the natural and logical sequence from the Offertory to the Consecration.

The placing of the Prayers before the Offertory has another advantage, in that it makes possible a full-rounded service of the Word that may be useful in situations and circumstances where there is no Communion, and where an alternative to Morning Prayer may be desired. In the general rubrics (page 20) specific provision is made for a Deacon, or a Lay Reader specially licensed by the Bishop, to lead this expanded Ante-Communion wherever there is "reasonable cause." Thus congregations without a settled priest need not be deprived of that Ministry of the Word which is built around the Eucharistic lectionary.[46]

The revision of the "Prayer for the Church" in *Prayer Book Studies IV* did not find much favor. Most of the criticisms had to do with its style—the awkward juxtaposition of sixteenth- and twentieth-century English. Some objections were also made to various details of its content. But there was widespread disappointment in the failure to produce an intercession in bidding or litany form, with responses by the people. The litany structure for this Prayer first appeared in Anglican rites in the Ceylon Liturgy of 1933, and has been recently adopted in the Indian, African, English, and New Zealand liturgies.

We do not know exactly what was the form of the Prayers in the Eucharist of the ancient Church, or whether a common form was universally used. Many scholars believe that it was something akin to the biddings-silence-collect sequences of the Good Friday rite in the Roman Missal. By the latter part of the fourth century, the litany form was almost universal in the East, and for a time it found its way in the Roman rite also. The recent reform of the Roman Mass in its vernacular versions has restored the "Prayers of the Faithful" before the Offertory. To date its structure is largely free of set forms, but it generally tends to consist of biddings followed by brief corporate responses. "The Prayer for the Church" in the *Lutheran Service Book and Hymnal* (1958)—one of the finest pieces of contemporary liturgical composition—is in litany form. On the other hand, the intercessions in the recent Presbyterian *Service for the Lord's Day* (1964) are patterned after the Roman Good Friday sequence of bidding-silence-collect.

The Commission decided to adopt a litany form, since this has been long familiar to and beloved by our people. Its basic model has been the Prayer Book Litany, though the opening of it, with its linkage of theme to the Peace, is reminiscent of the litanies in the Eastern rites. All of the concerns of the present "Prayer

---

46. It may be readily seen that by the use of Psalms and Canticles, the Ante-Communion of this draft may contain all the elements of worship found in the Daily Offices, with a Sermon in addition. Our proposal should not, however, be taken in any way as a rival designed to eliminate or displace Morning (or Evening) Prayer. The Ante-Communion is a catechetical and missionary service; the Daily Offices are ascetical. The rationale of the two orders of service of the Word is quite different. This should be obvious from the distinctive way each service utilizes the Psalter and from the differing principles of their respective lectionaries. Moreover the Ante-Communion is not designed primarily as a daily office.

for the Church" and many of its phrases are preserved in the new form. But unlike the intercession in *Prayer Book Studies IV*, it is not a revision of the "Prayer for the Church" but a new formulary. Yet we believe that it will "sound" familiar to the ears of our congregations, and that they will find in it not only all the values of the old prayer, but a real enrichment of them. Some of the advantages of this new form, as we see them, are:

a. It is a general litany such as the Prayer Book Litany, and is not confined to the "Church" or tied specifically to the Eucharistic Offertory such as the "Prayer for the Church" in our present rite. Thus it may be employed on other occasions of worship, in the same way as the Litany or the Bidding Prayer.

b. It is formal without being inflexible. It allows the insertion of petition for immediate or local concerns, without disturbing the larger perspective and balance of the prayer.

c. It includes, in addition to the time-honored supplications for Church and State, the needy and afflicted, and the departed, reference to wider concerns both of our churchly and communal life: the mission of the Church; the vocations of men and women in commerce and industry, arts and sciences, school and home; and the proper use of the created order. A special penitential petition is also included; and the petition for the departed allows for specific reference to any particular commemorations of the day.

d. The congregational responses are direct and simple—invariable except for the last two. In places where it may be desired to sing this Litany, easy adaptations of the familiar musical responses of the Prayer Book Litany can be made.

6. The Offertory

The basic actions of the Offertory are such as need no change or revision. The Table must be set, the gifts presented, and the elements of bread and wine prepared. We have not attempted to describe in detail how these actions may or must be performed, for they necessarily vary according to circumstances from place to place. We have, however, sought to clarify certain ceremonies that were left obscure in the rubrics of *Prayer Book Studies IV*:

a. The People are to stand, at least for the announcement of the Offertory and the presentation of the gifts. (They may sit, of course, during the time of receiving the gifts and hearing the permissive hymn or anthem.) This posture simply recognizes that the Offertory is essentially the People's action.

b. Representatives of the congregation must be involved in the bringing of the gifts to the Table—whether servers or persons in the nave. We have not spelled out any details of an "Offertory Procession"—a ceremony that is becoming increasingly effective in so many congregations. The rubrics do assume, however, that the celebrant must have someone from the congregation assist in the Offertory actions. He should not do them all by himself, whether the congregation is large or small. Where a Deacon is present, he is the preferred intermediary between priest and people in the receiving of the gifts.

c. The ancient ceremony of the *Lavabo* or washing of the celebrant's hands is not mentioned, for it is not universally observed in our churches. But there is nothing to prevent this ceremony taking place at the customary times—at the beginning of the Offertory, or before or after the formal Presentation, according to the wishes of the celebrant.

Some textual enrichments have been made. There is a fixed bidding to the Offertory that attempts to summarize succinctly the meaning and purpose of the action. In addition, the priest may read one or more Offertory Sentences. These are placed in an appendix, so as not to impede the ready following of the rite by the congregation. Many of the familiar ones have been retained; all of the new ones proposed in *Prayer Book Studies IV* have been included except Psalm 50:14. In its place we have added St. Matthew 5:23-24. We have eliminated the suggested classifications of *Prayer Book Studies IV* as unnecessary. The texts have been conformed, with only a few minor variations, to the Revised Standard Version. Suitable Presentation Sentences have been separated from the other Sentences, as in *Prayer Book Studies IV*, but they are permissive. We have arranged them in versicle-response form, though obviously they may be sung as a whole by the congregation, if it wishes to do so. A new one is suggested, taken from the New Testament—Revelation 4:11.

7. The Consecration

Once the Table is set and prepared, it is logical to proceed without delay to the Giving of Thanks. The restoration of this ancient order and sequence, the Commission considers to be of great importance. It still obtains in the Roman rite, and it is a feature of many recent revisions—South India, Taizé, the *Liturgy for Africa*, and the New Zealand rite. It is also characteristic of the latest revisions in the liturgies of the Presbyterian and Congregational Churches. It makes sense. One does not normally gather at a banquet table that is prepared, and then wait through a long discourse before the table grace is offered.

We have directed that the People remain standing through the Preface and *Sanctus*, after which they may kneel or remain standing throughout the Prayer. The latter posture may not be common in our Anglican Churches, but it has been maintained since ancient times in the Eastern and Roman Churches. The *Sursum corda*, Preface and *Sanctus* are the greatest acts of praise in all the liturgy; only hymns such as the *Gloria* and *Te Deum* can be compared with them. It would seem only proper for the people to stand with the celebrant during this outburst of laud and thanksgiving—this *Eucharist* in the strictest sense.

In recent years there has been much learned discussion regarding the primitive form of the Eucharistic or Consecration Prayer. It is agreed on all sides that the form is directly descended from Jewish blessings, whose form consisted of an address to God in praise and thanksgiving, followed by a laudatory recital of his mighty acts in creation, providence, and redemption, a petition for the fulfillment of his ultimate purposes, and a concluding doxology. This form, translated into Christian terms, is readily recognizable in the oldest Table Thanksgivings of the Church known to us today; namely the formularies in the *Didache* (*ca.* A.D. 100).[47] It conforms also to the descriptions of the Thanksgiving Prayer at the Eucharist in the first *Apology* of Justin Martyr, composed at Rome *ca.* 150. In the same context Justin refers to the Words of Institution, but does not make clear whether they were actually incorporated in the Prayer. Our next witness comes from the text in the *Apostolic Tradition* of Hippolytus, generally dated *ca.* 200, and probably composed also in Rome. Hippolytus' form has influenced all the later liturgies of the East and West; but we do not possess its original Greek text, but only translations and adaptations made in the fourth and fifth centuries.[48]

The Hippolytan text has the *Sursum corda* followed by a recital of God's mighty acts in creation and redemption that leads into the Words of Institution. (There is no *Sanctus*, though we know from other sources, stemming from Egypt and North Africa, that many churches included the *Sanctus* at this time.) The Institution narrative is then followed by a summary *Anamnesis* (or Memorial), an Oblation of the gifts, and an Invocation of the Holy Spirit, with prayer for the fruits of communion, before concluding in a doxology. This structure is basically the same as that of the Consecration Prayers of the later Greek and Latin rites (with the notable exception of the Roman Canon), except that the *Sanctus* has been inserted in the recital of God's acts immediately before the recalling of our Lord's redemptive life and work. The many problems connected with the origin and structure of the Roman Canon, which cannot be traced in any case before the latter part of the fourth century, do not concern us here. We may note, however, that it has no overall recital of the works of God comparable to the fuller outlines of the Eastern liturgies, but distributes many themes of it in the various Proper

---

47. A fundamental study is that of J. P. Audet, O.P., "Literary Forms and Contents of a Normal Εὐχαριτία in the First Century," *Studia Evangelica*. Papers presented to the International Congress on "The Four Gospels in 1957" held at Christ Church, Oxford, 1957. Edited by Kurt Aland and others. (Texte und Untersuchungen, 73; Berlin: Akademie-Verlag, 1959), pp. 643-62.

48. For English readers the best texts of the *Apostolic Tradition* are those edited by Burton Scott Easton (Cambridge University Press, 1934) or by Dom Gregory Dix (London: S.P.C.K., 1937).

Prefaces of the Christian Year. The history of the influence of the Roman Canon, and later of the Eastern liturgies, upon the pattern of the Prayer Book Consecration Prayer has been recounted in full in *Prayer Book Studies IV*.[49] Suffice it to say that at present our Consecration Prayer follows in the main the outline of the Eastern rites, with the single exception of the use of Proper Prefaces.

Some sixteen years ago, one of the most eminent liturgical scholars of the Church of England, Professor E. C. Ratcliff of Cambridge, published a technical and closely argued study of the Hippolytan Eucharistic prayer, in which he sought to prove that in its original form it must have been one long recital of thanksgiving for all God's acts of creation, redemption, and final consummation, concluding with the *Sanctus*. The versions of it which have come down to us represent later revisions, which eliminated the *Sanctus*, revamped the *Anamnesis* with an Oblation, and modified the Invocation of the Spirit.[50] Dr. Ratcliff's study remains a hypothesis, but one that has found favor with other liturgical scholars. We mention it here because it has recently exercised considerable influence in the revision of two recent Anglican rites—*A Liturgy for Africa* and the proposed New Zealand liturgy.[51] In such a scheme there is no place or need for a Proper Preface.

Our Commission has felt the attractiveness of this new theory about the ancient form of Consecration. But since it is a theory, and not as yet an established fact, we have decided to maintain the tradition which we have received regarding the primary structure of the Consecration Prayer; and indeed, we have re-enforced it by a considerable addition to and extension of the Proper Prefaces, including a special Preface for Sundays when there is no special one for the season.

Since the Proper Prefaces—like the Offertory Sentences—concern the celebrant and are variable with time and occasion, we have printed them also in an appendix to the basic service, with the single exception of the Sunday Preface. In preparing these Prefaces we have given close attention to those in *Prayer Book Studies IV* (and the reactions to them submitted to the Commission) as well as to those which are printed in synoptic form and gathered from all the Anglican liturgies in Bernard Wigan's *The Liturgy in English*. A few comments on our present proposals may be helpful:

a. *Advent.* This is a new composition of the Commission, not found in other rites, though some of the phrasing has been suggested by the Advent Preface of the Book of Common Order (Church of Scotland).

---

49. See Vol. 1, pp 142 ff.

50. "The Sanctus and the Pattern of the Early Anaphora," *The Journal of Ecclesiastical History*, I (1950), 29-36, 125-34. See also the acceptance of Ratcliff's thesis by A. H. Couratin, "The Sacrifice of Praise, The Church's Thanksgiving in New Testament Times," Theology. 58 (1955), 285-91; and by G. A. Michell, *Landmarks in Liturgy* (London: Darton, Longmann and Todd, 1961).

51. See Appendix 2, Nos. 8 and 13.

b. *Christmas.* This is a revision of the one appointed in the Prayer Book. The result clause exhibits a shift of emphasis from the theme of atonement to that of adoption.

c. *Epiphany.* The same as the present form, with the addition of "the" before "substance."

d. *Incarnation.* The same as our present Prayer Book form.

e. *Lent.* The form in *Prayer Book Studies IV* was more closely woven from the text of Hebrews 4:15. We have altered the latter portion, reminiscent of 2 Corinthians 5.15, more in the manner of the Preface in the Book of Common Order (Church of Scotland). Cf. also the Preface in the Scottish Prayer Book. We considered it important to link the Lenten discipline with the Easter hope.

f. *Passiontide.* This is a condensation of the one in the Scottish Prayer Book—the basis also of the one in *Prayer Book Studies IV*. It is based on John 12:32 and Hebrews 5:8-9.

g. *Easter.* A revision of the present Prayer Book Preface, mainly in matters of linguistic style. But the doctrinal implication in the substitution of "given" for "restored" was deliberately intended by the Commission.

h. *Ascension.* A slight stylistic modification of the present Prayer Book form.

i. *Whitsuntide.* A further shortening of the revision of the present form in *Prayer Book Studies IV*. There has been much objection to overly lengthy Prefaces. Note that this Preface is also allowed on Feasts of Apostles.

j. *Trinity Sunday.* This is a new composition of the Commission and is not derived from any other liturgy. The one in our present Prayer Book is a textbook definition, useful in pedagogy. But it is not praise. The Commission considered that a Proper Preface should be an act of worship. Doctrinally, the Preface makes no less clear the unity, equality, and co-eternity of the Triune God.

k. *All Saints.* The same as the present Preface, with a slight modernizing of the English of the last phrase.

l. *Apostles and Ordinations.* A revision and shortening of the one in *Prayer Book Studies IV*, which in turn had been suggested by the Embertide Preface in the Scottish Prayer Book. It is based on Hebrews 3:20 and Matthew 29:19-20. The exceptions noted, for the use of this Preface, are due to the fact that the seasonal Prefaces that replace it, respectively, are also suitable to the commemoration of Apostles or concern for the Ministry.

m. *Commemoration of the Departed.* The effort to translate the great Preface at Requiems in the Roman Missal, which was made in *Prayer Book Studies IV*, was ingenious. But many critics pointed out that it was cumbersome in length and complicated in subject matter. We have sought here not to make a translation, but a paraphrase (after the manner of many of Cranmer's so-called "translations") that preserves the basic substance of the great Latin Preface but simplifies the communication of what it has to say. This should be welcome particularly to those who mourn.

The text of the Consecration Prayer following the *Sanctus* has in the main followed the directions of revision characteristic of *Prayer Book Studies IV*—namely, in the attempt to give a fuller recital of the mighty works of God in the whole history of salvation, rather than a concentration mainly upon the death and sacrifice of our Lord; and in the excision of repetitious, and therefore tedious, expressions in the present form. The end result is a prayer that is richer in content and shorter in length.[52] We have, however, been less sparing of the familiar wording than was the case in *Prayer Book Studies IV*, and we have sought, where possible, to break up overly long sentences. Certain new features should be pointed out:

a. Reference at the beginning is made to the Creation and the Fall of man, as a background for the thanksgiving for the Incarnation and Atonement.

b. The recalling of our Lord's sacrifice is enlarged, and not confined solely to the concept of a "sacrifice for sin." His sacrifice involves also his total taking upon himself of our nature and his perfect obedience.[53]

c. While retaining the traditional Prayer Book conflation of Matthew and 1 Corinthians, the Words of Institution have been conformed to the style of Revised Standard Version. The Fraction of the bread at this point is omitted (as in *Prayer Book Studies IV*).

d. We have returned to the present Prayer Book structure of having the *Anamnesis* follow the Oblation of the Gifts. And the *Anamnesis* has itself been enriched by reference to the Coming again of our Lord—a restoration which many modern revisions have made after the model of the Eastern liturgies. The Oblation of the worshippers is then conjoined to the Oblation of the Gifts, and not separated by the Invocation. The reference to the heavenly Altar, another ancient dimension restored in *Prayer Book Studies IV*, met with much opposition because of the imagery. We have sought to avoid this problem by reference instead to the eternal mediation of our Lord, who ever lives to make intercession for us (cf. Hebrews 7:25). The unity of our Eucharist with the worship of heaven is thus indicated not only in the Preface but in this taking up of our life and offering by our Lord Redeemer and Mediator.

e. The Invocation paragraph has been very much rewritten. The double blessing of the Word and the Holy Spirit is maintained from our present rite. For

---

52. The present Prayer has 545 words; the form in *Prayer Book Studies IV* has 425 words; this one, 430 words.

53. See the work of one of our Commission members: Bonnell Spencer, O.H.C., *Sacrifice of Thanksgiving* (West Park: Holy Cross Publications, 1965).

the Word no less than the Spirit is re-creative in his function. Sanctification is sought for ourselves as well as for "these holy Mysteries," so that the totality of what is here present, what is here done, and what is here offered, may be caught up in the new creation of the Word and Spirit. We have attempted to avoid any notion of a "moment of consecration" or any definition of how consecration is effected.[54] We affirm only the reality and the effectual fruits of this sanctification, and the final end to which it points. The eschatological note that rounds off the prayer returns us to the opening "Lift up your hearts"—indeed to the very opening of the liturgy itself: "Blessed be his Kingdom, now and forever."

f. In the final Doxology, the phrase "in whom" has been restored from the Roman Canon, on which this Doxology is based (cf. Romans 11:36). For some unknown reason, Cranmer left it out of the First Prayer Book.

g. The "now" in the bidding to the Lord's Prayer has been shifted. At present, it sounds very much like a punctuation mark! In its new position it has force. By virtue of all that has been recited concerning our redemption, we may "now" have confidence in addressing God as Our Father.

8. The Breaking of the Bread and Communion

These two parts of the "four-action" shape of the Eucharist are so intimately bound together that we have placed them both under one major caption. The restoration of the Fraction to its ancient and proper position was already proposed in *Prayer Book Studies IV*, and received favorable comment, especially from the laity. Its use, however, may be a mere piece of ceremonialism, so long as small wafer breads are customary. The example of Clare College, Cambridge, of restoring a real "loaf" has been taken up by some parishes, but it cannot as yet be called a "trend." The Commission senses nonetheless an undercurrent of reaction to the widespread use of small, individualized wafers, which in many cases cannot be chewed and are virtually tasteless. Roman Catholics are experimenting with a larger whole wheat wafer that can be broken easily into at least two pieces and which must be chewed in order to be eaten.

The Fraction was, of course, a utilitarian ceremony in origin. The one loaf had to be broken if it was to be shared. Symbolically it was an obvious reference to the Lord's own broken body. The contemplation of the mystery here of "breaking for sharing," and so of making expendable for the life of many, calls for more than a passing attention. The rubric therefore requires that "silence shall be kept for a space."

---

54. Note that all references to the elements from the Words of Institution to the end of the Prayer are capitalized.

Just as there should be no long interruption between the Offertory and the Giving of Thanks, so there should not be extended pre-Communion devotions separating the Breaking of the Bread from the Communion. We have attempted a new approach to Communion—one that is less penitential and more expectantly joyous. Hence with some reluctance we have omitted the familiar Prayer of Humble Access, since its principal themes have been taken care of elsewhere in the service—in the Prayers of Intercession and in the conclusion of the Consecration Prayer. In its place we have put responsive anthems that summon the congregation to the feast with joy and thanksgiving, and link the Eucharistic climax to the Easter mystery. The versicles from 1 Corinthians 5:7-8 recall the Easter anthem (Prayer Book, page 162). Their use here was suggested by the paraphrase in the First Prayer Book of 1549 at this place. The *Benedictus qui venit* has its ancient place as a pre-Communion acclamation of the Lord who comes to us in this intimate meeting.[55] The invitation to Communion combines the primitive "Holy things to the holy," so characteristic of the Eastern rites, with the theme of our Prayer Book sentences of administration. The general rubrics allow also a hymn or anthem at the Communion time, and here the popular Agnus Dei may be sung or other suitable hymns of varying approaches of devotion. We have thus attempted to leave flexible the moods and emphases of access to Communion, placing over them a few brief acclamations that define the festal nature of the Banquet. We believe that Christians should be happy about the reconciliation of Communion.

The words of administration have been shortened, so that they may be said to each communicant without prolonging the time of Communion. From our limited experiment with them, we have found them less monotonous and tedious than the shorter form provided in *Prayer Book Studies IV*.

We have continued the directives of Study IV concerning Intinction, Reservation, and Ablutions, since they seem to have been received with general satisfaction.

The directive concerning reconsecration is new, and to some may appear to be a startling innovation. There is little or no evidence about such a practice in ancient and medieval times, since the need for reconsecration would be unlikely to occur. In the ancient Church, the loaves were larger and could easily be divided into smaller pieces; and the consecrated Chalice was poured into larger cups containing unconsecrated wine, for purposes of Communion. During medieval times, the Communion of the people became infrequent. Extra hosts, as needed,

---

55. We recognize that the developed liturgies of East and West, and those Anglican rites which have restored the *Benedictus qui venit*, place it after the *Sanctus*. But the oldest sources use it as a Communion acclamation. Our experiments with *Prayer Book Studies IV* and this draft have convinced us of its appropriateness at this place. See *Prayer Book Studies IV*, Vol. 1, pp. 297-303.

were supplied from the reserved Sacrament, and from the twelfth century on the Chalice was withdrawn altogether from the people.[56]

Thus the problem became acute only at the time of the Reformation, with the increasing numbers of communicants and the more frequent occasions when they were encouraged to receive. Moreover the chalices inherited from the medieval Church were often too small for administering the consecrated Wine to a large congregation. Probably for this reason, *The Order of the Communion* (1548) provided for a reconsecration of the wine alone by reciting the second half of the Words of Institution. But no provision was made for supplementary consecration in the Books of 1549 and 1552.[57] The Scottish Book of 1637, followed by the English 1662 Book, directed a supplementary consecration of either element by the Words of Institution alone.

The Scottish Non-Jurors in their rite of 1764, influenced as they were by the Eastern emphasis upon the consecratory character of the Invocation, introduced the provision of supplementary consecration by recital of the Institution, Oblation, and Invocation paragraphs of the Consecration Prayer. From them the custom passed to the American Church, and in recent times to many other Anglican liturgies—in varying combinations of their revised Consecration Prayers, and with provision in some cases for reconsecration of a single element.[58] A few Anglican liturgies have no directives at all. The Liturgy of the Church of South India allows reconsecration either by use of the Words of Institution, or by a factual statement: "Obeying the command of our Lord Jesus Christ, we take this bread (wine) to be set apart for his holy use, in the name of the Father and of the Son and of the Holy Spirit. Amen."

In the light of these uncertainties in our tradition, the Commission has suggested in this draft what it believes to be a simple and sufficient method of supplementary consecration that avoids the cumbersome method now in use. It is a

---

56. Medieval Missals and Canons were more concerned with the problem of defect or accident with regard to the elements to be consecrated. As one would expect, the recital of the Words of Institution was considered sufficient for the consecration of proper or newly supplied elements. See the evidence in W. E. Scudamore, *Notitia Eucharistica*, 2nd ed., (London: Rivingtons,1876), pp. 760 ff. Cf. also *Dictionnaire de droit canonique*, ed. by R. Naz, (Paris, 1957), VI, 862-63.

57. Scudamore, *Notitia Eucharistica*, 2nd ed., (London: Rivingtons,1876), pp. 762-73, cites the case of a priest in the time of Elizabeth I, who was condemned by the High Commission for not consecrating new wine supplied for Communion. Some of the Continental Reformers opposed reconsecration. In a communication of Peter Martyr to Bucer, concerning the 1549 Book's provision for reservation of the Sacrament for the sick, he wrote: "the words of the Supper belong more to the man than to the bread, or to the wine. . . . And it is really amazing how they dislike saying those words in the presence of the sick man, to whom they are especially profitable, when they are willing to repeat the same [words] uselessly when during communion in the church the wine happens to run short in the cup—[uselessly,] since the persons who are present and receive the sacraments have already heard them." Quoted in C. H. Smyth, *Cranmer and the Reformation under Edward VI* (Cambridge University Press, 1926), pp. 243-44.

58. See the important summary in Wigan, *The Liturgy in English*, pp. 252-54, which supplements Scudamore, *op. cit.*

brief prayer addressed to God—not a statement or a formula—that asks specifically for the sanctification of the additional element or elements, with a Trinitarian reference, and with a positive acknowledgment of the result desired by such sanctification. It is thus a synopsis of the entire Consecration Prayer.[59]

9. The Final Thanksgiving and Dismissal

The climax of the Liturgy, both formally and psychologically, is Communion. Almost all of the comments sent to the Commission regarding *Prayer Book Studies IV* favored a shortening of the post-Communion. In many of our parishes this has happened at most celebrations by the dropping of the *Gloria* and substitution of a doxology or short hymn. The experiments with this draft at our Commission meetings have confirmed our continuing assent to this overwhelming desire to let the service end quickly after Communion.

We have revised slightly the present final Thanksgiving, chiefly in matters of style, and made it a corporate act—hence the capitalizations at the beginning of phrases. The practice is already very common today of congregations reciting this prayer with the celebrant, after the analogy of the General Thanksgiving at the conclusion of the Daily Offices. It is responsive to an instinctive desire of the people to express audibly their praise for God's grace and gifts. And it is all the more needful in this draft inasmuch as the *Gloria* has been transferred to the introductory portion of the rite.

The ancient liturgies concluded the Eucharist with a dismissal (usually given by the Deacon), comparable to the dismissal of the catechumens after the Ministry of the Word. The Communion itself was considered the final Blessing of the service. At a later time, when frequency of communion by the laity began to decline, it became customary for the Bishop or celebrant to bless the non-communicating faithful—often just before Communion—as a sort of substitute for their Communion. After the rite was over, the Bishop would give a personal blessing to the people as he passed on his way out of the church. This final blessing was added to the Latin rite in the Middle Ages, and extended as a privilege of the priest-celebrant. But the ancient dismissal (the *Ite missa est*) remained as the formal conclusion of the liturgy. The priestly blessing was an appendage, and continued to function as a substitute for a largely non-communicating congregation.

The early Prayer Books dropped the dismissal and kept the Blessing (enriching it by an opening "Peace" from Philippians 4:7). This has been characteristic of all Anglican rites to the present time.

---

59. The problem usually occurs with insufficient, consecrated Wine. The Commission has not felt it expedient to adopt the suggestion of some that the Chalice be "increased" either by adding water (for which there is no precedent) or by the addition of unconsecrated wine (for which there is good ancient precedent). We have no clear tradition in our Anglican Churches regarding a consecration by commixture.

There is, however, a distinct trend in recent revisions and experimental rites to return to the ancient custom—to consider Communion as the Blessing, and to end the liturgy with a Dismissal. This is true of the Taizé rite, *A Liturgy for Africa*, and the new proposal of the Church of New Zealand. We have decided to join this "trend," for we believe that a Blessing placed so nearly after Communion is redundant. But we have allowed the Bishop when present to dismiss the people as he wishes, with or without a personal blessing. The form we have chosen is a shorter version of the Dismissal provided in the English 1928 Book for the conclusion of Confirmation. It is reminiscent of several New Testament passages: 2 Timothy 2:1, Ephesians 6:10, 1 Thessalonians 5:21, Acts 2:46. The force of the Dismissal is that it sends the Eucharistic assembly out on its mission.

10. Other Considerations

A. Language

There has been much discussion throughout the Church of late, reflected in our own Commission's concerns, about the modernization of the English of the Prayer Book. The problem of Prayer Book English lies much deeper than its scattered archaisms, whether in the meaning of individual words and phrases or in quaint and outmoded grammatical constructions. (Many of these were changed in *Prayer Book Studies IV*, not to speak of a number of revisions in this area made in the 1928 Book.) It involves at least the predominantly "Latin" style of the sentence-structure—for example, the Collects, with their involved subordinate clauses, or the Consecration Prayer, with its parentheses and participial constructions. The Prayer Book prefers long sentences, which, however beautiful in balance, modulation, and rhythm, make difficult a comprehension by modern congregations of its wondrous communication of the gospel. As the months and years go by, more and more clergymen testify to the difficulty of more and more of our people in grasping the teaching of the Prayer Book.[60]

We have officially as a Church acknowledged the problem by canonical changes that allow the use of the Revised or the Revised Standard Versions of the Bible and The New English Bible (New Testament) to be read in the Daily Offices. But in the lectionary of the Eucharist we are still bound to the Authorized (or King James) Version, and in the Psalter and many of the Scriptural sentences of the liturgy to the Great Bible of 1539. In the 1928 Book we admitted many new prayers written by persons living in our own century—albeit in the

---

60. We now have a thorough and scientific study of Prayer Book language and style in Stella Brook's *The Language of the Book of Common Prayer* (Oxford University Press, 1965). This work should be required reading for all revisers of the liturgy.

older form of sentence-structure of the Collects—without any feeling of their inappropriateness or disturbance to the older materials.[61]

It is only fair to acknowledge also, with humility and gratitude, that the liturgical revisions now going on in other Churches are pressing us in the Episcopal Church to a more critical examination of our inheritance. Our Prayer Book is no longer "copied" by the Protestant Churches in their recovery of liturgical worship. The English vernacular now introduced in the Roman Catholic Church has been a shock—perhaps a providential stimulus. There is no good reason to suppose that there is a single, proper "style" of liturgical expression, much less any particular value in every Church's exhibiting the same "style" in its liturgical vernacular. Today, however, the increasing number of opportunities and occasions of an ecumenical sharing in worship among the several traditions calls for some common formularies if we are to avoid confusion and frustration. Especially is this true of those texts which we all possess and constantly use, such as the Lord's Prayer, the Creeds, the great hymns of the Gloria and Te Deum, and doubtless also the Psalter. A great step forward in this direction has been the official approval by the Roman Catholic Church of the Revised Standard Version of the Bible.[62]

The hold of our Anglican inheritance of liturgical speech from the sixteenth century is very strong among us, and understandably so. Hence most Anglican revisions in recent years have not risked any tampering with it, other than necessary changes in words that have lost their original meaning or reference, or in awkward grammatical constructions no longer in common use. More surprising perhaps is the hesitancy of these revisions in finding fresh expressions for certain themes and subjects, such as the contemporary relations of the Church to the State, and the mission of the Church in our modern international, technological, and urban society. Only *A Liturgy for Africa* has ventured in this uncharted territory, and also, with a startling directness of language, the new proposed liturgy for New Zealand.

In this proposal, we have endeavored to take several steps towards a more contemporary language (if not style), and a wider outlook towards the world about us today:

a. We have retained the archaic use of the second person singular (Thou, thee, thy) in all formularies addressed directly to God. But we have consistently

---

61. For their sources, see James Arthur Muller, *Who Wrote the New Prayers in the Prayer Book?* (Church Historical Society Publications, No. 20, 1946).

62. At the present writing plans are under way for some conference and consultation on the matter of the vernacular: 1) Among Roman Catholics, Lutherans, and Anglicans, with respect to the common forms of their related liturgies; and 2) in projected study by the newly formed Commission on Worship of the Churches involved in the Consultation on Church Union. The Standing Liturgical Commission hopes to encourage, and participate in, all such ventures.

substituted the modern "you" and "yours" in all exchanges with or biddings to the congregation. This follows the usage of the Revised Standard Version.

b. We have sought to eliminate archaic words, such as "quick" for "living," "very" for "true" or "truly," "Ghost" for "Spirit." A few remain, however: for example, "Very God of Very God" in the Creed, and "meet" in the *Sursum corda*.

c. By use of verse lines, paragraphing, and shorter sentences, we have sought to lighten some of the load on the attention and comprehension of the worshipper.

d. Biblical citations have been generally made from the Revised Standard Version. Where we have departed from it, the reason has been one of rhythm of phrase.

e. We have introduced into the Prayers of intercession new themes, particularly with reference to men's vocations in the world of today, and to the proper use of God's created order. The penitential petition has a wider range than sins of commission.

f. We have sought to increase the corporate and dramatic character of the rite, and to reenforce the note of joy and praise.

It is essential to the effectiveness of this proposed rite that the Biblical lessons be drawn from a contemporary translation of the Scriptures. We therefore propose that the Revised Standard Version, at least, be permitted for these lessons in any experimental use.

B. Length of the Service

The pace and taste of modern life demand shorter services than those enjoyed by our forefathers. And in many parishes and missions, the very practical problem of schedules for several congregations on a Sunday morning necessitate attention to the problem. Others see a need for a short Eucharist on weekdays that can be managed within the limited period of business recess for the lunch hour. On page 23 of this Study we have given a table that illustrates the flexibility of our present proposal.

The apparent, undue length of our present rite is partly a matter of structure. There are too many long "monologues" by the celebrant, not enough action and corporate response by the people. We believe that our proposal largely overcomes this "psychological" tedium. For attention and interest are not so much due to length of time as to the impact of movement and participation. It is quite possible that the present rite when celebrated with hymns and a sermon, and perhaps with the additional Old Testament lesson, will take as much time as the present Prayer Book liturgy. But it will not seem to be so long.

In most cases, the time span of the liturgy is directly related to the numbers who must be communicated. In proportion to the total service, the Communion is likely to be the "longest stretch" and hence the portion of the service that is most wearisome to congregations. This is not so much a liturgical problem, as it is an engineering one. It can be resolved only by an increase of assisting ministers, or by better deployment of the interior space where the communicants gather. Wider aisles, more open and free circulation about the sanctuary are helps. The Roman Catholics, who have an even greater problem than we do, because of the larger numbers of communicants, are experimenting with the use of several "stations" (often side altars) in addition to the main altar where people can receive Communion. They have also introduced the ceremonial of standing to receive. Should they restore the Cup to the people—and this is not unlikely—it is generally thought that they will do so by way of Intinction, a method used in many of our parishes.

C. *The Use of Silence*

We have made provision for two specific places where silence is to be kept "for a space"—immediately before the General Confession, and at the time of the Fraction. The values of periods of silence in corporate worship need no argument. They can also be dramatic moments of punctuation, as is the rest in music. Of course, officiants can find other suitable places when desired—in *ex tempore* prayers after the Sermon, between the several intercessions, during the Offertory or the Communion time when the actions may speak louder than words.

D. *The Ministers*

Attention has already been called to the general rubric on page 2. We would simply underscore here our aim of utilizing more imaginatively, and in accordance with ancient tradition, a wider ministry of both clergy and laity in the Eucharist. In particular, we have sought to restore the time-honored ministry of the Diaconate—especially so, now that so many of our parishes have a regular service of one or more Deacons. We believe also that laymen should have responsibilities as lectors, bearers of the oblations, and, where effective, leaders in prayer. Above all, the Bishop should be acknowledged as the liturgical president and primary teacher of his flock, whenever it is possible for him to be present in the Eucharistic assembly.

Appendices

I. The Structure and Contents of the Eucharistic Liturgy

[A Document of an Inter-Anglican Committee by The Most Rev. Dr. Leslie Brown, Archbishop of Uganda.]

The Liturgical Consultation in Toronto decided to implement Lambeth Resolution 76 and the Archbishop of Rupert's Land, the Bishop of Singapore and

Malaya, Dr. Massey Shepherd and I were chosen "to prepare recommendations for the structure of the Holy Communion service which could be taken into consideration by any Church or Province revising its Eucharistic rites, and which would both conserve the doctrinal balance of the Anglican tradition and take account of present liturgical knowledge." Agreement has now been reached on an outline of the structure and contents of the Eucharistic liturgy.

There are five phases in the celebration of the full Eucharistic rite. They are:

1. The Preparation
2. The Service of the Word of God
3. The Great Intercession
4. The Service of the Lord's Supper
5. The Dismissal

1. *The Preparation:* This section should not be too long, but must be adequate for a congregation which may have no other opportunity of confession and explicitly and liturgically receiving God's forgiveness. This starting section ought to be, following Cranmer, subdued in tone, but ending with praise and adoration before hearing the Word of God in the next section. A suggested order is:

> A prayer and psalm or hymn of approach;
> Confession and Absolution;
> Psalm (or portion thereof) or hymn of praise.

The first prayer might well be the so-called "Collect for Purity." An appropriate Psalm of approach might be Psalm 43, 95, or 100. The Commandments in some form or *Kyrie* could be used before the Confession. The hymn of praise at the end might be *Gloria in excelsis* or *Te Deum.*

The Preparation has to be somewhat flexible depending on local needs.

2. *The Service of the Word of God.* This should include a prayer focusing the thoughts of the congregation on the message God is giving through His Word on that particular day, and readings from the Old Testament, or a sermon followed by the recitation of the Creed. Psalmody or canticles can well be included in this part of the service between the readings.

3. *The Great Intercession.* This should normally be in litany form and should be not only for the Church but for the world which the Church is called to serve.

4. *The Service of the Lord's Supper.* This should include the placing of the gifts on the Lord's Table and the ancient form of Sursum corda. The consecration prayer should be in the form of a thanksgiving for creation and for God's mighty acts in Christ and in sending the Holy Spirit. There should be a recital of the words

and acts of the Lord at the Last Supper and a prayer for the communicants. The Lord's Prayer makes a fitting ending to this prayer. The Breaking of the Bread follows, and the Communion of clergy and people.

5. *The Dismissal.* The Dismissal should be short. There seems a psychological need for some corporate expression of praise when all have received Communion and returned to their places and there should be a simple sending out, without a blessing.

February, 1965

II. Recent Consecration Prayers

1. The Apostolic Tradition *of Hippolytus*

This work is ancient, and comes from the Church in Rome about the year A.D. 200. But our knowledge of it has only been recovered in modern times. Its Eucharistic rite has influenced all recent revisions since the 1930's. The following text of the Consecration Prayer is taken from the edition of Burton Scott Easton, *The Apostolic Tradition of Hippolytus* (Cambridge University Press, 1934). It was used (with adaptations) for the 19th Ecumenical Student Conference on the Christian World Mission, of the National Christian Student Federation, held at Ohio University, Athens, Ohio, December 27, 1963-January 2, 1964.

[Sursum corda]:

We give thee thanks, O God, through thy beloved Servant Jesus Christ, whom at the end of time thou didst send to us a Saviour and Redeemer and the Messenger of thy counsel. Who is thy Word, inseparable from thee; through whom thou didst make all things and in whom thou art well pleased. Whom thou didst send from heaven into the womb of the Virgin, and who, dwelling within her, was made flesh, and was manifested as thy Son, being born of the Holy Spirit and the Virgin. Who, fulfilling thy will, and winning for himself a holy people, spread out his hands when he came to suffer, that by his death he might set free them who believed in thee.

Who when he was betrayed to his willing death, that he might bring to nought death, and break the bonds of the devil, and tread hell under foot, and give light to the righteous, and set up a boundary post, and manifest his resurrection, taking bread and giving thanks to thee said: Take, eat: this is my body which is broken for you. And likewise also the cup, saying: This is my blood, which is shed for you. As often as ye perform this, perform my memorial.

Having in memory, therefore, his death and resurrection, we offer to thee the bread and the cup, yielding thee thanks, because thou hast counted us worthy to stand before thee and to minister to thee.

And we pray thee that thou wouldest send thy Holy Spirit upon the offerings of thy holy church; that thou, gathering them into one, wouldest grant to all thy saints who partake to be filled with the Holy Spirit, that their faith may be confirmed in truth, that we may praise and glorify thee. Through thy Servant Jesus Christ, through whom be to thee glory and honour, with the Holy Spirit in the holy church, both now and always and world without end. Amen.

2. The Church of South India

"The Service of the Lord's Supper or The Holy Eucharist" of the Church of South India was first published in 1950. It has been several times revised.

The definitive edition is contained in *The Book of Common Worship As Authorized by the Synod 1962* (Oxford University Press, 1963). It is also included in Wigan's *The Liturgy in English* (see Bibliography).

[Sursum corda.

Preface:] It is verily meet, right, and our bounden duty, . . . Almighty and Everlasting God;

THROUGH Jesus Christ thy Son our Lord, through whom thou didst create the heavens and the earth and all that in them is, and didst make man in thine own image, and when he had fallen into sin didst redeem him to be the first fruits of a new creation.

Therefore with angels . . . saying [Sanctus and Benedictus].

TRULY holy, truly blessed art thou, O heavenly Father, who of thy tender love . . . [continues through Words of Institution as in the Prayer Book].

Amen. Thy death, O Lord, we commemorate, thy resurrection we confess, and thy second coming we await. Glory be to thee, O Christ.

Wherefore, O Father, having in remembrance the precious death and passion, and glorious resurrection and ascension, of thy Son our Lord, we thy servants do this in remembrance of him, as he hath commanded, until his coming again, giving thanks to thee for the perfect redemption which thou hast wrought for us in him.

We give thanks to thee, we praise thee, we glorify thee, O Lord our God.

And we most humbly beseech thee, O merciful Father, to sanctify with thy Holy Spirit us and these thine own gifts of bread and wine, that the bread which we break may be the communion of the body of Christ, and the cup which we bless the communion of the blood of Christ. Grant that, being joined together in him, we may all attain to the unity of the faith, and may grow up in all things unto him who is the Head, even Christ, our Lord, by whom and with whom in the unity of the Holy Spirit, all honour and glory be unto thee, O Father Almighty, world without end. Amen.

[Lord's Prayer.]

3. The Reformed Church of France

The National Synod of the Reformed Church of France approved for trial use in 1948 the Sunday Service (*Service dominical*), which was revised in 1951. The French text may be found in: *Eglise Reformée de France: Liturgie* (Paris: Editions Berger-Levrault, 1963), p. 39. The English translation is from *Venite Adoremus* (Geneva: World's Student Christian Federation Prayer Book, 1951), p. 177.

[Lord's Prayer.
Sursum corda, Preface, Sanctus, Benedictus.
Words of Institution—according to 1 Cor. 11:23-26.]

HOLY and righteous Father, in commemorating here the one perfect sacrifice made by our Lord Jesus Christ once for all upon the Cross, and while we joyfully await his coming, we offer ourselves to thee as a living and holy sacrifice.

O thou, who knowest the hearts of men, purify us now and renew in us the assurance of thy pardon and the presence of our Risen Lord, that he may live in us and we in him.

Send down upon us thy Holy Spirit, so that in eating this bread and drinking this cup we may partake of the body and blood of our Lord Jesus Christ, since it is through him that thou createst, sanctifiest, dost raise to life and bless, and dost give us all good things.

Even as the ears of corn which were once scattered through the fields and the grapes which grew in the vineyards are now brought together on this table in the bread and wine, so may thy Church, O Lord, be soon gathered together from the ends of the earth into thy kingdom. Come, Lord Jesus! Amen.

4. The Community of Taizé, France

The Taizé Community is a Protestant monastic Order, founded in 1948, whose members are especially concerned with Christian unity and mission. Their *Liturgie Eucharistique* (1959) has been published in English translation: *The Eucharistic Liturgy of Taizé*, With an Introductory Essay by Max Thurian, Translated by John Arnold (London: The Faith Press, 1962). (For the following, see pp. 255-256.)

[Sursum corda, Preface, Sanctus, Benedictus:]

Epiclesis

OUR Father, God of the hosts of heaven, fill with thy glory this our sacrifice of praise.

Bless, perfect and accept this offering as the figure of the one and only sacrifice of our Lord.

Send thy Holy Spirit upon us and our Eucharist: Consecrate this bread to be the Body of Christ and this cup to be the Blood of Christ; that the Creator Spirit may fulfil the word of thy well-beloved Son.

Institution

WHO, in the same night, . . .

Memorial

WHEREFORE, O Lord, we make before thee the memorial of the Incarnation and the Passion of thy Son, his Resurrection from his sojourn with the dead, his Ascension into glory in the heavens, his perpetual intercession for us; we await and pray for his return.

All things come of thee and our only offering is to recall thy gifts and marvellous works.

Moreover we present to thee, O Lord of glory, as our thanksgiving and intercession, the signs of the eternal Sacrifice of Christ, unique and perfect, living and holy, the Bread of life which cometh down from heaven and the cup of the feast in thy Kingdom.

In thy love and mercy, accept our praise and our prayers in Christ, as thou wast pleased to accept the gifts of thy servant Abel the righteous, the sacrifices of our Father Abraham, and of Melchizedek, thy high Priest.

Invocation

ALMIGHTY God, we beseech thee, that this prayer may be borne by the hand of thine angel to thy altar in thy presence on high; and when we receive, communicating at this Table, the Body and Blood of thy Son, may we be filled with the Holy Spirit and endowed with grace and heavenly blessings, through Christ our Saviour.

Conclusion

BY whom, O Lord, thou ever dost create, sanctify, quicken, bless and give us all thy benefits.

By whom, and with whom, and in whom, be unto thee, O Father Almighty, in the unity of the Holy Spirit, all honour and glory, world without end. *Amen.*

[Lord's Prayer.]

5. *The Lusitanian Church, Catholic, Apostolic, Evangelical*

The Lusitanian Church of Portugal is one of the Churches of the Wider Episcopal Fellowship, in full communion with the Episcopal Church. For several years it has been engaged in revising its liturgy. The *Eucaristia ou Ceia do Senhor*, authorized for experimental use, was published in Porto: Imprensa Social, 1963. The following translation is from "The Order for the Eucharist or Lord's Supper According to the Revised Rite of the Lusitanian Church," Prepared by The Diocese of East Carolina, Wilmington, N.C.

[Sursum corda, Preface, Sanctus.]

ALL glory and thanksgiving unto thee O almighty God, maker of heaven and earth; who by thy great love didst send thy Son, who took upon himself human nature and wrought our redemption. And we do give thanks unto thee that by his one oblation of himself once finished upon the cross, he did offer a perfect and sufficient sacrifice for the sins of the whole world. And likewise, we give thee thanks because he did institute and in his holy Gospel command us to continue this perpetual memorial of his redeeming sacrifice, until his coming again.

FOR in the night . . . [After each of the Words of Institution, the congregation responds Amen.]

THEREFORE, O heavenly Father, we thy humble servants, according to the commandment of thy beloved Son, desire to show forth his death until his coming again; remembering his blessed passion and precious death, his mighty resurrection and glorious ascension; and we render unto thee most hearty thanks for the innumerable benefits procured unto us by the same. And now we present unto thy divine majesty these thy gifts, humbly beseeching thee to pour thy Holy Spirit upon the oblation of thy Church, that we who come to thy Table may worthily receive the most sacred Body and Blood of thy dear Son, the holy Bread of everlasting life and the cup of eternal salvation; that we may be filled with thy grace and heavenly benediction, and made one body in Jesus Christ our Saviour.

MERCIFULLY accept, we pray thee, this our sacrifice of praise and thanksgiving, granting that by the merits and death of thy Son Jesus Christ and by faith in his blood, we and thy whole Church may obtain remission of our sins and all other benefits of his passion, THROUGH JESUS CHRIST OUR LORD; BY WHOM AND WITH WHOM, IN THE UNITY OF THE HOLY GHOST, ALL HONOR AND GLORY BE UNTO THEE, O FATHER ALMIGHTY, WORLD WITHOUT END. *Amen.*

[Lord's Prayer.]

6. The Lutheran Church in America

Eight Lutheran bodies in the United States cooperated in the production of a common Service Book and Hymnal, which was finally issued by their respective publishing houses in 1958, after ten years of trial use of the Holy Communion rite.[63]

[Sursum corda, Preface, Sanctus, Benedictus.]
HOLY art thou, Almighty and merciful God. Holy art thou, and great is the Majesty of thy glory.
Thou didst so love the world as to give thine only-begotten Son, that whosoever believeth in him might not perish, but have everlasting life; Who, having come into the world to fulfill for us thy holy will and to accomplish all things for our salvation, IN THE NIGHT ..
REMEMBERING, therefore, his salutary precept, his life-giving Passion and Death, his glorious Resurrection and Ascension and the promise of his coming again, we give thanks to thee, O Lord God Almighty, not as we ought but as we are able; and we beseech thee mercifully to accept our praise and thanksgiving, and with thy Word and Holy Spirit to bless us, thy servants, and these thine own gifts of bread and wine, so that we and all who partake thereof may be filled with heavenly benediction and grace, and, receiving the remission of sins, be sanctified in soul and body, and have our portion with all thy saints.
And unto thee, O God, Father, Son, and Holy Spirit, be all honor and glory in thy holy Church, world without end. Amen.
[Lord's Prayer.]

7. *The Presbyterian Churches in America*

The Joint Committee on Worship, established in 1957, represents a common endeavor of the Presbyterian Church in the United States and the United Presbyterian Church in the United States of America. In 1959 it published a revised Directory for Worship, and is now engaged on the basis of principles laid out in the Directory upon a revision of the Book of Common Worship. In 1964 the Committee issued for experimental use a "Service for the Lord's Day and Lectionary for the Christian Year" (Philadelphia: Westminster Press).

[Sursum corda.]
O HOLY Lord, Father Almighty, Everlasting God:
We thank thee for commanding light to shine out of darkness, for stretching out the heavens, and laying the foundations of the earth; for making all things through thy Word. We thank thee for creating us in thine image and for

---

63. It may be noted that classic Lutheran rites have traditionally contained no formula between Sanctus and Lord's Prayer except the Words of Institution. This revision marks a major change in Lutheran Eucharistic prayers. The above form is a skillful weaving together of ideas and phrases, whose sources are: *The Apostolic Tradition* of Hippolytus, the Liturgy of St. Chrysostom, the Canon of the Roman Mass, and the Consecration Prayer of the (American) Book of Common Prayer.

keeping us in thy steadfast love. We praise thee for calling us to be thy people, for revealing thy purpose in the Law and the Prophets, and for dealing patiently with us in our disobedience.

Great and wonderful are thy deeds. Just and true are thy ways. We glorify thy name, O Lord, for thou alone art holy:

[Sanctus.]

ALL glory be to thee, O God our Father, for Jesus Christ thy Son, who was born of Mary and lived among us full of grace and truth, who died on the cross in obedience to thee, and rose from the dead by thy power to be Lord of creation and head of the church.

We thank thee that the Lord Jesus on the night when he was betrayed ... [Words of Institution.]

Remembering the Lord Jesus Christ, we take this bread and this cup, proclaiming his death for the sins of the world, and confessing his resurrection until he comes again.

[Benedictus.]

GRANT, O Lord, that thy Holy Spirit may come among us; that the bread we break and the cup we share may be for us a means of grace; that, receiving them, we may be made one with Christ and he with us, and remain faithful members of his body until we feast with him anew in his Kingdom.

O God, who hast called us from death to life, we offer ourselves to thee, and with thy church through all ages, we thank and praise thee for thy redeeming love in Christ Jesus our Lord. Amen.

[Lord's Prayer.]

8. A Liturgy for Africa

In 1961 the Archbishops of the five Provinces of the Anglican Communion in Africa authorized the preparation of a common liturgy—primarily for use in the African vernaculars. This Liturgy was referred to the Liturgical Commissions of all the Anglican Churches, and discussed at the Consultation held following the Anglican Congress in Toronto, August 1963. It was published as *A Liturgy for Africa* (London: S.P.C.K., 1964).

[Sursum corda.]

IT is most meet and right that we should at all times and in all places give thanks unto thee, O Lord, Holy Father, Almighty, Everlasting God, through Jesus Christ our Lord, through whom thou hast made and dost sustain the worlds. We praise thee for the order of thy creation, and for all the material blessings of our life.

But chiefly we praise thee for thy love for fallen man in giving thy Son to take our nature upon him, to die for our sins and to be raised from the dead for our justification. We praise thee, O God, who hast set him in glory at thy right hand, where he ever lives to make intercession for us, who draw near to thee through him.

Again, we praise thee, O Father, for sending to us the promised Holy Spirit, through whom thou dost pour out upon us thy manifold gifts of grace and hast made us a royal priesthood, to set forth thy praises who hast called us out of darkness into the glory of thy light.

Therefore with angels ...

[Sanctus.]

ALL glory be to thee, O heavenly Father, who in thy tender mercy didst give thine own Son Jesus Christ that all who believe in him might have eternal life. Hear us, O merciful Father, we humbly beseech thee, and grant that we receiving this Bread and this Cup, in remembrance of the death and passion of thy Son our Saviour Jesus Christ, may be partakers of his most blessed Body and Blood: for in the same night that he gave himself to death ...

[Words of Institution.]

His death, O Father, we proclaim. His resurrection we confess. His coming we await. Glory to thee, O Lord.

WHEREFORE, O Father, we do this as thy Son commanded, offering to thee, with this holy Bread and Cup, our praise and thanksgiving for his one sacrifice once offered upon the cross, for his mighty resurrection and glorious ascension. Accept us in him, we beseech thee, and grant that all we who are partakers of this holy communion may be filled with thy Holy Spirit and made one in thy holy Church, the body of thy Son Jesus Christ our Lord, through whom and in whom, in the unity of the Holy Spirit, all honour and glory be to thee, O Father Almighty, for ever and ever. Amen.

[Lord's Prayer.]

9. Diocese Of Hong Kong and Macao

The following is taken from "An Order for Holy Communion" authorized for experimental use in the Diocese of Hong Kong and Macao for bilingual Celebrations and other special occasions, with the concurrence of the Bishops of the Council of the Church of South East Asia. It is published by The Anglican Literature Society, Hong Kong, December 1965.

[Sursum corda.]

It is very meet ...

Who having loved his own that were in the world loved them unto the end: and on the night before he suffered, sitting at meat with his disciples, did institute these holy mysteries: That we redeemed by his death and quickened by his resurrection might be partakers of his divine nature.

Therefore with angels ... [Sanctus; Benedictus.]
TRULY holy, truly blessed art thou, O heavenly Father, who of thy tender love towards mankind didst give thine only Son Jesus Christ to take our nature upon him and to suffer death upon the cross for our redemption; who made there ... [continues as in Prayer Book through the Words of institution].
WHEREFORE, O Lord and heavenly Father, we thy humble servants, having in remembrance the precious death and passion of thy dear Son, his mighty resurrection and glorious ascension, do celebrate and set forth before thy Divine Majesty with these thy holy gifts, the memorial which he hath willed us to make, rendering unto thee most hearty thanks for the innumerable benefits which he hath procured unto us.
WE most humbly beseech thee, O merciful Father, to sanctify with thy Holy Spirit us and these thy gifts of bread and wine, that the bread which we break may be the communion of the body of Christ, and the cup which we bless the communion of the blood of Christ.
AND we entirely desire thy fatherly goodness to accept this our sacrifice of praise and thanksgiving; most humbly beseeching thee to grant, that by the merits and death of thy Son Jesus Christ, and through faith in his blood, we and all thy whole Church may obtain remission of our sins, and all other benefits of his passion.

And here we offer and present unto thee, O Lord, ourselves, ... [as in Prayer Book, through the *Amen.*]

[Lord's Prayer after the Communion.]

10. The Church of England

The Church of England Liturgical Commission has produced "An Order for Holy Communion," which has been amended and passed by the Convocations and is to be considered by the House of Laity on February 13, 1967, with a view to authorization for experimental use for three years from that date. (London: S.P.C.K., December, 1966.)

[Sursum corda.]
IT is very meet ... through Jesus Christ, thine only Son, our Lord; Because through him thou hast created all things from the beginning, and fashioned us men in thine own image;
Through him thou didst redeem us from the slavery of sin, giving him to be born as man, to die upon the cross, and to rise again for us;
Through him thou hast made us a people for thine own possession, exalting him to thy right hand on high, and sending forth through him thy holy and life-giving Spirit;

Through him therefore, with angels ... [Sanctus].

Hear us, O Father, through Christ thy Son our Lord; through him accept our sacrifice of praise; and grant that these gifts of bread and wine may be unto us his body and blood;

Who in the same night ... [Words of Institution].

Wherefore, O Lord, having in remembrance his saving passion, his resurrection from the dead, and his glorious ascension into heaven, and looking for the coming of his kingdom, [we offer unto thee this/give thanks to thee over] bread and this cup; and we pray thee to accept this our duty and service, and grant that we may so eat and drink these holy things in the presence of thy divine majesty, that we may be filled with thy grace and heavenly blessing;

Through the same Christ our Lord, by whom, and with whom, and in whom, in the unity of the Holy Spirit, all honour and glory be unto thee, O Father Almighty, from the whole company of earth and heaven, throughout all ages, world without end. *Amen.*

[Benedictus...]

[Lord's Prayer, immediately before Communion.]

11. "An Experimental Liturgy"

One of the most influential essays in liturgical revision has been the study *An Experimental Liturgy*, by G. Cope, J. G. Davies, and D. A. Tytler (Ecumenical Studies in Worship No. 3; London: Lutterworth Press; Richmond: John Knox Press, 1959).

[Sursum corda.]

Holy art thou, eternal Father; holy in thy redeeming Son; holy in thy life-giving Spirit. Therefore with Angels ... [Sanctus.] ...

It is very meet right and our bounden duty that we should at all times and in all places give thanks unto thee, O Lord, Holy Father, Almighty, Everlasting God, through thy beloved Son Jesus Christ, by whom thou madest all things, whom thou didst send in the fullness of time to take our nature upon him and to suffer death upon the Cross for our redemption.

Who in the same night that he was betrayed ... [Words of Institution.]

Therefore, O Father, we thy humble servants recall the blessed passion and death of thy beloved Son, his mighty resurrection and glorious ascension, until his coming again; and we here present unto thee, through thy Holy Spirit, this bread of eternal life and this cup of everlasting salvation that, being made one Body in him, we may receive the forgiveness of our sins and the joy of thy kingdom;

And we beseech thee to accept this our sacrifice of praise and thanksgiving through the mediation of thy most dearly beloved Son, and so to renew us through thy Holy Spirit that he may bring forth in us the fruits of our redemption, and confirm us unto the end; through him who is the beginning and the end; even Jesus Christ thy Son our Lord, by whom and with whom, in the unity of the Holy Spirit, all honour and glory be unto thee, O Father Almighty, world without end.

Salvation unto God who sitteth upon the throne, and unto the Lamb. Blessing and glory and wisdom and thanksgiving, and honour and power and might be unto our God for ever and ever. Amen.

By the Spirit of adoption we are bold to say,
[The Lord's Prayer.]

12. "An Order of Holy Communion"

In the summer of 1963, Professor Keith Watkins published in *Encounter*, Vol. 24, No. 3, "An Order of Holy Communion for Use Every Sunday," with a symposium of comment. The service was proposed for the use of "free" Churches. The Eucharistic Prayer, pp 312-13, is as follows:

[Sursum corda.]

HOLY art thou, eternal Father; holy in thy redeeming Son; holy in thy life-giving Spirit. Therefore with Angels ... [Sanctus].... .

HOLY Lord, Father Almighty, Everlasting God, we lift up our hearts and praise thee for all thy mercies. We bless thee that through Jesus Christ our Lord thou, the Creator of heaven and earth, didst make us in thine own image; and that, when we had fallen away from thee through sin, thou of thine infinite mercy and love didst send thy Son to be our Savior. We thank thee that we have redemption through his blood, the forgiveness of our sins; that by him we have access to the throne of thy majesty on high, and are made thy children by adoption and grace; and that we are called this day to eat and to drink at this table. For these, and all thy mercies, we laud and magnify thy holy name; and with thy whole church in heaven and on earth, we praise and adore thee.

O GOD our Father, grant unto us, we humbly beseech thee, thy glorious presence, and the powerful working of thy Spirit in us; and so sanctify these elements of bread and wine, and bless thine own ordinance, that we may receive by faith the body and blood of Jesus Christ, crucified for us, and so feed upon him, that he may be one with us, and we with him.

MOST gracious God, accept our sacrifice of praise and thanksgiving, and receive the offering and consecration which we now make of ourselves, our souls and bodies, unto thee; through Jesus our Lord, by whom and with whom, in the unity of the Holy Spirit, all honor and glory be unto thee, O Father Almighty, world without end. Amen.

[Lord's Prayer.]

13. *The Church of the Province of New Zealand*

The General Synod of the Church in the Province of New Zealand authorized in 1966 a revised order of "The Liturgy or Eucharist," for experimental use "subject to the direction of the Bishop of any Diocese." It is the first Anglican liturgy to be phrased in modern contemporary English.

The Lord be with you.
And with you also.
Lift up your hearts.
We lift them to the Lord.
Let us give thanks to the Lord our God.
It is right indeed that we should do so.

It is most right and proper, holy Lord, almighty Father, everlasting God, that we should at all times, and in all places, give thanks to you through Jesus Christ, your only Son, our Lord; through whom you have created all things from the beginning and made man in your own image; through whom in the fullness of time you redeemed us, when we had fallen into sin, giving him to be born as man; to die on the Cross and to rise again for us; setting him in glory at your right hand; through whom you have made us a holy people by sending forth your holy and lifegiving Spirit; through him therefore with the faithful who rest in him and all the glorious company of heaven, joyfully we praise you and say:

Holy, Holy, Holy, Lord God of Hosts, heaven and earth are full of your glory. Glory to you, Lord most high.

Blessed is he who comes in the name of the Lord. Hosanna in the highest.[64]

All glory to you, heavenly Father, who in your tender mercy gave your only Son Jesus Christ that all who believe in him might have eternal life. Hear us, merciful Father, and grant that receiving this bread and this wine in remembrance of the death and passion of your Son our Saviour Jesus Christ, we may be partakers of his most blessed body and blood; who, the night before he gave himself to death, took bread, and when he had given thanks he broke it and gave it to his disciples, and said, Take, eat, this is my body which is given for you; do this in remembrance of me. In the same way after supper he took the cup, and when he had given thanks he gave it to them, and said, Drink this, all of you, for this is my blood of the new covenant which is shed for you and for many, for the forgiveness of sins; do this, as often as you drink it, in remembrance of me.[65]

---

64. The Benedictus is optional.

65. The traditional manual acts of Anglican liturgies are retained during the Words of Institution, except that there is no Fraction at this place.

His death, Father, we show forth, his resurrection we proclaim, his coming we await. Glory to you, Lord most high.

Therefore, Father, we do this as your Son commanded, offering to you our praise and thanksgiving for his one perfect sacrifice made on the cross for the sin of the world, for his mighty resurrection and glorious ascension, which we recall before you in this sacrament of the bread of life and the cup of salvation. Accept us, in him, we pray, with this our sacrifice of praise and thanksgiving, and grant that all we who are partakers of this holy communion may be filled with the Holy Spirit and made one in your holy Church, the body of your Son, Jesus Christ our Lord, through whom and in whom, in the unity of the Holy Spirit, all honour and glory be to you, almighty Father, for ever and ever. *Amen.*
As our Lord has taught us, we say:
[The Lord's Prayer.]

III. A Select Bibliography

Anglican Rites

Brightman, F. E., *The English Rite*. Being a Synopsis of the Sources and Revisions of The Book of Common Prayer. With an Introduction and an Appendix. 2 vols. London: Rivingtons, 1915.

> The standard edition of the texts of the English Prayer Books 1549-1661, with their medieval sources, and detailed notes of changes in all editions to 1662.

McGarvey, William, *Liturgiae Americanae* or The Book of Common Prayer as used in the United States of America ... Philadelphia, 1895.

> A definitive reference to texts of the American Prayer Book, through the revision of 1892.

Wigan, Bernard, *The Liturgy in English*. Second Edition. Oxford, 1964.

> A collation of all Anglican Eucharistic rites in current use, including other English rites in Britain and South India. Supersedes J. H. Arnold, Anglican Liturgies (Oxford, 1939). Since publication there have appeared the following revised Anglican rites:

A Liturgy for Africa. London: S.P.C.K., 1964. [Prepared under the direction of the Archbishops of the five Anglican Provinces in Africa; intended for experimental use as authorized, especially in the African vernaculars.]

An Order for Holy Communion. Authorized for experimental use in the Diocese of Hong Kong and Macao for bilingual Celebrations and other special occasions (with the concurrence of the Bishops of the Council of the Church of South East Asia). Hong Kong: The Anglican Literature Society, 1965.

The Church of England Liturgical Commission, *Alternative Services. Second Series*. Recommended by the Archbishops of Canterbury and York to be Introduced to the Convocations and the House of Laity. London: S.P.C.K., 1965.

The Liturgy or Eucharist of the Church of the Province of New Zealand. An alternative Order approved for experimental use upon certain conditions by the General Synod, 1966. [Printed at Auckland by The Pelorus Press Ltd.]

Various cathedral and college uses in England:

The Holy Communion. Clare College, Cambridge. [For exposition, see J. A. T. Robinson, *Liturgy Coming to Life*; London: Mowbray, 1960.]

The Communion in Coventry Cathedral. Hodder and Stoughton.

Holy Communion in Southwark Cathedral. [Privately printed.]

Semi-official and unofficial revisions by commissions and individuals of the Anglican Communion:

Prayer Book Studies. IV: The Eucharistic Liturgy. The Standing Liturgical Commission of the Protestant Episcopal Church in the United States of America. New York: The Church Pension Fund, 1953. See Chapter I of this study.

Baptism and Confirmation. A Report submitted by the Church of England Liturgical Commission to the Archbishops of Canterbury and York in November 1958. London: S.P.C.K., 1959.

Cope, G. F., Davies, J. G., and Tytler, D. A., *An Experimental Liturgy*. (Ecumenical Studies in Worship, No. 3.) London: Lutterworth Press; Richmond, Va.: John Knox Press, 1958. (See also *An Experimental Liturgy as Televised by BBC Television*. London: BBC Television Network, 1959.) Cf. J. G. Davies, "Criticisms of 'An Experimental Liturgy,'" *Theology*, 62 (1959), 274-79.

Gavitt, L. N., "What Do Catholics Want in Prayer Book Revision," *American Church Quarterly*, 3 (1963), 83-118. [A study to which is appended "The Order for the Administration of the Lord's Supper or Holy Communion."]

Spencer, Bonnell, O.H.C., "A Functional Liturgy," *Anglican Theological Review*, 43 (1961), 333-69. [See also his critique, "What's Wrong with the Rite?" *American Church Monthly*, 3 (1963), 14-25.]

Ceremonial:

The Chichester Customary. The Rites of the Church as Observed Throughout the Year in Chichester Cathedral, With an Introductory Essay by A. S. Duncan-Jones. (Alcuin Club Collections No. XXXVI.) London: S.P.C.K., 1948.

Before the Holy Table. A Guide to the Celebration of the Holy Eucharist, Facing the People, According to the Book of Common Prayer. Edited by Massey H. Shepherd, Jr., John H. Keene, John O. Patterson, and John R. Bill, with the assistance of other members of The Associated Parishes, Inc. Greenwich: The Seabury Press, 1956.

Ritual Notes. A Comprehensive Guide to the Rites and Ceremonies of the Book of Common Prayer of the English Church interpreted in accordance with the latest revisions of the Western Use. Compiled by the present editor of 'The Order of Divine Service,' and 'Anglican Services.' Tenth Edition. London: W. Knott and Son Ltd., 1956.

The Parson's Handbook. Practical Directions for Parsons and others according to the Anglican Use, as set forth in the Book of Common Prayer on the Basis of the twelfth edition by Percy Dearmer. 13th edition, revised and rewritten by C. E. Pocknee. Oxford University Press, 1965.

Special Studies:
The Lambeth Conference 1958. The Encyclical Letter from the Bishops together with the Resolutions and Reports. London: S.P.C.K.; Greenwich: The Seabury Press, 1958.
Prayer Book Revision in the Church of England. A Memorandum of the Church of England Liturgical Commission. London: S.P.C.K., 1957. A special report prepared for the Lambeth Conference.
Principles of Prayer Book Revision. The Report of a Select Committee of the Church of India, Pakistan, Burma, and Ceylon appointed by the Metropolitan to review the Principles of Prayer Book Revision in the Anglican Communion. London: S.P.C.K., 1957. A special report prepared for the Lambeth Conference.
Brook, Stella, *The Language of the Book of Common Prayer*. Oxford University Press, 1965.
Brooks, Cleanth, "Prayer Book Revision: Literary Style," *Anglican Theological Review*, 44 (1962), 18-32.
Couratin, A. H., "The Sacrifice of Praise, The Church's Thanksgiving in New Testament Times," *Theology*, 58 (1955), 285-91.
_____, "The Service of Holy Communion, 1552-1662," *Church Quarterly Review*, 163 (1962), 431-42.
_____, "The Holy Communion 1549," *Church Quarterly Review*, 164 (1963), 148-59.
Davies, J. G., "The 1662 Book of Common Prayer: its virtues and vices," *Studia Liturgica*, 1 (1962), 167-74.
Dugmore, C. W., *The Mass and the English Reformers*. London: The Macmillan Co. Ltd., 1958.
Every, Brother George, S.S.M., *A Study in the Structure of the Eucharistic Prayer*. London: The Faith Press, 1961.
Gibbard, S. M., "Prayer Book Revision," *Church Quarterly Review*, 160 (1959), 71-76.
Grisbrooke, W. Jardine, "The 1662 Book of Common Prayer: its history and character," *Studia Liturgica*, 1 (1962), 146-66.
_____, "Oblation at the Eucharist. II. The Liturgical Issues," *Studia Liturgica*, 4 (1965), 37-55.
Hettlinger, R. F., "Worship in the Anglican Communion," *Anglican Theological Review*, 40 (1958), 169-81.
Hinchcliff, Peter, *The South African Liturgy, The Story of the Revision of the Rite and Its Consecration Prayer*. Oxford University Press, 1959.
Jones, Bayard Hale, *Dynamic Redemption*. Reflections on the Book of Common Prayer. Greenwich: The Seabury Press, 1961.
Lash, William Quinlan, *The Indian Liturgy*. Oxford University Press, 1949. Lewis, Ewart, Prayer Book Revision in the Church of Wales. Penarth: The Church of Wales Provincial Council for Education, 1958.
Lowrie, Walter, *Action in the Liturgy, Essential and Unessential*. New York: Philosophical Library, 1953.
Mascall, E. L., *Corpus Christi*. Essays on the Church and the Eucharist. London: Longmans, Green and Co., 1953.
Minchin, Basil, *Covenant and Sacrifice*. (Worship in the Body of Christ.) London: Darton, Longmann and Todd, 1958.
_____, *Every Man in His Ministry*. (Worship in the Body of Christ.) London: Darton, Longman and Todd, 1960.
_____, *Outward and Visible*. (Worship in the Body of Christ.) London: Darton, Longmann and Todd, 1961.

Nicholls, William, *Jacob's Ladder*. The Meaning of Worship. (Ecumenical Studies in Worship No. 4.) London: Lutterworth Press; Richmond: John Knox Press, 1958.

Paton, David M. (ed.), *The Parish Communion Today*. The Report of the 1962 Conference of Parish and People. London: S.P.C.K., 1962.

Ratcliff, E. C., "The English Usage of Eucharistic Consecration, 1548-1662," *Theology*, 60 (1957), 229-36, 273-80.

Sansbury, C. Kenneth, "Revisions of the Eucharistic Rite in the Anglican Communion," *Theology*, 57 (1954), 123-28, 163-69.

_____, "Recent Revisions of the Eucharistic Prayer," *Theology*, 59 (1956), 281-88.

_____, "Revising the Liturgy," *Church Quarterly Review*, 161 (1960), 163-74.

Shepherd, Massey H., Jr., *The Liturgical Renewal of the Church*. Perspectives and Prospects. (The Bohlen Lectures 1959). Oxford University Press, 1961.

_____, *Liturgy and Education*. New York: The Seabury Press, 1965.

Spencer, Bonnell, O.H.C., *Sacrifice of Thanksgiving*. West Park, N.Y.: Holy Cross Publications, 1965.

Wright, Nathan, *One Bread, One Body*. Greenwich: The Seabury Press, 1962.

Roman Catholic Reforms

The vast literature on the subject may be conveniently checked in the bibliography of the annual *Yearbook of Liturgical Studies*, edited by John H. Miller, C.S.C., and others. University of Notre Dame Press, 1960-.

The Constitution on the Sacred Liturgy of the Second Vatican Council, and the subsequent Instruction on the Constitution for its implementation, are fundamental documents. For English translations, see:

Abbott, Walter M., S.J. (ed.), *The Documents of Vatican II*. In a New and Definitive Translation, With Commentaries and Notes, etc. Translations Directed by Joseph Gallagher. New York: Herder and Herder, Association Press, 1966. Also available in paperback edition.

Other useful translations in pamphlet form published by The Liturgical Press, Collegeville, Minn. (Latin and English); The National Catholic Welfare Conference, Washington (English only); and The Paulist Press, Glen Rock, N.J., with Commentary by Gerard S. Sloyan.

Commentaries:

Bugnini, A., C.M., and Braga, C., C.M. (ed.), *The Commentary on the Constitution and on the Instruction on the Sacred Liturgy*. By a Committee of Liturgical Experts. Translation by Vincent P. Mallon, M.M. New York: Benziger Brothers, 1965.

Flannery, Austin, O.P. (ed.), *Vatican II: The Liturgy Constitution*. 3rd edition. Dublin: Scepter Books, 1964.

The Liturgy Constitution. A Chapter by Chapter Analysis of the Constitution on the Sacred Liturgy. Glen Rock, N.J.: The Paulist Press (Deus Books), 1964.

Other Documents:

Seasoltz, R. Kevin, *The New Liturgy*. A Documentation, 1903-1965. New York: Herder and Herder, 1966.

Service Books in Vernacular:

Our Parish Prays and Sings. A Service Book for Liturgical Worship, with official texts, hymns, psalms and paraliturgies. Collegeville, Minn.: The Liturgical Press, 1965.

The Book of Catholic Worship. Washington: The Liturgical Conference, 1966.

Special Studies:

Concilium. Theology in the Age of Renewal. Glen Rock: The Paulist Press.
  Vol. 2: *The Church and the Liturgy.* 1965.
  Vol. 12: *The Church Worships.* 1966.
Crichton, J. D., *The Church's Worship.* New York: Sheed and Ward, 1964.
Diekmann, Godfrey, O.S.B., *Come, Let Us Worship* (Benedictine Studies). Baltimore: Helicon Press, 1959.
Jungmann, Joseph A., *The Mass of the Roman Rite: Its Origins and Development.* 2 vols. New York: Benziger Brothers, 1951-55. The fundamental study of the history of the Roman Mass. A single one-volume, abridged edition is also available.
McGowan, Jean C., R.S.C.J., *Concelebration: Sign of the Unity of the Church.* New York: Herder and Herder, 1964.
McManus, Frederick R. (ed.), *The Revival of the Liturgy.* New York: Herder and Herder, 1963. Essays in honor of Dom Godfrey Diekmann.
Miller, John H., C.S.C., *Signs of Transformation in Christ* (Foundations of Catholic Theology Series.) Englewood Cliffs, N.J.: Prentice-Hall, Inc. 1963.
Reinhold, R.A., *Bringing the Mass to the People.* Baltimore: Helicon Press, 1960.
Sheppard, Lancelot (ed.), *True Worship.* London: Darton, Longmann and Todd, 1963.
_____, *Blueprint for Worship.* Westminster, Md.: The Newman Press, 1964.
Sloyan, Gerard S., *Worship in a New Key.* What the Council Teaches on the Liturgy. The Liturgical Conference. New York: Herder and Herder, 1965.
Vagaggini, Cipriano, *Theological Dimensions of the Liturgy.* Translated by Leonard J. Doyle. Collegeville, Minn.: The Liturgical Press, 1959.

Protestant Worship

Liturgies:

Service Book and Hymnal. Authorized by the Lutheran Churches cooperating in The Commission on the Liturgy and Hymnal. Philadelphia: United Lutheran Publishing House, 1958.
The Book of Common Order of the Church of Scotland. By Authority of the General Assembly. New Impression with New Lectionary. Oxford University Press, 1957.
The Book of Common Worship. Approved by the General Assembly of the Presbyterian Church in the United States of America. Philadelphia: Board of Christian Education, 1946.
Service for the Lord's Day and Lectionary for the Christian Year. Philadelphia: The Westminster Press, 1964. [Presbyterian]
A Book of Public Worship compiled for the use of Congregationalists, by John Huxtable, John Marsh, Romilly Micklem, and James Todd. London: Oxford University Press, 1948.
A Book of Worship for Free Churches. Prepared under the direction of the General Council of the Congregational Christian Churches in the United States. New York: Oxford University Press, 1948.

The Lord's Day Service, With Explanatory Notes. Boston-Philadelphia: The United Church Press, 1964.

The Book of Worship for Church and Home. With orders of worship, services for the administration of Sacraments, and aids to worship according to the usages of The Methodist Church. Nashville: The Methodist Publishing House, 1964, 1965.

Christian Worship: A Service Book. Edited by G. Edwin Osborn. St. Louis: Christian Board of Publication, 1953. [Disciples of Christ]

The Church of South India. The Book of Common Worship. As authorized by the Synod, 1962. Oxford University Press, 1963.

The Eucharistic Liturgy of Taizé. With an Introductory Essay by Max Thurian. Translated by John Arnold. London: The Faith Press, 1962.

Special Studies:

Abba, Raymond, *Principles of Christian Worship.* With Special Reference to the Free Churches. London: Oxford University Press, 1957.

Benoit, Jean Daniel, *Liturgical Renewal.* Studies in Catholic and Protestant Developments on the Continent. (Studies in Ministry and Worship.) London: SCM Press Ltd., 1958.

Bowmer, John C., *The Lord's Supper in Methodism.* London: Epworth Press, 1961.

Clark, Neville, *Call to Worship.* (Studies in Ministry and Worship.) London: SCM Press Ltd., 1960.

Davies, Horton, *Christian Worship: Its History and Meaning.* New York. Abingdon Press, 1957.

———, *Worship and Theology in England.* Princeton University Press.
Vol. 3: *From Watts and Wesley to Maurice, 1690-1850.* 1961.
Vol. 4: *From Newman to Martineau, 1850-1900.* 1962.
Vol. 5: *The Ecumenical Century, 1900-1965.* 1965.

Garrett, T. S., *Worship in the Church of South India.* (Ecumenical Studies in Worship, No. 2.) London: Lutterworth Press; Richmond: John Knox Press, 1958.

Hagemann, Howard G., *Pulpit and Table.* Some Chapters in the History of Worship in the Reformed Churches. Richmond: John Knox Press, 1962.

Hahn, Wilhelm, *Worship and Congregation.* Translated by Geoffrey Buswell. (Ecumenical Studies in Worship, No. 12.) London: Lutterworth Press; Richmond: John Knox Press, 1963.

Hammond, Peter, *Liturgy and Architecture.* New York: Columbia University Press, 1961.

Hardin, H. Grady, Quillian, Joseph D., Jr., and White, James F., *The Celebration of the Gospel.* A Study in Christian Worship. New York-Nashville: Abingdon Press, 1964.

Hedley, George, *Christian Worship.* Some Meanings and Means. New York: The Macmillan Co., 1953.

Keir, Thomas H., *The Word in Worship.* Preaching and Its Setting in Common Worship. London: Oxford University Press, 1962.

Koenker, Ernest B., *Worship in Word and Sacrament.* St. Louis: Concordia Publishing House, 1959.

MacLeod, Donald, *Presbyterian Worship.* Its Meaning and Method. Richmond: John Knox Press, 1965.

Osborn, G. Edwin, *The Glory of Christian Worship.* Indianapolis: The Christian Theological Seminary Press, 1960.

Reed, Luther D., *The Lutheran Liturgy*. A Study of the Common Liturgy of the Lutheran Church in America. Revised edition. Philadelphia: Muhlenberg Press, 1947.
_____, *Worship*. A Study of Corporate Devotion. Philadelphia: Muhlenberg Press, 1959.
Shands, Alfred R., *The Liturgical Movement and the Local Church*. Revised edition. London: SCM Press, Ltd.; New York, Morehouse-Barlow Co., Inc., 1959.
Taylor, Michael J., S.J., *The Protestant Liturgical Renewal*. A Catholic Viewpoint. Westminster, Md.: The Newman Press, 1963.
Thurian, Max, *The Eucharistic Memorial*. (Ecumenical Studies in Worship, Nos. 7-8.) 2 vols. London: Lutterworth Press; Richmond: John Knox Press, 1960-61.
Vajta, Vilmos, *Luther on Worship*. An Interpretation. Translated by U. S. Leupold. Philadelphia: Muhlenberg Press, 1958.
von Allmen, J. J., *Preaching and Congregation*. (Ecumenical Studies in Worship, No. 10.) London: Lutterworth Press; Richmond: John Knox Press, 1962.
_____, *Worship, Its Theology and Practice*. New York: Oxford University Press, 1965.
Watkins, Keith, "An Order of Holy Communion for Use Every Sunday," *Encounter*, 24 (1963), 303-13. See also "A Symposium" that follows this article, pp. 314-29.
Winward, Stephen F., *The Reformation of our Worship*. (W. T. Whitley Lectures, 1963.) London: Carey Kingsgate Press, 1964.

Acknowledgments

GRATEFUL ACKNOWLEDGMENT is made of permissions to republish in Appendix II, "Recent Consecration Prayers," the forms copyrighted by the following publishers and editors:

No. 1. Cambridge University Press, New York, N. Y.

No. 2. Oxford University Press, New York, N. Y.

No. 3. World's Student Christian Federation, Geneva, Switzerland, and M. le Pasteur Paul Bourguet of Paris.

No. 4. The Rev. Frère Max Thurian, for *Les Presses de Taizé*.

No. 5. Mr. Walker Taylor, Jr., for the Diocese of East Carolina.

No. 6. The Rev. Dr. William R. Seaman, Secretary of the Commission on Liturgy and the Hymnal.

No. 7. The Westminster Press, Philadelphia, Pa.

No. 8. The Trustees of the S. P. C. K., London.

No. 9. The Bishop of Hong Kong.

No. 10. The Registrars of the Convocations of Canterbury and York.

No. 11. The Rev. Dr. J. G. Davies.

No. 12. The Managing Editor of *Encounter*.

No. 13. The Rt. Rev. G. R. Monteith, Auckland, New Zealand.

The Liturgy of the Lord's Supper

THE CELEBRATION OF HOLY EUCHARIST AND MINISTRATION OF HOLY COMMUNION

The Ministers of the Liturgy

At celebrations of the Holy Eucharist, it is fitting that the officiating Minister, whether a Bishop or Priest, be assisted by other clergymen and laymen, in accordance with the Canons and customs of the Church.

When the BISHOP is present, it is his prerogative to preside as officiant at the Lord's Table and to preach the Gospel.

When PRIESTS other than the officiant are present, it is appropriate that they stand with the officiant at the Holy Table as fellow ministers of the Sacrament, and join in the Offering and Consecration of the gifts at the altar, in the Breaking of the Bread, and in the ministering of the Communion.

A DEACON, if present, should read the Gospel and lead the Prayer of Intercession. Deacons should also assist the officiant in preparing the elements of bread and wine at the Offertory, and in the ministration of the Sacrament to the people. In the absence of a Deacon, his duties may be performed by an assisting Priest.

LAY PERSONS from the congregation, appointed by the Priest, should normally be assigned the reading of the Old Testament Lesson and the Epistle. And in the absence of a Deacon, they may lead the Prayer of Intercession.

THE CELEBRATION OF HOLY EUCHARIST AND MINISTRATION OF HOLY COMMUNION

A Psalm or Hymn may be sung during the Entrance of the Ministers.

The Priest or Minister appointed shall say,

BLESSED BE GOD: Father, Son, and Holy Spirit.

People

And blessed be his Kingdom, now and forever. Amen.

Priest

ALMIGHTY GOD, unto whom all hearts are open, all desires known, and from whom no secrets are hid: Cleanse the thoughts of our hearts by the inspiration of thy Holy Spirit, that we may perfectly love thee, and worthily magnify thy holy Name; through Christ our Lord. *Amen.*

Priest or Deacon

Our Lord Jesus Christ says,

The first commandment is this:
  "Hear, O Israel: The Lord our God is one Lord; and you shall love the Lord your God with all your heart, and with all your mind, and with all your strength."
  The second is like it,
  "You shall love your neighbor as yourself."
  There is no other commandment greater than these. On these two commandments depend all the Law and the Prophets.

Then this Hymn may be sung or said,

Kyrie eleison.
Christe eleison.
Kyrie eleison.

  or,

Lord, have mercy upon us.
Christ, have mercy upon us.
Lord, have mercy upon us.

  or this,

Holy God, Holy Mighty, Holy Immortal,
Have mercy upon us.

  Here, when appointed, shall be sung or said the Hymn,

Gloria in Excelsis

GLORY BE TO GOD ON HIGH:
  and on earth peace, good will towards men.
We praise thee, we bless thee, we worship thee,
  we glorify thee, we give thanks to thee for thy great glory.
O Lord God, heavenly King, God the Father Almighty.

O LORD, the only-begotten Son, Jesus Christ:
O Lord God, Lamb of God, Son of the Father,
  who takest away the sin of the world,
    have mercy upon us.
Thou who takest away the sin of the world,
  receive our prayer.
Thou who sittest at the right hand of God the Father,
have mercy upon us.

For thou only art holy,
Thou only art the Lord.
Thou only, O Jesus Christ, with the Holy Spirit,
　　art most high in the glory of God the Father. Amen.

or the Hymn,

Te Deum Laudamus

The Ministry of the Word

Then the Priest shall say,

The Lord be with you.
And with your spirit.
Let us pray.

The Collect

The People shall be seated for the following Lessons.

The Old Testament Lesson
The Epistle

The person who reads the Lesson (if there be one appointed) and the Epistle shall stand in a pulpit or some other suitable place, and face the People, first saying,

The Word of God,
　　written in the Book of _____

or,

written in the Epistle _____

After the Lesson and after the Epistle, a Psalm or Hymn may be sung.

The Gospel

Then, all the People standing, the Deacon (or a Priest) shall face the People and read the Gospel from a pulpit or some other suitable place, first saying,

The Holy Gospel of our Lord and Saviour Jesus Christ,
 according to Saint _____

And the People shall say,

Glory be to thee, O Lord.

After the Gospel, the People shall say,

Praise be to thee, O Christ.

Then follows

The Sermon

On all Sundays and festivals, there follows, the People standing,

The Nicene Creed

WE BELIEVE IN ONE GOD
 the Father Almighty, Maker of heaven and earth,
 and of all things visible and invisible.

And in one Lord, Jesus Christ,
 the only-begotten Son of God,
 begotten of the Father before all worlds:
God, of God: Light, of Light: Very God, of very God:
 begotten, not made,
 being of one substance with the Father,
 and through whom all things were made:
Who for us men and for our salvation came down from heaven,
 and was incarnate by the Holy Spirit of the Virgin Mary,
 and was made man:
And was crucified also for us under Pontius Pilate;
 he suffered and was buried:
And the third day he rose again
 in accordance with the Scriptures:
And ascended into heaven,
 and is seated at the right hand of the Father:
And he shall come again, with glory,
 to judge both the living and the dead;
 his kingdom shall have no end.

And we believe in the Holy Spirit, the Lord:
    The Giver of Life,
        proceeding from the Father:
Who with the Father and the Son together
    is worshipped and glorified;
    who spoke by the Prophets.
And we believe in one holy Catholic and Apostolic Church:
We acknowledge one Baptism for the remission of sins:
And we look for the resurrection of the dead,
    and the life of the world to come. Amen.

Here on occasions, and as appointed, follows

The Penitential Order

(see page 294)

Then the Priest and People shall exchange one with another

The Peace

The Peace of the Lord be always with you.
And with your spirit.

After which, the Deacon or Priest, or some other person appointed, shall lead the People in

The Prayer of Intercession

IN PEACE, let us pray to the Lord:

For the peace from above, for the salvation of mankind: that righteousness, mercy, and truth may prevail among all peoples and nations,
Hear us, good Lord.

For the well-being of thy holy Catholic Church in every place: that thou wilt confirm it in the truth of thy holy Word, and grant to all Christians to live in unity, love, and concord,
Hear us, good Lord.

For Bishops and other Ministers, especially for N., our Presiding Bishop, N (N)., our Bishop (s), and those who serve thee in this place: that both by their life and teaching, they may set forth thy true and life-giving Word, and faithfully administer thy holy Sacraments,
Hear us, good Lord.

For all who bear authority in this and every land, and especially for the President of the United States [*or,* of this Nation]: that in thy holy fear they may govern the peoples in wisdom, justice, and peace,
Hear us, good Lord.

For all who spread the Gospel among the nations, and who minister to the suffering, the friendless, and the needy: that they may have strength and courage to fulfill thy holy will,
Hear us, good Lord.

For all who labor in commerce and industry, especially those whose work is dangerous or burdensome; for all who are engaged in the arts and sciences, and those who teach and study in schools of good learning; for all who keep house and train children: that they may be worthy of their calling to serve thee and their fellow men,
Hear us, good Lord.

For those who farm the fields and tend the woods; for all who gather the harvest of the lands and of the waters; and for our faithful use of thy creative bounty: that mankind, being delivered from famine and disaster, may acknowledge thy glory in all thy works,
Hear us, good Lord.

> [*Here may be inserted any particular bidding, according to times and occasions, or at the special request of the Congregation.*

For _____, and more especially _____: that *they* may _____, according to thy will,
Hear us, good Lord.]

For all who in this transitory life are in danger, trouble, sorrow, need, sickness, or any other adversity [and especially for thy servants NN.]: that they may have comfort and relief according to their necessities,
Hear us, good Lord.

For all thy people, and especially those who worship in this place: that with faith, reverence, and godly fear, they may serve thee with a glad mind and ready will all the days of their life,
Hear us, good Lord.

Have mercy upon us, most merciful Lord, and deliver us from all affliction, strife, and catastrophe: in thy compassion forgive us all our sins and failures, known and unknown, things done and left undone: and so uphold us by thy Spirit, that we may end our days in peace, trusting in thy mercy at the day of judgment,
Have mercy upon us.

We commend to thy keeping all thy servants departed this life in thy faith and fear [and especially thy servant(s), N(N).]: that thou wilt grant them mercy, light, and peace. May we with all thy saints [and especially N., whose faith and devotion we commemorate this day], be partakers of thine everlasting kingdom: through the mercies and merits of thy Son, Jesus Christ, our only Mediator and Advocate.

To thee be honor, glory, and dominion, now and forever. Amen.

If there is no Communion, all that is before appointed may be said, concluding with THE LORD'S PRAYER *and* THE GRACE.

The Offertory

The Priest shall go to the Holy Table and begin THE OFFERTORY *as follows, the People standing.*

LET US WITH GLADNESS present the offerings and oblations of our life and labor unto the Lord.

The Priest may read one or more of the Offertory Sentences. (See pages 295-296.)

Representatives of the Congregation shall receive the alms and other offerings of the People. Both the alms and the oblations of bread and wine shall be brought to the Deacon or Priest. The Priest shall present and offer the alms and oblations, and place them upon the Holy Table, the People standing.

One of the following Sentences[66] may be said or sung at

The Presentation

Thine, O Lord, is the greatness, and the power, and the glory, and the victory, and the majesty:
For all that is in the heaven and in the earth is thine.
Thine is the kingdom, O Lord,
And thou art exalted as head above all.

or this,

---

[66]. Ed. Note: There seems to have been some organizational confusion as to where these sentences should be located. They are printed here, but also appear again in the later section between the Offertory Sentence options and the Proper Prefaces.

All things come of thee, O Lord:
And of thine own have we given thee.

or this,

Worthy art thou, our Lord and God, to receive glory and honor and power,
For thou hast created all things, and by thy will they exist and were created.

The Consecration

The Priest shall face the People, still standing, and shall sing or say,

The Lord be with you.
And with your spirit.

Lift up your hearts.
We lift them up unto the Lord.
Let us give thanks unto our Lord God.
It is meet and right so to do.

It is truly meet, right, and our bounden duty, that we should at all times and in all places, give thanks unto thee, O Lord, Holy Father, Almighty, Everlasting God:

On Sundays

Through Jesus Christ our Lord, who on this day overcame death and the grave, and by his glorious resurrection opened to us the way of everlasting life:

Or the Proper Preface, as appointed (Spoken: pages 296-299; Sung: pages 299-311):

Spoken Prefaces: [Advent] [Christmas] [Epiphany] [Incarnation] [Lent] [Passiontide] [Easter] [Ascension] [Whitsuntide] [Trinity] [All Saints] [Apostles] [Commemoration of the Departed]

Sung Prefaces: [Advent] [Christmas] [Epiphany] [Incarnation] [Lent] [Passiontide] [Easter] [Ascension] [Whitsuntide] [Trinity] [All Saints] [Apostles] [Commemoration of the Departed]

Therefore with Angels and Archangels, and with all the company of heaven, we laud and magnify thy glorious Name, evermore praising thee and saying,

Priest and People

HOLY, HOLY, HOLY, Lord God of Hosts: Heaven and earth are full of thy glory. Glory be to thee, O Lord most high.

Here the People may kneel; and the Priest shall continue,

ALL GLORY BE TO THEE, Almighty God, Holy Father, Creator of heaven and earth, who didst make us in thine own image. And when we had fallen into sin, thou of thy tender mercy didst give thine only-begotten Son Jesus Christ, to take our nature upon him, and to suffer death upon the Cross for our redemption: Who made there, by his one oblation of himself once offered, a full and perfect sacrifice for the whole world: And instituted and commanded us to continue this perpetual memorial of his precious death and sacrifice, until his coming again.

FOR IN THE NIGHT in which he was betrayed, he took bread; *[Here the Priest is to lay his hands upon all the bread]* and when he had given thanks to thee, he broke it, and gave it to his disciples, and said, "Take, eat: This is my Body which is given for you. Do this in remembrance of me."

In the same way also, after supper, he took the cup; *[Here he is to lay his hand upon every vessel of wine to be blessed]* when he had given thanks, he gave it to them and said, "Drink this, all of you: For this is my Blood of the New Covenant, which is poured out for you and many for the forgiveness of sins. Do this, as often as you drink it, in remembrance of me."

WHEREFORE, O LORD AND HOLY FATHER, we thy people do celebrate here before thy Divine Majesty, with these thy holy Gifts, which we offer unto thee, the memorial of the blessed Passion and precious Death of thy dear Son, his mighty Resurrection and glorious Ascension, looking for his Coming again in power and great glory. And herewith we offer and present unto thee, O Lord, ourselves, which is our bounden duty and service. And we entirely desire thy fatherly goodness mercifully to accept, through the eternal mediation of our Saviour Jesus Christ, this our sacrifice of praise and thanksgiving.

WE PRAY THEE, GRACIOUS FATHER, of thine almighty power, to bless and sanctify us and these holy Mysteries with thy Life-giving Word and Holy Spirit. Fill with thy grace all who partake of the Body and Blood of our Lord Jesus Christ. Make us one Body, that he may dwell in us and we in him.

And grant that with boldness we may confess thy Name in constancy of faith, and at the last Day enter with all thy saints into the joy of thine eternal kingdom:

Through the same Jesus Christ our Lord; by whom, and with whom, and in whom, in the unity of the Holy Spirit, all honor and glory be unto thee, O Father Almighty, world without end.

AMEN.

As our Saviour Christ has taught us, we are now bold to say:

Priest and People

Our Father, who art in heaven, Hallowed be thy Name. Thy kingdom come. Thy will be done, On earth as it is in heaven. Give us this day our daily bread. And forgive us our trespasses, As we forgive those who trespass against us. And lead us not into temptation; But deliver us from evil. For thine is the kingdom, and the power, and the glory, for ever and ever. Amen.

The Breaking of the Bread

Here the Priest shall break the consecrated Bread, and silence shall be kept for a space.

Then shall be said or sung the following Anthem, or some other proper Hymn. From Easter Day to Trinity Sunday,

Alleluia

may be sung or said before and after the Anthem.

Christ our passover is sacrificed for us:
Therefore let us keep the feast.

Blessed is He who comes in the Name of the Lord.
Hosanna in the highest.

Then the Priest shall face the People and say,

Holy things for the People of God: Take them in remembrance that Christ gives himself for you, and feed on him in your hearts by faith, with thanksgiving.

The Minister who delivers the Bread shall say,

The Body of our Lord Jesus Christ keep you unto everlasting life.

The Minister who delivers the Cup shall say:

The Blood of our Lord Jesus Christ keep you unto everlasting life.

Opportunity shall always be given to every communicant to receive the consecrated Bread and Wine separately. But the Sacrament may be received in both kinds simultaneously, in such manner as is authorized by the Ordinary, in which case the Minister shall say,

THE BODY AND BLOOD of our Lord Jesus Christ keep you unto everlasting life.

When all have communicated, the Priest shall say,

Let us give thanks to the Lord.

Priest and People

ALMIGHTY AND EVERLIVING GOD, we most heartily thank thee, That thou dost feed us in these holy Mysteries, With the spiritual food of the most precious Body and Blood of our Saviour Jesus Christ, Assuring us thereby of thy favor and goodness towards us; And that we are truly members incorporate in the mystical Body of thy Son, The blessed company of all faithful people; And heirs, through hope, of thine everlasting kingdom. And we humbly pray thee, O heavenly Father, so to assist us by thy Holy Spirit, That we may continue in that holy fellowship, And do all such good works as thou hast prepared for us; Through Jesus Christ our Lord, To whom, with thee and the same Spirit, be all honor and glory, world without end. Amen.

Then shall the Priest or Deacon dismiss the People as follows. But if the Bishop is present, he shall dismiss the People and give them his blessing.

GO FORTH INTO THE WORLD IN PEACE. Be strong and of good courage. Hold fast that which is good. Love and serve the Lord with gladness and singleness of heart, rejoicing in the power of his Spirit. *Amen.*

The Order for Celebration of Holy Eucharist

The Holy Table shall be spread with a fair white cloth during the celebration.

The officiant shall begin the service, standing before the Holy Table or at some other suitable place.

A Psalm or Canticle may always be sung in place of a Hymn.

The Kyrie eleison may be sung or said in threefold, sixfold, or ninefold form. The Trisagion may be said or sung three times.

The Gloria in excelsis or the Te Deum Laudamus shall be sung or said on all Sundays and other festivals, except the Sundays in Advent, Pre-Lent, and Lent, and may be omitted on the Sundays after Trinity.

The Collect of the Season or of the Octave, if any is appointed, shall be said first, and after that the Collect of the Day.

A Lesson from the Old Testament may be read after the Collect and before the Epistle, according to the Table of "Psalms and Lessons for the Christian Year."

At the end of the Lesson or of the Epistle, the reader shall say, "Here ends the Lesson," or "Here ends the Epistle."

Before the Sermon, or after the Nicene Creed, notice shall be given of what Holy Days in the week following are to be observed, of the celebrations of the Holy Eucharist, of the Banns of Matrimony, and other proper matters to be published. And prayers set forth by authority may be used.

The Nicene Creed may be omitted, except on Sundays and festivals.

The Penitential Order shall be said on the First Sunday in Advent, Ash Wednesday, the First Sunday in Lent, Passion Sunday, and the First Sunday after Trinity, and at other times at the discretion of the Priest. Where desired, the Order may be said before the Liturgy, or after the Summary of the Law.

If there is no Communion, all that is appointed through the Prayer of Intercession may be said, concluding with The Lord's Prayer and The Grace. For reasonable cause, a Deacon, or a Lay Reader specially licensed by the Bishop, may say all that is appointed through the Prayer of Intercession, except the Absolution in the Penitential Order.

During the Offertory, and also at the time of ministration of the Communion, Hymns or Anthems may be sung.

While the People are coming forward to receive the Holy Communion, the Priest shall first receive the Sacrament in both kinds himself. Then the same shall be delivered into the hands of the Bishops, Priests, and Deacons, assisting at the Holy Table; and after that to the People.

When the officiant is assisted by a Deacon or another Priest, it is customary for the officiant to minister the consecrated Bread, and the assistant to minister the Chalice. When several Deacons or Priests are present, some may minister the Bread, others the Wine, as the officiant may direct.

If the consecrated Bread or Wine be spent before all have communicated, the Priest is to consecrate more of either, or both, saying,

> HEAR US, O heavenly Father, and with thy Word and Holy Spirit bless and sanctify this Bread (*or,* Wine) that it also may be the Sacrament of the precious Body (*or,* Blood) of thy Son Jesus Christ our Lord. *Amen.*

If any of the consecrated Bread or Wine remain, apart from any which may be required for the Communion of the Sick, or of others who for weighty cause could not be present at the celebration, the Priest (or Deacon) and other communicants shall reverently eat and drink the same, either immediately after the Communion of the People or after the Dismissal.

The Penitential Order

The People standing, a Deacon or Priest shall say this INVITATION:

YOU THAT TRULY and earnestly repent you of your sins, and are in love and charity with your neighbors, and intend to lead a new life, following the commandments of God, and walking hereafter in his holy ways: Draw near with faith to receive the holy Sacrament, and make your humble confession to Almighty God, in the presence of his Church, devoutly kneeling.

Here silence may be kept for a space.

Then this GENERAL CONFESSION shall be led by the Deacon, or a Priest, and repeated with him by all who intend to receive the Holy Communion, humbly kneeling.

ALMIGHTY GOD, Father of our Lord Jesus Christ, Maker of all things, Judge of all men:

We acknowledge and confess our manifold sins and wickedness, Which we have committed against thy Divine Majesty, by thought, word, and deed. We do earnestly repent, and are heartily sorry for these our misdoings.

Have mercy on us, Have mercy on us, most merciful Father: For thy Son our Lord Jesus Christ's sake, Forgive us our sins and offenses. And grant that we may ever hereafter, Serve and please thee in newness of life:

To the honor and glory of thy Name; Through the same Jesus Christ our Lord. Amen.

Here the Priest, standing up and facing the People, may say,

Hear the Word of God to all who truly turn to him:

> COME UNTO ME, all who travail and are heavy laden, and I will refresh you. [*St. Matthew 11:28.*]
>
> God so loved the world, that he gave his only-begotten Son, that whoever believes in him should not perish, but have eternal life. [*St. John 3:16.*]
>
> Faithful is the saying and worthy of full acceptance, that Christ Jesus came into the world to save sinners. [*1 Timothy 1:15.*]

If any one sin, we have an advocate with the Father, Jesus Christ the righteous; and he is the expiation for our sins, and not for ours only but also for the sins of the whole world. [*1 John 2:1-2.*]

Then shall the Bishop, if he is present, or the Priest, say this ABSOLUTION*:*

ALMIGHTY GOD, our heavenly Father, who of his great mercy has promised forgiveness of sins to all those who turn to him with true repentance and sincere faith: Have mercy upon you. Pardon and deliver you from all your sins. Confirm and strengthen you in all goodness, and bring you to everlasting life; through Jesus Christ our Lord. *Amen.*

Offertory Sentences

To be used at THE OFFERTORY of the Holy Eucharist, and on other occasions of public worship when the offerings of the People are to be received.

GIVE TO THE LORD the glory due his Name; bring an offering and come into his courts. [*Psalm 96:8.*]

Walk in love, as Christ loved us and gave himself up for us, an offering and sacrifice to God. [*Ephesians 5:2.*]

I pray you, brethren, by the mercies of God, to present your bodies as a living sacrifice, holy and acceptable to God, which is your spiritual worship. [*Romans 12:1.*]

If you are offering your gift at the altar, and there remember that your brother has something against you, leave your gift there before the altar and go; first be reconciled to your brother, and then come and offer your gift. [*St. Matthew 5:23-24.*]

Remember the words of the Lord Jesus, how he said, "It is more blessed to give than to receive." [*Acts 20:35.*]

As we have opportunity, let us do good to all men, and especially to those who are of the household of faith. [*Galatians 6:10.*]

God is just; he will not overlook your work and the love which you have showed for his sake in serving the saints, as you still do serve. [*Hebrews 6:10.*]

If any one has the goods of this world and sees his brother in need, yet closes his heart against him, how does God's love abide in him? [*1 John 3:17.*]

The King will answer them, "Truly, I say to you, as you did it to one of the least of these my brothers, you did it to me." [*St. Matthew 25:40.*]

How are men to call upon him in whom they have not believed? And how are they to believe in him of whom they have never heard? And how are they to hear without a preacher? And how can men preach unless they are sent? [*Romans 10:14.*]

Jesus said to them, "The harvest is plentiful, but the laborers are few; pray therefore the Lord of the harvest to send out laborers into his harvest." [*St. Luke 10:2.*]

At the Presentation

Thine, O Lord, is the greatness, and the power, and the glory, and the victory, and the majesty. For all that is in the heaven and in the earth is thine. Thine is the kingdom, O Lord, and thou art exalted as head above all. [*1 Chronicles 29:11.*]

All things come of thee, O Lord, and of thine own have we given thee. [*1 Chronicles 29:14.*]

Worthy art thou, our Lord and God, to receive glory and honor and power; for thou hast created all things, and by thy will they exist and were created. [*Revelation 4:11.*]

Spoken Proper Prefaces

Advent

> *From the First Sunday in Advent until Christmas Day, except on Ember Days and Saints' Days.*

BECAUSE thou didst send thy well-beloved Son to redeem us from sin and death, and to make us sons and heirs in him of everlasting life: that when he shall come again in power and great triumph to judge the world, we may without shame or fear rejoice to behold his appearing:

Christmas

> *From Christmas Day until the Epiphany.*

BECAUSE thou didst give Jesus Christ, thine only Son, to be born as at this time for us; who, by the mighty power of the Holy Spirit, was made perfect Man of the flesh of the Virgin Mary his mother: that we, being delivered from the bondage of sin, might receive power to become the sons of God:

Epiphany

> *From the Epiphany until Septuagesima, except on Saints' Days.*

Through Jesus Christ our Lord; who, in the substance of our mortal nature, manifested forth his glory: that he might bring us out of darkness into his own marvelous light:

The Incarnation

Upon the Feasts of the Presentation, Annunciation, Visitation, and Transfiguration.

Because in the Mystery of the Word made flesh, thou hast caused a new light to shine in our hearts, to give the knowledge of thy glory in the face of thy Son Jesus Christ our Lord:

Lent

From Ash Wednesday until Passion Sunday, except upon Ember Days, the Annunciation, and major Saints' Days.

Through Jesus Christ our Lord; who knows our infirmities, for he was in every way tempted as we are, yet did not sin; by whose grace we are able to triumph over every evil, and to live no longer unto ourselves, but unto him who died for us and rose again:

Passiontide

From Passion Sunday through Maundy Thursday, except on the Annunciation. This Preface may also be used on the Feast of the Holy Cross.

Through Jesus Christ our Lord; who for our sins was lifted up on the Cross, that he might draw all men to himself; who, although a Son, learned obedience through his sufferings; and, being perfected, became the Author of eternal salvation to all who obey him:

Easter

From Easter Day until Ascension Day, except on major Holy Days.

But chiefly are we bound to praise thee for the glorious Resurrection of thy Son Jesus Christ our Lord; for he is the Paschal Lamb, who was offered for us, and has taken away the sin of the world; who by his death has overcome death, and by his rising to life again has given to us everlasting life:

Ascension

From Ascension Day until Whitsunday.

THROUGH thy most dearly beloved Son Jesus Christ our Lord; who, after his most glorious Resurrection, openly appeared to all his Apostles, and in their sight was taken into heaven, to prepare a place for us: that where he is, thither we might also ascend, and reign with him in glory:

Whitsuntide

On Whitsunday and six days after. This Preface (without the words "at this time") may be used on Feasts of the Apostles.

THROUGH Jesus Christ our Lord; according to whose true promise, the Holy Spirit came down at this time from heaven upon the disciples, to teach them and to lead them into all truth; giving them boldness with fervent zeal constantly to preach the Gospel to all nations:

Trinity Sunday

WHOM with thy co-eternal Son and Holy Spirit we worship as one God and one Lord, in Trinity of Persons and in Unity of Being; and we celebrate the one and equal glory of thee, O Father, and of the Son, and of the Holy Spirit:

All Saints

On All Saints' Day and seven days after; and upon other Saints' Days, except those of Apostles and those in Christmastide and Ascension-tide.

WHO, in the multitude of thy saints, hast compassed us about with so great a cloud of witnesses: that we, rejoicing in their fellowship, may run with patience the race that is set before us; and, together with them, may receive the crown of glory that never fades away:

Apostles and Ordinations

To be used on Feasts of the Apostles, the Ember Days, and at the time of conferring Holy Orders: except the days from Christmas through the Epiphany, from Ascension Day through Trinity Sunday, and in the Octave of All Saints.

THROUGH the great Shepherd of thy flock, Jesus Christ our Lord; who after his Resurrection sent forth his Apostles to preach the Gospel, and to teach all nations; and did promise to be with them always, even unto the end of the ages:

The Liturgy of the Lord's Supper

Commemoration of the Departed

THROUGH Jesus Christ our Lord; who has brought to light the living hope of a blessed resurrection: that we may not grieve because of mortal death, but may rejoice in full assurance of our change into the likeness of his glory; for when our earthly habitation is dissolved, he has prepared for us a dwelling place eternal in the heavens:

Conclusion

After any of the Proper Prefaces, the Priest shall conclude, saying,

THEREFORE with Angels and Archangels, and with all the company of heaven, we laud and magnify thy glorious Name, evermore praising thee and saying,

Priest and People

HOLY, HOLY, HOLY, Lord God of Hosts: Heaven and earth are full of thy glory: Glory be to thee, O Lord most high.

Sung Proper Prefaces

Advent

From the First Sunday in Advent until Christmas Day, except on Ember Days and Saints' Days.

ADVENT

Christmas

From Christmas Day until the Epiphany.

CHRISTMAS

The Liturgy of the Lord's Supper 301

Mary his mother: that we, being delivered from the bondage of sin, might receive power to become the sons of God: Therefore, with Angels . . .

Epiphany

From the Epiphany until Septuagesima, except on Saints' Days.

EPIPHANY

O Lord, Holy Father, Almighty, Everlasting God: Through Jesus Christ our Lord; who, in the substance of our mortal nature, manifested forth his glory: that he might bring us out of darkness into his own marvelous light: Therefore, with Angels . . .

302 PRAYER BOOK STUDIES XVII

The Incarnation

Upon the Feasts of the Presentation, Annunciation, Visitation, and Transfiguration.

THE INCARNATION

O Lord, Holy Father, Almighty, Everlasting God: Because in the Mystery of the Word made flesh, thou hast caused a new light to shine in our hearts, to give the knowledge of thy glory in the face of thy Son Jesus Christ our Lord: Therefore, with Angels . . .

The Liturgy of the Lord's Supper 303

Lent

From Ash Wednesday until Passion Sunday, except upon Ember Days, the Annunciation, and major Saints' Days.

LENT

O Lord, Holy Father, Almighty, Everlasting God: Through Jesus Christ our Lord; who knows our infirmities, for he was in every way tempted as we are, yet did not sin; by whose grace we are able to triumph over every evil, and to live no longer unto ourselves, but unto him who died for us and rose again: Therefore, with Angels ...

304 PRAYER BOOK STUDIES XVII

Passiontide

From Passion Sunday through Maundy Thursday, except on the Annunciation. This Preface may also be used on the Feast of the Holy Cross.

PASSIONTIDE

Easter

From Easter Day until Ascension Day, except on major Holy Days.

EASTER

O Lord, Holy Father, Almighty, Everlasting God: But chiefly are we bound to praise thee for the glorious Resurrection of thy Son, Jesus Christ our Lord; for he is the Paschal Lamb, who was offered for us, and has taken away the sin of the world; who by his death has overcome death, and by his rising to life again has given to us everlasting life: Therefore, with Angels . . .

306 PRAYER BOOK STUDIES XVII

Ascension

From Ascension Day until Whitsunday.

ASCENSION

O Lord, Holy Father, Almighty, Ever-lasting God: Through thy most dearly beloved Son Jesus Christ our Lord; who, after his most glorious Resurrection, openly appeared to all his Apostles, and in their sight was taken into heaven, to prepare a place for us: that where he is, thither we might also ascend, and reign with him in glory: Therefore, with Angels . . .

Whitsuntide

On Whitsunday and six days after. This Preface (without the words "at this time") may be used on Feasts of the Apostles.

WHITSUNTIDE

O Lord, Holy Father, Almighty, Ever-last-ing God: Through Je-sus Christ our Lord; ac-cording to whose true pro-mise, the Holy Spirit came down at this time from heaven upon the dis-ci-ples, to teach them and to lead them in-to all truth; giv-ing them boldness with fer-vent zeal con-stantly to preach the Gos-pel to all na-tions: There-fore, with Angels . . .

308 PRAYER BOOK STUDIES XVII

Trinity Sunday

The Liturgy of the Lord's Supper 309

SUNDAYS

O Lord, Holy Father, Almighty, Ever-last-ing God: Through Je-sus Christ our Lord; who on this day overcame death and the grave, and by his glorious re-sur-rect-ion opened to us the way of ev-er-last-ing life: There-fore, with Angels . . .

All Saints

On All Saints' Day and seven days after; and upon other Saints' Days, except those of Apostles and those in Christmastide and Ascension-tide.

ALL SAINTS

O Lord, Ho-ly Fa-ther, Al-might-y, Ev-er-last-ing God: Who, in the multitude of thy saints, hast compassed us about with so great a cloud of wit-ness-es: that we, rejoicing in their fel-low-ship, may run with patience the race

310 PRAYER BOOK STUDIES XVII

Apostles and Ordinations

To be used on Feasts of the Apostles, the Ember Days, and at the time of conferring Holy Orders: except the days from Christmas through the Epiphany, from Ascension Day through Trinity Sunday, and in the Octave of All Saints.

APOSTLES AND ORDINATIONS

Commemoration of the Departed

COMMEMORATION OF THE DEPARTED:

O Lord, Holy Father, Almighty, Everlasting God: Through Jesus Christ our Lord; who has brought to light the living hope of a blessed resurrection: that we may not grieve because of mortal death, but may rejoice in full assurance of our change into the likeness of his glory; for when our earthly habitation is dissolved, he has prepared for us a dwelling place eternal in the heavens: Therefore, with Angels . . .

www.ingramcontent.com/pod-product-compliance
Lightning Source LLC
Chambersburg PA
CBHW070746020526
44116CB00032B/1990